Schoenberg/a critical biography

Schoenberg a critical biography

Willi Reich

Translated by Leo Black

PRAEGER PUBLISHERS

New York · Washington

BOOKS THAT MATTER

Published in the United States of America in 1971
by Praeger Publishers, Inc., 111 Fourth Avenue,
New York, N.Y.   10003

First published in 1968 under the title
SCHÖNBERG *oder Der Konservative Revolutionär*
© 1968 in Austria by Verlag Fritz Molden, Vienna

English translation © 1971 in England by Longman Group Limited,
London

Library of Congress Catalog Card Number: 73-134527

Printed in Great Britain

In memoriam Gertrud Schoenberg

Contents

Illustrations

Plates

Drawings

Acknowledgements

We are grateful to the following for permission to reproduce copyright material:

Faber and Faber Limited for extracts from Arnold Schoenberg: *Letters* translated by Ernst Kaiser and Eithne Wilkins and edited by Erwin Stein, and *Style and Idea* translated by Leo Black and edited by Leonard Stein; the proprietors of *The Musical Quarterly* for extracts from 'Schoenberg in America' by Walter H. Rubsamen from *The Musical Quarterly*, October, 1951; Lawrence A. Schoenberg for extracts from letters and notes by Arnold Schoenberg; Thames and Hudson Limited and Harcourt Brace Jovanovich, Inc, for extracts from *Alban Berg* by Willi Reich, translated by Cornelius Cardew.

Photographic credits are gratefully extended to: Baerenreiter Verlag (plates facing pp. 85, 149 *top*, 213), Österreichische Nationalbibliothek (52, 84, 116, 117, 149 *bottom* and the line-drawings on pp. 54, 89, 178), USIS (both photographs facing page 212) and private owners (53, 148, 180).

Foreword

This book tries to do something not previously attempted: to give a comprehensive account of Schoenberg's career and personality, drawing on all the material available to me. In order not to be suspected of one-sidedness or fanatical over-enthusiasm, I have advanced as much documentary evidence as possible to back up what I say. So that the text shall also be intelligible to non-musicians, I have done without technical analyses and musical examples, trying rather to describe as precisely and clearly as possible the spiritual atmosphere in which Schoenberg's creative work was conducted.

I received indispensable help from Mrs Gertrud Schoenberg, who not merely allowed me to quote at will from her husband's printed utterances, but also provided me with unpublished material, either in the form of photocopies or else written out in her own hand. It goes without saying that this book is dedicated to the memory of Mrs Schoenberg, who died in February 1967.

The book's appearance in English, so soon after the original German edition, causes me great satisfaction, for I find it very important that English-speaking circles, among whom Schoenberg's work is becoming ever more widely and better known, should also know more of his career and personality. I am particularly grateful to Mr Leo Black. He has not only provided a very faithful and readable English translation: in letters and personal meetings, he has made a number of valuable suggestions, which I have adopted, to the benefit of the English edition.

Zürich, October 1969   Willi Reich

1 Romantic Beginnings

Arnold Schoenberg was born on 13 September 1874 at No. 57 (No. 393 according to the old numbering), Obere Donaustrasse, in the second district of Vienna. His father, Samuel Schoenberg (1838–90), after coming to Vienna from Pressburg at the age of fourteen, had gradually worked his way up from apprentice to owner of a small shoe-shop. In 1870 he married a girl from Prague, Pauline Nachod (1848–1921).

Only a few remarks about his parents have come to light among Schoenberg's posthumous papers: 'The marriage seems to have gone quite normally and well, with nothing worse than economic worries to disturb it'. His mother was 'devoted, altruistic, selfless, modest, and I could possibly have inherited from her a certain hard-working quality and sense of duty'. Were his parents musical? All one can gather is that they enjoyed music—vocal music especially—but without taking part in any artistic activities. When young, his father had belonged to an amateur choir, but Schoenberg described his father's sensitivity to music as 'in no way surpassing that possessed by any Austrian who does not actually dislike music'. Two members of the family were professional singers—Hans Nachod, a cousin of the composer, who sang the role of King Waldemar when Franz Schreker conducted the first performance of the *Gurrelieder*, and Heinrich Schoenberg, the composer's brother, who became a bass at the German Theatre in Prague.

In a memoir of his life written in 1949[1], Schoenberg tells us: 'Of the seventy-five years of my life I have devoted almost ninety per cent to music. I began studying the violin at eight, and almost immediately started composing.'

Schoenberg also tells of the intellectual stimulus provided by his uncle on his mother's side, Fritz Nachod. This uncle was 'of a dreamy temperament, wrote lyric poetry, harboured high-liberal enthusiasms, taught his nephew French, and recited Schiller's poems to him'. But neither this art-loving uncle nor Schoenberg's parents paid serious attention to his musical talent, which showed itself at an early age. Schoenberg later remarked: 'At home, there may indeed have been some talk, which I cannot remember, of my being musically inclined, for it occurs to me that I quite early read a life of

1 Originally for the Mexican periodical *Nuestra Musica*, which published it (August 1949) in a Spanish translation. Schoenberg gave a slightly extended version of it as a lecture at the University of California, Los Angeles, and this was published posthumously, under his title 'My creative evolution', in the *Musical Quarterly* (October 1952). The memoir thus exists in two original versions—one in German, the other in the highly characteristic and inimitable English of Schoenberg's last years in America. Rufer's catalogue lists the memoir as *Rückblick—My Evolution*. L.B.

Mozart, which prompted me to write my compositions without the aid of an instrument.'

Schoenberg has given an account of his early musical activities in the following autobiographical sketch reprinted in 1959, eight years after his death, as part of the programme book for a series of concerts in Milwaukee, at which the Pro Arte (Kolisch) Quartet performed his four published string quartets and the String Trio, Op. 45, each concert also including music by one of the great Viennese classical composers. (Such concert series by the Kolisch Quartet were a feature of the composer's late years in America.)

As a child of less than nine years, I had started composing little and, later, larger pieces for two violins, in imitation of such music as I used to play with my teacher or with a cousin of mine. When I could play violin duets of Viotti, Pleyel and others, I imitated their style. Thus I progressed in composing in the measure I progressed in playing. After all, I came so far as to compose once a kind of symphonic poem, after Friedrich von Schiller's drama *Die Räuber*, that is *The Robbers*, which I called *Die-Räuber-Phantasie*.

Decisive progress took place when, a few years later, I found a classmate who possessed a viola and could play it. At once I started writing trios for two violins and viola, though there was no model for imitation available. Next, with money I had earned for teaching German to a Greek, I bought, secondhand, a few scores of Beethoven: the third and fourth symphonies, two Rasoumovsky string quartets and the Great Fugue for string quartet, Op. 133. From this minute, I was possessed by an urge to write string quartets.

Yet this desire did not find satisfaction until I had acquired a friend, Oscar Adler, who was to play a great role in my evolution. I am obliged to him for a great many matters he taught me. Not only did he teach me elementary harmony, he also stimulated me in the direction of exercising my ear in order to strengthen my memory of pitches. Besides, our repertory of trios was augmented by his arrangements of violin sonatas for this ensemble.

We wanted to play quartets of Mozart and Beethoven, so Adler procured a large viola, furnished with zither strings, which produced pitch and compass of the cello. This instrument I was to play, which, knowing no better, I played by using the fingering of the viola. Soon thereafter I purchased a cello, and this also I played with the same fingering with which I had played the violin, viola and the (as I called it) violincello. This went on for quite a time, until Adler had been told by a real cellist that the fingering on the cello is different. The rest I had to find out myself. At once, of course, I started writing string quartets. In the meantime, *Meyers Konversations-Lexikon* (an encyclopedia, which we bought on installments) (*sic*) had reached the long-hoped-for-letter 'S', enabling me to learn under 'Sonate' how a first movement of a string quartet should be constructed. At that time I was about eighteen years old, but had not obtained any other instruction than that which Oscar Adler had given me.

Elsewhere, Schoenberg admitted that all his compositions written before his seventeenth year were no more than imitations of the music to which he had then had access, and the sole sources on which he could draw had been violin duets and arrangements (for two violins) of opera potpourris, and the music played by military bands at concerts in the public parks.

The manuscripts of a number of these early compositions, from the posthumous papers of Hans Nachod, were auctioned in Basel in June 1966: ten complete pieces and many fragments, also arrangements, for two violins, of music by other composers (including the Viennese *Fiakerlied*). One such work, of which only the second-violin and viola parts have survived, is worth mentioning for its elegantly-phrased title: *Romance en ré mineur, pour deux violons et alto par Arnaude Schoenberg, Op.* 1 (81 bars); another was a musical setting of a favourite quotation from Goethe's *Götz von Berlichingen*.[1]

In 1924, in the special Schoenberg issue of *Musikblätter des Anbruch*, the Viennese writer and music critic David Josef Bach vividly described what went on around those 'military bands in the public parks':

In front of the Erste Kaffeehaus, in the main alley of the Prater, there stood a group of young onlookers, one of whom was a young lad in a short overcoat of bright yellow, talking loudly about music and remarking, among other things, on the sounds that swept to us from the bandstand in the Café park. That is my earliest recollection of Arnold Schoenberg, an initial impression that the long years since have been unable to blur.

[1] The German equivalent of Eliza Doolittle's famous line, though one that proved even more shocking in its time. Götz, a rebel commander in one of Goethe's early plays, answers the commander of the besieging forces to the effect that 'greatly though I respect you, when you demand that I give up this fortress you may kiss my arse!' (*Leckt mich im Arsch.*) In all early editions of the play the crucial word was replaced by asterisks. L.B.

All of us, seventeen- and eighteen-year-olds, used to stand near the dividing hedge, so as to hear music for nothing. A young conductor—his name was Grossmann, unless I am mistaken—used to perform excerpts from Wagner—once, in 1891 or 1892, even from the *Mastersingers*. . . . For most of us, this was our only chance of hearing a little real music, and Schoenberg, too, made the most of the opportunity, while still a grammar-school boy—and, indeed, later, when he had run away from school before even taking his final examination. We were poor devils, but young, hungry for life, and confident about the future.

Apart from these two early friends, Oskar Adler and David Josef Bach, there was Alexander von Zemlinsky who was two years older (born in Vienna in 1872, died in 1942, in Larchmont, New York). As Schoenberg himself admitted, he owed to Zemlinsky 'almost all he knew about the technique and problems of composition'. Zemlinsky had received his musical education at the Vienna Conservatoire, from Robert Fuchs (1847–1927); even as a student he had been outstanding in all fields of music because of his wealth of invention and his sure touch in all matters to do with form and the technique of composition. One of his youthful pieces of chamber music aroused the interest of Brahms, who invited Zemlinsky to visit him, gave him valuable advice, and followed his further creative career with a kindly interest.

Schoenberg came to know Zemlinsky in the amateur orchestra *Polyhymnia*. In his *Recollections of my Youth*, Zemlinsky recorded:

The orchestra had chosen me as its conductor. It was not large: a few violins, one viola, one cello, one double-bass—or only half a one, really. Demanding though we were in all other respects, we were very pleased with the results we achieved. We were all young and hungry for music, and once a week we got together and let fly, for better or worse. Now, such societies had always existed—there was nothing unusual about it. However, at the single cello desk sat a young man, fervently ill-treating his instrument—not that the instrument deserved any better; it had been bought with three painfully saved-up Gulden at Vienna's so-called Tandelmarkt. This cellist was none other than Arnold Schoenberg. At that time Schoenberg was still a junior bank clerk, but he was not overzealous in his profession, preferring music paper to the paper-money at the bank. Thus I came to know Schoenberg, and our acquaintanceship soon developed into intimate friendship.

Schoenberg taught himself to play the cello while still at grammar school. The *Polyhymnia*, of which his performance then made him such a striking member, awarded him his first composition prize, for a work composed in 1893 (*Schilflied*— Song of the Reeds—after Nikolaus Lenau, the Austrian romantic poet).

Schoenberg worked in a small private bank from 1891 to 1895. Bach vividly describes the termination of this employment: one day Schoenberg returned home and announced to his entire family, 'I'm so happy, I've lost my job!' Ignoring the general consternation, he went on, 'You see, my boss has gone bankrupt; no one will ever get me inside a bank again!'

A year before this 'catastrophe', he had paid a visit to the blind Viennese composer Joseph Labor (1842–1924), a pupil of Simon Sechter. Labor listened while Oskar Adler and some friends performed a movement from a still unpublished C-major string quartet by Schoenberg. Bach reports: 'When the movement was finished, Labor said very calmly, 'You must become a musician!' He would not be swayed in his judgment by any objections—that Schoenberg could not play the piano, and that he was entirely self-taught.'

It was probably this string quartet that gave rise to the following anecdote, which Schoenberg used to tell in later years: when the young man showed his string quartet to a publisher, the publisher is said to have refused it with the following words: 'You seem to believe that if the second subject consists of the first subject turned upside down and played backwards, the work is all right, come what may!'

The publisher's remark does at least suggest the work's strict contrapuntal style, evidence of Schoenberg's great reverence for Brahms. This reverence expressed itself in short piano pieces (solos and duets), composed in 1895 at the suggestion of the composer and music critic Richard Heuberger (1850–1914), a member of Brahms' Viennese circle.

In *My Evolution* Schoenberg tells how his acquaintance with Zemlinsky widened his musical horizons: 'I had been a "Brahmsian" when I met Zemlinsky. His love embraced both Brahms and Wagner, and thereafter I became an equally confirmed addict. No wonder that the music I composed at that time mirrored the influence of these masters, to which a flavour of Liszt, Bruckner, and perhaps also Hugo Wolf was added.'

And in his *Thoughts about Zemlinsky* (Prague, 1921), which deal with him principally as an operatic composer, Schoenberg began by saying:

The worldly-wise, should they wish to establish exactly how much my assessment of Zemlinsky can contribute to their stock of common knowledge, would have to subtract as follows: he was my teacher, I became his friend, later his brother-in-law, and in the many years that have since gone by, he has remained the man whose behaviour I try to imagine when I need advice.

The 'instruction' which Schoenberg received from Zemlinsky until about 1900 must have consisted of Zemlinsky's explaining the classical rules of composition technique, and of Schoenberg's showing him his own compositions, which they would discuss in a friendly way. Schoenberg's String Quartet in D major, composed in the autumn of 1897, but not published until 1966, illustrates the latter point.[1] On Zemlinsky's advice Schoenberg completely reworked the first two movements, also changing many details of the finale. Only the third movement remained unaltered (Andante con moto with five variations, and two further variations which Schoenberg later struck out).

With this quartet Schoenberg first presented himself to a wider Viennese musical public. At that time Zemlinsky was on the committee of the Wiener Tonkünstlerverein, whose honorary president was Brahms, and he secured a performance at a private musical evening of the society in the 1897–8 season. Although the work was probably performed in its unrevised version by members of the society, it made so strong an impression that it was successfully repeated—in the new version—by the much-respected Fitzner Quartet at one of the society's subscription concerts.

[1] A few months earlier Schoenberg had prepared the vocal score of Zemlinsky's first opera, *Sarema*; the opera had received the Luitpold Prize in 1896 and was first performed in Munich two years later. W.R.

This encouraged Zemlinsky to take further steps, as he tells in *Reminiscences of my Youth*:

In the summer of 1899 (during a holiday together in Payerbach) Schoenberg composed a sextet, after a poem by Richard Dehmel. So far as I know, this was the earliest programme-music for chamber ensemble.[1] I again tried to persuade the committee of the Tonkünstlerverein to perform the work, but this time I had no luck. The piece was 'examined', and the results were utterly negative. A member of the jury pronounced his judgment in the following words: 'It sounds as if someone had smeared the score of *Tristan* while it was still wet!' Now, this sextet, *Transfigured Night*, has come to be one of the most frequently performed works of Schoenberg, or, indeed, in the whole literature of modern chamber music.[2] Schoenberg was not swayed by this apparent setback—a few strong and whimsical words about his critic, and the matter was over and done with for someone of his temperament, which at that time was still uncommonly cheerful and optimistic.

Not until 1903 was the work given its first performance—by the Rosé Quartet, at one of the Tonkünstlerverein's concerts.

The sheer sound of the work is undoubtedly reminiscent of late Wagner—though it does not exactly sound as if the score of *Tristan* had been smeared—but in its internal structure the influence of Brahms is stronger than any other. In *My Evolution* Schoenberg discussed this 'double nature' of the work that marks the real beginning of his instrumental output, and is therefore crucially important for a study of his entire artistic development. Among other things, Schoenberg states:

The thematic construction is based on Wagnerian 'model and sequence'-technique above a moving harmony, on the one hand, and on Brahms' technique of developing variation, as I call it, on the other. The imparity of measures[3] must also be ascribed to Brahms. . . . But the treatment of the instruments, the manner of composition, and much of the sonority were strictly Wagnerian. I think there were also some Schoenbergian elements to be found in the length of some of the melodies . . . in the sonority, in contrapuntal and motival combinations, and in the semi-contrapuntal movement of the harmony and its basses against the melody. Finally, there were already some passages of

1 Smetana's quartet *From my Life*, completed in 1879, does not follow any precise programme, but simply reflects, in its various movements, general moods and situations from the composer's life—the only exception being one particular passage in the finale. W.R.

2 Both in its original version for six solo strings, and in the version for string orchestra which Schoenberg prepared in 1917. W.R.

3 Phrases constructed with an odd number of bars, or including half bars. L.B.

7

unfixed tonality which may be considered premonitions of the future.

The work's five-section structure is very convincingly derived from the 'programme', that is to say, from the text, which is the first poem in Richard Dehmel's book of poems *Weib und Welt* (Woman and World), published in 1896. To facilitate understanding, and to help in assessing this first piece of programmatic chamber music, here is a summary of the poem's five sections.

1   Six lines.
A man and a woman walk through a bare cold wood. The moon moves along with them above the sharply pointed oak trees. The night sky is cloudless. The woman speaks:

2   Twelve lines: musically, from 'etwas bewegter', page 5 of the published score.
She had given up hope of true happiness, and, to satisfy her deep desire for a purpose in life, sought the qualified fulfilment motherhood would bring. She is with child by a man she did not love: 'now, life has had its revenge—I have met you. Walking beside you, I am guilty—toward myself and toward you.'

3   Four lines: page 25 and first 7 bars of page 26.
She walks unsteadily. As she looks up into the moon, the dark despair in her eyes is suffused with light. The man speaks:

4   Eleven lines: page 27, last two bars, to page 44, figure U.
'Don't let the thought of the child oppress you. Look at the brilliance of the universe! Everything is radiant. We are floating on a cold ocean, but there is a unique warmth uniting us that will transfigure your child and make it mine. You have brought brightness into my life: through you, I have again become as a child.'

5   Three lines.
He embraces her and they kiss each other. Then they walk on, through the 'bright, lofty night'.

The sextet was published by the Berlin firm of Dreililien in 1899, as Op. 4. It was the first of Schoenberg's works to be printed. In 1904 the same publishers brought out three sets of songs composed earlier: Two Songs for baritone and piano, Op. 1 (poems by Karl von Levetzow); Four Songs for voice and piano, Op. 2 (three songs to poems by Dehmel, the fourth to a poem by Johannes Schlaf); and Six Songs for medium voice and piano, Op. 3 (poems by Gottfried Keller, Dehmel, Jens Peter Jacobsen, and Hermann Lingg, and from *Des Knaben Wunderhorn*). Some of the songs were performed at a concert in 1898 by the Viennese singing teacher Eduard Gärtner; Zemlinsky was the accompanist. Egon Wellesz reports that after the performance there was a disturbance— a minor 'scandal' in the hall. Recalling the event in later years, Schoenberg told Wellesz, 'And since then the scandal has never stopped!'

Apart from his close contact with Zemlinsky, Schoenberg found much intellectual stimulus in lively discussions, mainly about the art of Wagner, with Viennese literary men and musicians of his own generation, whom he used to meet regularly, above all in the Café Landtmann, next door to the Burgtheater. (The Café Griensteidl, prominently mentioned in several biographies, cannot have been a possible place for these gatherings after 1896, since it was demolished that year. Karl Kraus wrote a satirical obituary of this literary café in his pamphlet *Die demolierte Literatur*, published in 1896.)

During these years about the turn of the century, Schoenberg's economic position was very precarious. The socialist music teacher Josef Scheu had secured him a position as conductor of the choir of the metal-workers' union at Stockerau, an industrial centre about twelve miles from Vienna, and this proved very satisfying artistically. He trained the choir to give faultless performances even of difficult pieces by Brahms—but it brought him in little money. His most important source of income was the orchestration of operettas, which came to him in draft, sometimes from well-known composers. He is said to have scored some thousands of pages of operetta scores about then, and a few years later he again had to devote himself to this 'creative' work.

At the end of 1899 he did however find a true creative

stimulus in a competition, instituted by the Tonkünstler-verein, for a song-cycle with piano. Zemlinsky reports:

Wishing to compete for the prize, Schoenberg composed just a few songs, after poems by Jacobsen. I played them to him. The songs were wonderfully beautiful and really original, but we both felt they were unlikely to win the prize, for that very reason. Undeterred, Schoenberg proceeded to set the whole of Jacobsen's cycle—but not for a solo voice; he added large choirs, a melodrama, preludes, interludes, and scored the whole thing for a gigantic orchestra.

The result? The *Gurrelieder*.

2 Intermezzo in Berlin

Hoping to improve his economic position, Schoenberg moved in December 1901 to Berlin where he had secured an engagement as musical director at the *Überbrettl*, part of the *Buntes Theater*,[1] founded the previous year by Ernst von Wolzogen (1855–1934). On 7 October 1901, just before the move, he married Mathilde von Zemlinsky, his friend's sister. Their first child, Gertrud, was born in Berlin in 1902. In 1921 Gertrud married Schoenberg's pupil Felix Greissle, and emigrated with him to America in 1938. She died in New York in 1947.

The leading spirits of the *Überbrettl*, apart from Wolzogen, were the poets Richard Dehmel (1863–1920), Karl von Levetzow (1871–1945), Frank Wedekind (1864–1918), and Otto Julius Bierbaum (1865–1910). The collection of poems published by Bierbaum in 1900 under the title *Deutsche Chansons* (*Brettl-Lieder*) conveys a clear idea of the kind of lyric customary at the *Überbrettl*. In his introduction to the chansons Bierbaum defines as follows the concept of 'applied lyricism' basic to the *Überbrettl's* activities:

I must admit that in placing our art at the service of the music-hall our intentions are entirely serious. We are firmly convinced the time has come for the whole of life to be permeated by art. Painters nowadays make chairs, and aim to make them not just the sort you can admire in museums but the sort you can park yourself in without discomfort to the portions of the anatomy concerned. In the same way we want to write poems that will not just be read amidst the bliss of solitude, but that can bear singing to a crowd hungry for entertainment.

Rufer's catalogue of Schoenberg's posthumous works[2] lists manuscripts of seven *Brettl*-songs by the composer: the poets were Wedekind, Bierbaum, Salus, Gustav Falke, Colly and Hochstetter. Rufer has reprinted the end of the Wedekind song 'Galathea' in facsimile facing page 80 of the catalogue.

His activities at the *Überbrettl* satisfied Schoenberg neither artistically nor materially. Once again he was obliged to spend his time scoring operettas and popular tunes. He tried several times to continue work on scoring the *Gurrelieder*, and finally abandoned the attempt. In Berlin, he made some degree of personal contact with Richard Strauss, and through the

1 Within this 'gaily coloured' theatre, itself quite small, the *Überbrettl* was an intimate theatre or cabaret. *Brettl* is the diminutive of *Brett* (board)—*die Bretten* = the boards.

2 Josef Rufer, *The works of Arnold Schoenberg* (London 1962).

latter's intervention he obtained a post as composition teacher at one of the city's most respected schools of music, the Stern Conservatoire. Strauss was also at pains to improve Schoenberg's economic position, by seeing to it that in 1902 he was awarded the Liszt Stipendium which was administered by the Allgemeiner Deutscher Musikverein.

The most valuable way in which Strauss helped Schoenberg, however, was to draw his attention to the play *Pelléas et Mélisande* (1892) by Maurice Maeterlinck (1862–1945), which struck him as promising material for an opera. Not knowing that Debussy had been working on the same subject from 1892 onward (the première of his opera was at the Paris Opéra Comique on 30 April 1902) Schoenberg began in July 1902 to set the story as a symphonic poem. In a note made in February 1950, supplementing a brief analysis of the work drawn up by him two months before, Schoenberg wrote:

I had first planned to convert *Pelléas and Mélisande* into an opera, but I gave up this plan, though I did not know that Debussy was working on his opera at the same time. I still regret that I did not carry out my initial intention. It would have differed from Debussy's. I might have missed the wonderful perfume of the poem; but I might have made my characters more singing.

On the other hand, the symphonic poem helped me, in that it taught me to express moods and characters in precisely formulated units, a technique that my opera would perhaps not have promoted so well.

Thus my fate evidently guided me with great foresight.

In 1920, fifteen years after Schoenberg had conducted the work's first performance (in Vienna), the publishers Universal Edition brought out a 'short thematic analysis' of it by Alban Berg, in which he demonstrated, with twenty extensive musical examples, that this symphonic poem was constructed in a strictly symphonic way, while still exactly matching the events of the drama. He showed the first part of the symphonic poem to be a sonata form exposition (with repeat): introduction (In the Forest), First subject (Golaud), second subject (Pelléas), and codetta with its own subject (awakening of love in Mélisande). Part 2: three pieces, representing scherzo and dramatic peripeteia (scene at the fountain, scene in the castle tower, scene in the subterranean vaults). An introductory passage, akin to a development, leads to Part 3: Quasi Adagio (Farewell and love scene between Pelléas and Mélisande). Part 4: recapitulation of Part 1, and reprise of the Adagio theme, leading to the scene at Mélisande's deathbed. Epilogue (in three parts: first subject, development of material from Parts 2 and 3, reprise of the opening of the epilogue).

Another feature worth mentioning is the lavish instrumental forces required (17 woodwind, 18 brass, 8 percussion, 64 strings, 2 harps); they are exceeded only by those in the *Gurrelieder*. It must have been about this time that the composer began to realise how pointless it would be to carry such lavishness any further. From 1904 onward Schoenberg's works show an ever more decided turn toward a new and looser instrumental style.

The things Schoenberg had to show for his stay in Berlin, which ended with his return to Vienna in July 1903, were, basically, the composition of one major work—the symphonic poem *Pelléas and Mélisande* (completed at the end of February 1903), and the first practical demonstration of his genius for teaching, which over the ensuing decade was to bring forth fruit a hundredfold.

3 Storm and Stress in Vienna

When Schoenberg returned to Vienna in 1903 the situation in the arts—and not only in the arts—was dominated by a philistinism which regarded anything new as automatically suspect. The first determined act of revolt against this state of affairs had been in 1897, when a number of important painters and sculptors founded the Secession, breaking away from the group of artists centred around the *Künstlerhaus* who were more anxious that their products should be commercially exploited than that they should develop in any progressive way. In 1903 the architect Adolf Loos (1870–1933) founded a periodical intended to break through the wall that shut off Austria from the new artistic ideas and movements in other countries; its title was *Das Andere. Ein Blatt zur Einführung abendländischer Kultur in Österreich: geschrieben von Adolf Loos* ('The Other: a paper for the introduction of Western Culture into Austria. Author Adolf Loos'). It ran to only two issues, extracts from which are reprinted in the second volume of Loos's collected writings (*Trotzdem*—'For all that'—Innsbruck, 1930). In 1903–4 the poet Peter Altenberg, an intimate friend of Loos, brought out an illustrated periodical with the title *Kunst. Halbmonatsschrift für Kunst und alles andere* ('Art; a fortnightly magazine for art and everything else[1]'). Almost all the contributions were by himself and Loos. The cover bore the motto 'Natura artis magistra'. The opening paragraph of Altenberg's introduction to the first number ran thus:

[1] Or everything 'other', 'different'. Cf above. L.B.

Art! Until now, you have been like a noble phantom, like a weird and wonderful ghost, rising up in the streets by the clear light of day, in front of people who are busy—all too busy. So far removed from their everyday existence, so unrelated to their ever-present, ever-effective instinct of self-preservation! A languid superfluous thing, created by grace of the superfluous artist! Luxurious trifling! We want to bring you to life, put you in contact with everyday life—Art, you anaemic, fleshless ghost! We want to let you loose during working hours, so that you fructify and enrich the lives of ordinary men!

After about eight issues, the periodical changed hands and became an advertising magazine for gramophones and photographic accessories.

The following lines from Paul Stefan's book *Das Grab in Wien* ('The Viennese Grave', Berlin 1913), may indicate the situation in literature and music:

Poets who had formerly been at the centre of Viennese youth only achieved wider recognition because of their Berlin publishers, and Berlin theatres. As ever, the plays of Hofmannsthal, Beer-Hofmann and Schnitzler would first be performed in Berlin, after which Vienna still did nothing. Often, so far as our theatre managements could see, they were not enough of a certainty, and the leading papers carried unfavourable reports about the experiments going on out there. One really learned very little about the various movements in the Empire, about Berlin, Munich, Paris, and what one did learn was mostly through uncomprehending, distorted reports from particularly clever or particularly facetious correspondents. Again, the decisive factor affecting musical performances and programmes was the taste of an outmoded literary dilettantism. The ranks of the damned began as early as Liszt, and Brahms had filled the last vacancy among the saints. Bruckner: a war-cry. His symphonies had, indeed, finally been performed by Mahler, even at the Vienna Philharmonic's concerts, and the newly formed Konzertverein, under Ferdinand Löwe, performed him most devotedly and assiduously at their musical evenings; these were cheap, and welcome as a release from the stranglehold of the Philharmonic. But the men in power strongly disapproved!

Young people in academic circles tried to fight this philistinism by founding various societies modelled on the Secession. An Academic Society for Art and Literature arranged performances of various stage-works not previously seen in Vienna. This auspicious venture came to an abrupt halt, however, when the directors of the Viennese theatres, fearing competition, forbade their actors to take part in the society's promotions.

The Ansorge Society, founded in 1903, devoted a considerable part of its activities to music. It was named after the pianist and composer Conrad Ansorge (1862–1930), who lived in Berlin; he was known to very few people in Vienna, and the Society set great store by encouraging him; but, *Sorge* being the German word for 'care', the name Ansorge also came to symbolise the Society's apprehensions about the future of the new art. The society's leading spirits were Paul Stefan and Wilhelm von Wymetal.

Some of Schoenberg's songs were performed by this Society early in 1904. It was the first time his music had been heard since his return from Berlin. The Society also planned to give the first performance of Schoenberg's sextet *Transfigured Night* but, as already mentioned (page 7), the performance was taken over by the *Tonkünstlerverein* and repeated shortly afterwards by Arnold Rosé at one of his chamber music evenings. This première also led to the first meeting between Schoenberg and Mahler. Rosé, Mahler's brother-in-law, used to rehearse with his colleagues in a room at the Court Opera. Mahler, having heard of the work from Rosé, came to a rehearsal and was strongly impressed. Schoenberg, who was introduced to him on this occasion, immediately won his sympathy. Time and again Mahler stood up for Schoenberg's art, although, as he himself confessed, he could not always follow his artistic development.

Shortly afterwards Schoenberg and Zemlinsky themselves took energetic measures to improve the musical situation in Vienna. They founded a Society of Creative Musicians, and persuaded Mahler not only to become Honorary President, but also to conduct at the Society's concerts. The foundation of the Society was announced in March 1904 in a circular, whose principal author was probably Schoenberg himself. Since this circular has not been quoted in any publication known to me, I here reproduce it in full. Passages here printed in italics were originally in bold print or double-spaced; the division into paragraphs is as in the original.

In Vienna's musical life, very little attention is given to the works of contemporary composers, especially Viennese ones. As a rule, new works are heard in Vienna only after doing the rounds of Germany's many musically active towns, great and small—and even then they usually meet with little interest, indeed with hostility.

There is a crass contrast between this state of affairs and Vienna's musical past, when she used to set the tone; the usual explanation is that the public seem to feel an insuperable distaste for everything new. Vienna is not the place for novelties—

that is the story, and the people who say so seem, at first glance, to be in the right if one disregards the operetta, a field in which our city does set the tone, beyond a doubt.

One thing, though: in musical life, since time immemorial, anything new has had to overcome greater and more passionate resistance than in other fields. Nearly all the works nowadays generally acclaimed—but particularly those one must regard as milestones in the development of music—met, when still new, with a cold or even hostile reception, and were felt to lack beauty, to be confused and incoherent. One need think only of Beethoven's *Eroica*, or Ninth Symphony, or late quartets; Bach's works, or those of Wagner and Brahms!

Now, this is not to say that every work received with indifference, or rejected, is of great and epoch-making importance. But a work does not have to be the Ninth Symphony in order to be misunderstood; the case of the Ninth Symphony proves that it is unsafe to base one's conclusions about a new work's artistic importance on first impressions, and that many a presentday work, rejected or laughed out of court at its first performance, *can* be liable, on closer acquaintance, to make one change one's mind completely.

After all, music of any kind can only make its effect if there is an inner relationship between the work and the listener; not only the work's qualities, but the listener's, too, are of decisive importance in producing this. The listener's powers of musical thought and feeling must be able to rise to the demands imposed by the work, just as the work must meet all one's own demands, be everything one asks of an artistic work.

So the most pressing need, if the musical public is to establish any kind of relationship with presentday music, is the need for familiarity with this music's special qualities—just as it took familiarity with classical music to bring about a relationship between such music and the public. There is, indeed, a small section of the public that is still completely uncultivated, so that for the moment its musical horizons stop short at light music; even today, it finds classical music boring.

All progress, all development, leads from the simple to the complex, and the latest developments in music are the very ones to increase all those difficulties and obstacles against which anything new in music has always had to battle; since this music is more complex, and its harmony and melody more concentrated, there are more obstacles, and they have increased in size, so that numerous, repeated, first-class performances are needed in order to overcome them, even assuming the listener to be receptive (and that is a matter both of ability and of willingness). Such performances need preparation which must be extraordinarily exact, and strictly in accordance with the composer's intentions.

But this will remain impossible, so long as the programmes of established concert-promoters continue to include the occasional new work merely as a kind of curiosity or monstrosity. These works need an artistic setting that would deal *exclusively* with presentday works; *a permanent home where the new would be fostered.*

Only regular performances of new works can show whether interest in the output of the present day can be awakened and kept awake in musical circles; whether the Viennese musical public, like that of many German musical centres, great and small, will sympathise with—or perhaps even take pleasure in—new works, which so far have either remained completely unknown in Vienna, or else have been laid aside after a single performance.

There are, however, further factors, of a more outward nature, that have up to now prevented presentday music from being intensively cultivated in Vienna.

Music differs from the visual arts in that, to attract a public, the creative artist requires the performing artist as middleman; but performers and their associations choose programmes primarily with their own artistic and material interests in mind, preferring for the most part to put on works of proven effectiveness, which the public has already taken to its heart; their sole guide, should they choose anything new, is their own insight, critical faculties, and—last but not least—good will. All this is understandable.

The possibilities of performing modern music are still further reduced because the existing concert agents and promoters, who are in most cases the middlemen between the artist and the public, likewise influence the choice of programmes as much as they can, with an eye to their own financial advantage; everything that seems unlikely to offer them an almost certain box office success they try to exclude. The free development of Viennese musical life finds its special enemies in such people; as a result of these 'factors', with their identical and never-changing programmes, the general public have already begun to stop being interested in music at all.

If all these outward obstacles to a free expansion of productive musical energies are to be removed, the people nearest to music—the creators—may not be permanently excluded from actual musical life. They must take steps to replace their indirect, distorted relationship with the public by one that will be *direct*, like the one the painters and sculptors long since achieved, to the great benefit of art.

And, just as in the latter case it took organisation, collective action, to achieve what no one could ever have achieved on his own—emancipation from the art dealers—so, too, do composers need to close their ranks and act together.

The majority of the creative musicians in Vienna have therefore resolved to found a society which aims

to create such a direct relationship between itself and the public; to give modern music a permanent home in Vienna, where it will be fostered; and to keep the public constantly informed about the current state of musical composition.

The society will pursue these aims by promoting public performances of artistically important new works, and of others which, it is convinced, Vienna has not yet assessed at their true value. It is to bear in mind Austrian and German composers particularly.

In choosing works to be performed, no 'movement'[1] or stylistic genre will be specially preferred; since a work's artistic stature has nothing to do with adherence to any movement or school, there will be performances of works from the classicist school and from the new-German, and works of Apollinian, as of Dionysian, tendencies, insofar as they manifest *a powerful artistic personality, expressing itself in a manner that is formally above reproach*.

As for the public, let them judge the works presented to them, not by whether they are easier or harder to comprehend, nor by how suave, or otherwise, their language is, but solely and simply *by the degree of artistry manifest in them; by the magnitude of the artistic achievement these works record*.

Apart from the circular's general importance in Vienna's cultural history, it has a threefold significance—as probably being Schoenberg's first published literary pronouncement; as the obvious prototype of the prospectus devised in 1919 by Berg for the Society for Private Musical Performances (cf page 120), which Schoenberg founded in Vienna in November 1918; and as a timeless document dealing with the encouragement of contemporary music. In this last respect it is still fully relevant even today.

The Viennese Society of Creative Musicians, announced

1 *'Richtung'*—literally 'direction'. L.B.

by the circular, in fact survived for one season only (1904–5), in the course of which it did, however, give two orchestral concerts and three chamber concerts. Among the works performed, with Mahler conducting, were Strauss's *Domestic Symphony* and Mahler's *Kindertotenlieder* and songs from *Des Knaben Wunderhorn*; and on 16 January 1905 Schoenberg conducted the first performance of his symphonic poem *Pelléas and Mélisande*.

For Schoenberg, back home again, it was very hard to get started on any new composition. A string quartet and a piece for men's voices—*Georg von Frundsberg*, a companion piece to the song from Op. 3, with the same title—got no further than preliminary sketches. However, the group of eight songs, Op. 6, for voice and piano (texts by Julius Hart, Dehmel, Paul Remer, Hermann Conradi, Gottfried Keller, John Henry Mackay, Kurt Aram and Nietzsche) was completed between 1903 and 1905, and he had meanwhile composed the six orchestral songs Op. 8 (1904: texts by Heinrich Hart, by Petrarch and from *Des Knaben Wunderhorn*); although these are still for a fairly large orchestra, there are already the first hints of a new approach to construction, favouring more transparent linear writing; this emerges particularly clearly from the piano scores prepared by Webern in 1911.

Schoenberg spent the summer of 1904 at Mödling, near Vienna, where he was later to settle permanently, and began work on his D minor string quartet (which he called his First String Quartet, Op. 7). He completed it at Gmunden, on the Traunsee, the following summer. It was first performed on 5 February 1907, in Vienna, by the Rosé Quartet. Paul Stefan reports:

To many people, the work seemed impossible, and they left the hall while it was being played; one particularly witty person left by the emergency exit. At the end, moreover, people could be heard hissing. Mahler was seated among them, and, immediately up in arms at this artistic injustice, he set upon one of the dissatisfied customers, telling him, with his wonderfully emotional involvement 'It's not for you to hiss!' The stranger, who would have been meek as a lamb in front of his own caretaker, was full of pride when faced by a spiritual monarch, and replied, 'I hiss at your symphonies too!' This scene was held very much against Mahler.

In the same year the work was played by the Rosé Quartet at a matinée during the Dresden festival of the German Society of Musicians. Here, too, it was loudly hissed. The *Neue Musik-Zeitung* (Stuttgart) took this as its cue to comment as follows:

The public had good reason to reject the work. After listening for three-quarters of an hour, most of which was highly painful, they were further provoked by insistent applause from a few of the composer's friends. They had been very patient, but this was too much, and the public forgot that at such music festivals the usual laws do not apply; a moment of irritation made them forget their manners which usually put many a critic to shame.

The astonishing thing about this severely adverse judgment is that the quartet Op. 7 carries on from Beethoven's works in a way that is emphatic and clearly audible even at a first hearing; it is thus directly in line with the traditions of the classics. For this reason Berg took his stand on this particular work when he added his tribute—'Why is Schoenberg's music so hard to understand?' (An article reprinted in my biography of Berg)—to the Schoenberg commemorative volume of 1924; he used the following words to justify his full and highly perceptive analysis of the work's first 28 bars.

I will be reproached with having proved something in this investigation where no proof was called for: namely the difficulty of the Quartet in D minor, a 'tonal' work that stopped being a problem long ago, a work in fact that has on the contrary been generally recognised and hence—understood! Well, even though the validity of that is questionable, I admit that the question at the head of this article would only really be answered if I were to demonstrate what I have shown on the basis of these few minor-key bars with reference to at least one example of so-called 'atonal' music. But it was not only a question of the difficulty but also—as readers of my analysis must have realised—a question of proving that the means of this music, despite the fact that much in it is felt to be particularly difficult to understand, are all right and proper: right and proper, naturally, in connection with the highest art! And it was of course easier to show this with regard to an example rooted in major/minor tonality, which nevertheless—an advantage in this connection—occasioned as much outrage in its day as 'atonal' music does today. [Trans. Cornelius Cardew]

In 1924 Berg was naturally concerned above all to show that the works which Schoenberg had composed since 1909 were so hard to understand not because of their so-called 'atonality', but—as before—because of their general structure: 'The wealth of artistic resources once again used throughout this so-called "atonal" style, the summing-up of all the possibilities offered the composer by the music of whole centuries: in a word, its immeasurable wealth.'

Consequently, the results of Berg's analysis of the Op. 7 quartet can be applied equally to the 'atonal' style of 1924 and to the absolutely tonal style of the 1905 quartet—the work that interests us at this point. One can, accordingly, sum up this work in Berg's words:

1 *Vielstufigkeit*: the presence of chords based on many different 'degrees' (*Stufen*) of the scale. The idea of 'degrees' was basic to Schoenberg's view of tonal harmony, as set down in the *Harmonielehre*. L.B.

Here too we find the same multiplicity in the harmony, the same multi-level definition[1] of the cadence; here too the unsymmetrical and completely free construction of themes, together with their unflagging motivic work; here too the art of variation, affecting both thematic work and harmonisation, both counterpoint and rhythm of this music; here too the same polyphony extending over the whole work, and the inimitable contrapuntal technique; here too, finally, the diversity and differentiation of the rhythms, of which we can only say again that besides being subject to their own laws, they are subject also to the laws of variation, thematic development, counterpoint, and polyphony. [Trans. Cornelius Cardew]

Among the sketches dating from about the time of the quartet, or just after, special mention should be made of a draft opening (36 bars of prelude and 31 bars of recitative) to an opera after Gerhart Hauptmann's legend *Und Pippa tanzt*. As we know, Berg, after completing *Wozzeck*, also planned to set *Und Pippa tanzt*, but he abandoned this plan in favour of *Lulu* in 1927.

Schoenberg's next major work was the First Chamber Symphony (Op. 9, in E major), which he completed in 1906.

He himself regarded this work as the climax of his first stylistic period, his reason being that here he had achieved 'the perfect amalgamation of melody with harmony, in that both of them participate equally in melting down more outlying tonal relationships to form a unity, and draw logical conclusions from the problems with which they have landed themselves; this means, at the same time, a major step toward the "emancipation of the dissonance" '.

This Chamber Symphony is of fundamental importance for Schoenberg's creative development also in two other respects. In the first place, its modest instrumental forces (flute, oboe, cor anglais, two clarinets, bassoon, contra-bassoon, two horns, and string quintet), used for the most part as in chamber music, show how emphatically Schoenberg had turned away from the gigantic orchestras of *Pelléas and Mélisande* and the *Gurrelieder*. Secondly, the systematic use of fourth-chords adds an important new harmonic element to Schoenberg's musical language. The composer himself explained this second point in his *Treatise on Harmony*, quoted here in the slightly simpler 1921 version:

Inspired by the desire to express riotous rejoicing, the fourths here form themselves into a resolute horn theme; they spread architectonically over the entire work, and leave their imprint on all that occurs. And so it is that, here, they no longer appear merely as melody or as purely impressionistic chordal effects; their special quality permeates the entire harmonic construction—they are chords like all the others.

The first Chamber Symphony is also important in that it prompted the composer to make his educational experiment of 1918 (cf pages 113–16).

This work is performed without a break, but has five distinct sections. Alban Berg examined its formal structure closely, quoting twenty-three examples from the score, in a thematic analysis published by Universal Edition in 1913. He arrived at two equally valid interpretations. In his first interpretation, he treats the five sections as elements of a symphony in several movements: 1. Sonata exposition (with first subject, transition, second subject, and codetta subject); 2. Scherzo; 3. Development of the thematic material presented in the exposition; 4. Quasi adagio; 5. Finale (recapitulation and coda). In Berg's second interpretation the work is seen as just one, the first, movement of a sonata, with exposition, development and recapitulation, the scherzo and the adagio being regarded as long episodes interpolated between, respectively, exposition and development, and development and recapitulation. Berg says:

> Whichever of these two explanations may be nearer the mark, it is in any case true that the work's form (one which seems to have been created in a single continuous access of inspiration, and which is that of a whole: articulated, indeed, but impossible to break down) results as much from the *constant* references back to earlier thematic components (not only in the closing section but also in the long development in the middle of the work, and elsewhere within the developing portions of each individual section)—these components being continually varied melodically, harmonically and contrapuntally—as from the dovetailing (done ever differently, but always most compellingly) of the individual sections within this single long movement (sections that are, obviously, also made to stand in a unified harmonic relationship with each other).

1 *Zusammenhang*, also translatable as 'unity' or 'relatedness'. L.B.

2 *Fasslichkeit*— literally, 'grasp-ability'. L.B.

These words of Berg's hinge on the idea of 'cohesion'[1] (or, as Schoenberg called it 'coherence') which, together with the idea of 'comprehensibility'[2], was crucial to Schoenberg's creative work as well as to his teaching. In *My Evolution* he pointed out certain particularly subtle thematic relationships in the Chamber Symphony, adding as a general remark:

Externally, coherence manifests itself through an intelligible application of the relationship and similarity inherent in musical configurations. What I believe, in fact, is that if one has done his duty with the utmost sincerity and has worked out everything as near to perfection as he is capable of doing, then the Almighty presents him with a gift, with additional features of beauty, such as he never could have produced by his talents alone.

Before we examine Schoenberg's further creative development, a few words should be said about his teaching, since his genius was as compellingly effective in this field as in his own creative activities.

Schoenberg began to teach in Vienna as early as 1904. At first he gave classes, using rooms made available to him by Dr Eugenie Schwarzwald at the girls' school she had founded in the Regierungsgasse (1st district of Vienna). Recalling the earliest days of the 'Viennese School', Egon Wellesz relates (*Österreichische Musikzeitung*, May 1960), that the majority of those attending were from the Institute of Studies in Musical History at Vienna University. Guido Adler, the director of the Institute, was an old friend of Mahler's, and it must have been Mahler who brought Schoenberg to Adler's attention. Schoenberg seems to have been dissatisfied with this teaching, because too few of his students had any talent for composition. After a year, he abandoned the classes, and the really talented pupils then came to him privately. Wellesz describes the scene, from his own experience:

It was an afternoon, in October 1905. A small, dark room facing onto the courtyard, at No. 68-70, Liechtensteinstrasse. Arnold Schoenberg, cigarette in hand, his head inclined, pacing ceaselessly to and fro. On a chest, a parcel of unusually large music paper—the still incomplete score of the *Gurre-lieder*. On the music desk of the piano, the recently published vocal score of Strauss's *Salome*, open at the first page. Schoenberg said, 'Perhaps in twenty years' time someone will be able to explain these harmonic progressions theoretically'. That was my first impression of him when, during the second year of my studies at the University, I visited him at his home for lessons in counterpoint.

A year before, in the autumn of 1904, Anton Webern (1883-1945), a student of musicology at the University since 1902, had become a pupil of Schoenberg. Alban Berg (1885-1935) went to him at almost the same time. Berg's brother Charly had heard about Schoenberg through a newspaper advertisement in which Schoenberg offered his services as teacher of musical theory and composition. Charly secretly got hold of some of his brother's songs and took them to Schoenberg who, after having looked at the compositions, invited Alban to visit him. Until then Berg had taught himself. Now Schoenberg took him on as his pupil. At first he taught him for nothing. And he did not accept any fee until the end of 1905, when the fortunes of the Berg family improved.

When working on my first book about Berg in 1936 I sent a copy of the manuscript to Schoenberg in Hollywood, asking him to honour the book with a preface. He was kind enough to agree straight away, but several months later I heard from him, indirectly, to the effect that pressure of his own work, and the rapidly approaching deadline, prevented him from getting his text ready in time. However, his posthumous papers contained an incomplete draft of this preface, which Mrs Gertrud Schoenberg made available to me; and I here reproduce a few passages, dealing with Berg's time as a pupil.

Two things emerged clearly even from Berg's earliest compositions, however awkward they may have been: first, that music was to him a language, and that he really expressed himself in that language; and secondly, overflowing warmth of feeling. . . . It was a pleasure to teach him. He was industrious, eager, and did everything in the best possible way. . . . I could do counterpoint with him in a manner rare amongst my pupils. . . . The instruction in composition that followed proceeded effortlessly and smoothly up to and including the Sonata. Then problems began to appear, the nature of which neither of us understood then. I know it today: obviously Alban, who had occupied himself extraordinarily intensively with contemporary music, with Mahler, Strauss, perhaps even Debussy whose work I did not know, but certainly with my music—it is sure that Alban had a burning desire to express himself no longer in the classical forms . . . but in a manner in accordance with the times, and with his own personality, which had been developing in the meantime. A hitch was apparent in his creative activity. . . .

That was the time when I moved to Berlin (1911) and he was left to his own devices. He has shown that he was equal to the task. [Trans. Cornelius Cardew]

To convey some idea of what Schoenberg gave his pupils during this, probably the most 'approachable' period of his teaching career, here are a few quotations from the book *Arnold Schoenberg*, dedicated to him (in 1912) 'with the deepest reverence', by his pupils, and by other artists who were in close contact with him.

ERWIN STEIN: Schoenberg teaches one to think. He prompts his pupil to open his eyes and see for himself, as if he were the first person ever to examine the phenomenon in question. Whatever has been thought so far is not to be the norm. Even if our way of thinking is no better than others', what matters is not absolute truth, but the search for truth.

ANTON WEBERN: People think Schoenberg teaches his own style and forces the pupil to adopt it. That is quite untrue—Schoenberg teaches no style of any kind; he preaches the use neither of old artistic resources nor of new ones. He says, 'What is the point of teaching how to master everyday cases? The pupil learns how to use something he dare not use if he wants to be an artist. But one cannot give him what matters most—the courage and the strength to find an attitude to things which will make everything he looks at into an exceptional case, because of the way he looks at it'.[1] But this 'thing that matters most' is what Schoenberg's pupils do indeed receive. Schoenberg demands, above all, that what the pupil writes for his lessons should not consist of any old notes written down to fill out an academic form, but should be something achieved as the result of his need for self-expression. So he has, in fact, to create—even in the musical examples written during the most primitive initial stages. Whatever Schoenberg explains with reference to his pupil's work arises organically from the work itself; he never has recourse to extraneous theoretical maxims.

So Schoenberg does in fact educate his student as a creator. With the utmost energy, he tracks down the pupil's personality, seeking to deepen it, to help it break through—in short, 'to give the pupil the courage and the strength to find an attitude to things which will make everything he looks at into an exceptional case, because of the *way* he looks at it'. It is an education in utter truthfulness with oneself.

KARL HORWITZ: 'Don't try to learn anything from this—rather learn from Mozart, Beethoven, and Brahms! Then, perhaps, some of the things contained here will strike you as worthy of consideration'. These words Arnold Schoenberg wrote down in my copy of his First String Quartet (Op. 7). I have discovered their meaning during my student years with him.

KARL LINKE: Here is the basis of Schoenberg's way of teaching: he lets the pupil find out. And only what one has found out for oneself is entirely one's own. What one has wrung from

1 Webern was quoting from Schoenberg's essay *Probleme des Kunstunterrichtes* (Problems in teaching art), which had appeared in 1911. W.R.

music, through zeal and hard work, one has for good, even if the composition concerned is a failure. One's strength has increased; what matter if ten, twenty battles are still needed before one wins? . . .

I once took to a lesson a song whose difficulty was my main reason for being so fond of it. Schoenberg said, 'Did you really think of it as this complicated?' A pupil always answers that kind of question in the affirmative, for he feels flattered. But Schoenberg was unrelenting: 'What I mean is, was this complicated kind of accompaniment unequivocally implied in your initial idea?' A pupil does not always answer that kind of question in the affirmative, because he realises how near the mark it is. I tried to remember what my first idea had been. However, Schoenberg, encouraged by my uncertainty, went on, 'Didn't you add this figure afterwards, to clothe a harmonic skeleton? Rather the way people stick façades onto houses?' He was right, too. It emerged that my idea had been merely a harmonic one, and not of the kind compellingly to create movement.

'Then, look, accompany the song simply harmonically, It will look primitive, but it will be more genuine. Because what you have here is decoration. Three-part inventions, decorated with a vocal part. But music must not decorate, it must simply be true. Wait patiently for an idea, one you are immediately aware of rhythmically, in the horizontal. You'll be amazed at the motive power an idea of that kind has. Look at the Schubert song *Auf dem Flusse*—the way one movement generates another! And another thing: nothing should ever seem difficult. What you compose must be as obvious to you as your hands and your clothes. You shouldn't put pen to paper before that. The simpler your things seem to you, the better they'll be. Some time, you should bring me the pieces of work you don't want to show anyone, because you find them too simple and artless. I'll prove to you that they're truer than these. You see, I can only start from things of that kind, things that are organic to you, that's to say self-evident. If you have written something you find very complicated, then you'd better doubt its genuineness straightaway.' After having been shown up like this a few times, the student is fanatically severe with his ideas. He hears his compositions through in an exact way, and that is what matters.

1 *bildet*—literally, 'forms'.
L.B.

HEINRICH JALOWETZ: Schoenberg *educates*[1] his pupils, in the deepest sense of the word; so compelling is the human contact he involuntarily establishes with every one that his pupils flock around him as the disciples around their Master. Others, too, have their indissoluble links with their teachers—some universal panacea to do with fingering, perhaps, or a new thorough-bass figuring. However we want to emphasize something quite different by calling ourselves 'Schoenberg-pupils'. We know, rather, that the essence of the man has affected the thoughts and feelings of all those who call themselves his pupils, and, because of this, we feel a certain spiritual bond between all of us. For anyone who has been his pupil, his name is no mere reminder of student days: it is one's artistic and human conscience.

A quotation from an essay, 'Unser Lehrer Arnold Schoenberg', published in the *Schweizerische Musikzeitung* by his pupil and son-in-law Felix Greissle on the occasion of Schoenberg's sixtieth birthday, shows that in his teaching Schoenberg continued to maintain this attitude of mind:

A while ago somebody asked me: what precisely had we learned from Schoenberg, and why should he be so famous as a teacher? At the time I found myself at a loss for an adequate answer. And yet one single sentence could have summed it up: *Schoenberg taught us to think straight.* To think straight—his basic demand, his criterion in judging what one had achieved. All the trouble he took with us boiled down, essentially, to teaching us to think straight. But not only as musicians. For it goes without saying: once a man can think straight—logically—he will always do so, whatever he is doing. To be able to think straight: is it not one of the hardest things, the prime and ultimate condition for the success of an enterprise? And, getting to the heart of the matter, does not the essence of Schoenberg lie in his strict, remorseless, unassailable logic? Even as we learned harmony and counterpoint from him, he passed on to us something far more valuable than mere specialist knowledge and technique. To him, music was simply and truly a pretext for teaching more important, fundamental things. He talked to us about the construction of a musical form, and suddenly we noticed that he had shown us the very laws of organic structure as such. We learned from him that, in the last event, it always comes down to the same thing; the conditions governing the creation of a work are the same in all branches of art, and they differ in no way from the conditions according to which a house or a machine is built. He himself once said to us, 'A really good musician must be able to pilot an aeroplane, even if he has never sat in one before!' Maybe this was a joke, but with him a joke was always the subtlest way of showing that he was serious.

Early in 1907, shortly after the first performance of the Op. 7 quartet (cf page 20), the Chamber Symphony Op. 9 also received its first performance. The Rosé Quartet joined forces with the wind principals of the Court Opera. Part of the public showed its displeasure by noisily leaving the large hall of the Musikverein during the performance. The Vienna correspondent of the Berlin *Vossische Zeitung* noted in his review that he had not taken part in the Vienna carnival season, but, 'so as not to lose touch completely with the spirit of Eternal Foolery, had listened to Mr Schoenberg's Chamber Symphony'. About the same time, however, an evening of songs at the Ehrbar Hall was highly successful, with singers from the Court Opera, accompanied by Zemlinsky in songs from Opp. 2, 3, and 6. The tickets carried a printed reminder that they only 'entitled the holder to listen quietly, and not to make his views known aloud (by applauding or hissing)'.

New works dating from this period are: the two ballads for voice and piano, Op. 12, *Der verlorene Haufen*[1] (words by Viktor Klemperer); *Jane Grey* (words by Heinrich Ammann), and the chorus for mixed voices, at times dividing into eight parts, *Friede auf Erden* (Peace on Earth), Op. 13, to words by Conrad Ferdinand Meyer. The first ballad was Schoenberg's (unsuccessful) entry for a competition in which the Berlin periodical *Die Woche* offered a prize for the best new ballad. Then, about the turn of the year 1907–8, he composed two songs for voice and piano Op. 14—*Ich darf nicht dankend an dir niedersinken* (words by Stefan George) and *In diesen Wintertagen* (words by Georg Henckell). The first of the songs is also noteworthy as, along with the third and fourth movements of the quartet Op. 10, it shows Schoenberg beginning to set poems by Stefan George.

Schoenberg himself described the two ballads Op. 12 as the direct forerunners of the second String Quartet, in F sharp minor, Op. 10, which leads to the second period in his creative career, the so-called 'atonal' period. In *My*

1 This title could be roughly translated 'The Dispensables': in the poem, legionaries take a last drink before going into battle. Their side will win, but they know that by the end of it most of them will be dead. L.B.

Evolution, Schoenberg said this about the quartet (which will be discussed at length later on):

In the first and second movements there are many sections in which the individual parts proceed regardless of whether or not their meeting results in codified harmonies. Still, here, and also in the third and fourth movements, the key is presented distinctly at all the main dividing points of the formal organisation. Yet the overwhelming multitude of dissonances cannot be balanced any longer by occasional returns to such tonal triads as represent a key. It seemed inadequate to force a movement into the Procrustean bed of a tonality without supporting it by harmonic progressions that pertain to it. This was my concern, and it should have occupied the mind of all my contemporaries also. That I was the first to venture the decisive step will not be considered universally a merit—a fact I regret but have to ignore.

Since, later on, 'atonality' itself will be discussed less than the transition from atonality to twelve-tone music, this seems the place to sum up the discussion of atonality, by quoting a contribution from Alban Berg. It has a rather strange history. Early in 1930 Berg was invited by the Vienna Radio to discuss, with an interviewer nominated by them, the question 'What is "atonal"?' Berg did not entirely trust this interviewer, and wished to present him, as far as possible, with a *fait accompli*. So he arranged with me a 'dress rehearsal' of the interview at his home, and hardly allowed me to get a word in. His words were taken down in shorthand by a lady-friend of mine, and were then given to the broadcaster to help him formulate his questions. Berg presented me with copies of the shorthand notes, and of the interview which took place on 23 April 1930. I printed the interview in my Viennese musical periodical *23*, in June 1936, and I appended the essential content of the shorthand notes to the memorial article I published in the *Schweizerische Musikzeitung* (February 1945) on the sixtieth anniversary of Berg's birth. As the war was still on, this text went almost unnoticed; excerpts are reprinted below. Apart from anything else, it is important as showing the strong sense of tradition that inspired Schoenberg and his pupils. I should point out, incidentally, that the invectives against 'atonal' music quoted and refuted by Berg were remarks that had in fact appeared in the Viennese press. What Berg said was, in essence, this:

The first use of the term 'atonal' can only have been to describe a kind of music whose harmonic course (as the word clearly suggests) did not conform to the laws of tonality familiar till then. It was doubtlessly meant to be a derogatory description, as in the case of the words a-rhythmic, a-melodic, a-symmetrical, which became current at the same time. But whereas these words could only be used to distinguish the occasional, special case, the term 'atonal' unfortunately became a portmanteau word indicating music that was assumed not only to be unrelated to a harmonic centre, but also to defy all the other musical requirements such as melody, rhythm, small-scale and large-scale formal articulation; so nowadays the term is really equivalent to 'non-music, no music at all'. And in fact people imagine 'atonal' music to be the opposite of everything previous understood by the word.

The impossibility of harmonically relating this so-called 'atonal' music to a major or minor key does not necessarily mean that the 'atonal' works of the last twenty-five years are without some harmonic centre—though, naturally, such a concept is not identical with the idea of the old-fashioned tonic. Even if, with the loss of major and minor, a few harmonic possibilities have been lost, all the other requirements for real and genuine music have remained.

The main thing to show—one may as well begin with the crucial point—is that the melody, the principal part, the theme, is the basis, or determines the course, of this, as of all other, music. Naturally, a melody allying itself to a harmony that is rich in degrees,[1] and bold—the two are much the same—can easily look 'crabbed' to a person who does not understand this harmonic explanation. That applies no less to strongly chromatic music; hundreds of passages in Wagner's music could serve as examples. But the melodic style of this so-called 'atonal' music seems to differ from that of previous music in yet another respect: I refer to asymmetry of melodic articulation. This art of asymmetrical melodic construction, which is very frequently found as early as Mozart, developed increasingly during the nineteenth century. Although four-bar periodic structure predominates in Wagner and his imitators, the tendency to rely less on such two- and four-bar structure is also particularly apparent about the same time. In this respect, a

[1] cf. note to p.22.
L.B.

straight line leads from Mozart, through Schubert and Brahms, to Reger and Schoenberg, and it is perhaps not without interest that both Reger and Schoenberg, when discussing the asymmetrical structure of their melodic lines, pointed out that it might roughly be compared to prose, whereas melody in strictly even barring would correspond rather to verse form.

This freedom of melodic formation is naturally accompanied by freedom of rhythmic articulation. Such music has more flexible rhythms—for instance, through the use of abbreviation, prolongation, and overlapping of time values, also through shifting the main accents, as is particularly evident in Brahms. This does not mean, however, that the laws of rhythm are abolished, and it is utter nonsense to describe as 'arhythmic' a process which, after all, represents merely a refinement of artistic resources. Then, this type of rhythm is occasioned particularly by the polyphonic character of the new music, and it seems appropriate in this context to point out that we seem to be going through a period very much like Bach's. Just as the appearance of J. S. Bach completed the transformation of pure polyphony and the imitative style—and the concept of the church modes—into the type of harmonic writing based on major and minor, so, at the moment, we are passing slowly but irresistibly from the harmonic period, which in fact dominated the entire Viennese classical period, into an epoch of predominantly polyphonic character. With this reference to polyphony, we have found a further distinguishing feature of all genuine music in so-called 'atonal' music.

I can say this much, on the basis of experience gained not only from my own creative work but also from that of artists to whom art is as sacred as it is to me—we, of the Viennese 'atonal' school are thoroughly unfashionable in that regard!—: there is in this music—our music—not one bar, be it never so complex harmonically, rhythmically, and contrapuntally, but has been subjected to the most severe aural checking, both by the inner ear and by actual listening. There is not one such bar for whose sense—in itself, and in its relation to the whole— we do not hold ourselves as responsible, artistically, as for the logic, immediately apparent even to the layman, of an entirely primitive structure—a simple motive, say, or a straightforward chord-progression.

Had the word 'atonal' occasioned the birth of an up-to-the-minute musical theory, standing outside the line along which the art of music has naturally evolved, then the opponents of this new music would be right in all the insinuations they make when they use the word 'atonal'—insinuations of being anti-musical, ugly, devoid of ideas, cacophonous and destructive; they would, moreover, have every reason to wail about musical anarchy, to complain that the long-standing treasury of music is being shattered, and that we are helpless and uprooted. But I think the origin of all this clamour for tonality is not so much the need to sense a relationship to a tonic, as a need for familiar chords: let us be frank, and say 'for the triad'; and I believe I have good reason to say that just so long as a certain kind of music contains enough such triads, it causes no offence, even if in other ways it most violently clashes with the sacred laws of tonality. But if these laws were not sacred to me, how could the likes of us, defying all the unbelievers in the world, amass the faith to believe in a *new* art, for which Antichrist in person could have devised no more devilish name than this word 'atonal'?!

The first sketch for the Second String Quartet, Op. 10, is dated 9 March 1907; the work was completed at Gmunden in July 1908. Schoenberg himself pointed out the special features of its compositional technique, which make it a transition to the period of absolute 'atonality' (cf pages 30–1). The only other thing that should be hinted at here is a 'secret programme'; this the composer would not make public, but there are various pointers to it. The texts used by Schoenberg as the basis of the last two movements (poems by Stefan George, from *Der Siebente Ring*, which had appeared in 1907), and, above all, the musical expressiveness given to the soprano line, show that the composer was going through a severe psychic crisis. For the time being, the opening lines of each poem should be enough to make some of this evident:

Third movement
Litanei

Litany

Tief ist die trauer,
die mich umdüstert,
Ein tret' ich wieder,
Herr! in dein haus . . .

Deep is the mourning
that lours about me,
I am entering again,
Lord!, into Thy house . . .

Lang war die reise,
matt sind die glieder,
Leer sind die schreine,
voll nur die qual. . . .

Long was the journey,
the limbs are weary,
The shrines are empty,
Anguish alone is full.

Fourth movement
Entrückung *Ecstasy* or *Transport*

Ich fühle luft von anderem planeten	I feel air from $\left\{\begin{array}{l}\text{the other}\\\text{another}\end{array}\right\}$ planet
Mir blassen durch das dunkel die gesichter	Through the dark, those faces fade upon my sight
Die freundlich eben noch sich zu mir drehten . . .	Which even now were turning to me kindly . . .

There is a further hint of the 'secret programme' in the quotation from the Viennese street song *O du Lieber Augustin, alles ist hin!*, in the trio of the scherzo (second movement). Dika Newlin, one of Schoenberg's American pupils, noted down a remark made to her by Schoenberg while discussing this passage: he said that Alles ist hin[1] was not to be taken symbolically, but in the true sense.

The work was first performed on 21 December 1908, at a subscription concert, by the Rosé Quartet, the soprano part being sung by Marie Gutheil-Schoder of the Court Opera. The scenes that took place during and after the performance were reported by a Viennese daily paper in its 'local news' section, which consisted mostly of 'accidents and crimes'. Here is part of the report:

The scenes last night between eight and nine o'clock, in the Bösendorfersaal, were unprecedented in Viennese musical history; there was a downright scandal, during the performance of a composition whose author had already caused a public nuisance with other products of his. But he has never gone so far as he did yesterday. You really would have thought you were in on a cats' concert. All the same, the public kept quiet. End of first movement. Then, from the standing-room at the back, shouts of approval. Cue for scandal, which grows like an avalanche, slackens off, picks up again, and finally reaches a fortissimo climax. . . . Ludwig Bösendorfer stood despairingly in the foyer—he sets such great store by propriety and becoming behaviour in his hall. One of his friends called out to him, 'Now they're going to play Beethoven, but have the hall ventilated first!'

1 It's all up, or all is lost, or everything's gone.

35

The music critic Richard Batka showed more goodwill in a general report for a Prague paper:

A violent clash of factions took place when Rosé and his colleagues and Mrs Gutheil-Schoder performed a new quartet by the ultraviolet musical secessionist Arnold Schoenberg. Even during the course of the various movements there were hisses and laughter. Suddenly the music critic Karpath stood up and shouted 'Stop it! That's enough!' His colleague Specht, on the other hand, shouted 'Quiet! Go on playing!' The majority of the public took against the work; various dissonances caused elegant ladies to utter cries of pain, putting their hands to their delicate ears, and elderly gentlemen to shed tears of excitement, while the figure of the composer rose up amid the tumult, with gestures of thanks and encouragement to his artists. . . . Not that one wishes to break a lance for Schoenberg's up-to-the-minute music, but one's sympathies, after such scenes, tend automatically to lie with the outraged artist. Rosé has, in any case, answered the opposition in the only way open to a man and an artist; on 8 January, he will give another performance of the questionable Opus.

There are no reports of any scandalous scenes during the repeat performance which formed part of a special Schoenberg Evening at the Ehrbar Hall, Auf der Wieden, Vienna; the tickets bore the precautionary inscription already mentioned.

After these and similar incidents Schoenberg's attitude to the Viennese music critics was understandably not of the friendliest. His immediate expression of his mood, apart from one or two personal polemics, was in an interview published in the *Neue Wiener Journal* on 10 January 1909. The history of this interview, and something of Schoenberg's general position vis-a-vis the public can be learned from letters he sent about then to his exact contemporary, the Viennese satirist and author Karl Kraus (1874–1936). (The quotations, here published for the first time, are from letters which I found among Karl Kraus's posthumous papers in 1946; the lady who owned them allowed me to transcribe them, and later I sent copies of the transcripts to Mrs Gertrud Schoenberg, who granted me the literary use of the texts.) In one of the first letters to Kraus, with whom he had been in friendly contact for several years, Schoenberg writes,

I still have to apologise to you for my interview in the *Neue Wiener Journal!* Really, apologise—for I do feel responsible to just a few people in Vienna. I only undertook this whole business for the sake of the last two sentences, and those they omitted! Here they are, and you can use them as you please: 'The Viennese music critics, with very few exceptions, are so incompetent and ignorant that one can judge them only by the degree of harm they do. Indeed, in that sense most of them understand their job aright, since they give publicity to an artist who is popular, or put people against one who is unpopular.' But even apart from that, everything I said was mangled, distorted, watered down!—by 'improvements', omissions, misquotation and similar well-directed measures. I was in utter despair—except that all this adversity has left me with rather a thick skin. I had, moreover, to worry about losing the respect of those few whom, to some degree, I do respect. Certainly, I could stay alive even without their respect. I am so little respected, and am forced to rely so much on my own good opinion of myself, that it would not[1] be easy. And I am, indeed, conscious—of my talent, and of being absolutely clean. And yet . . . you, of all people, will understand, for you surely did not become isolated out of mere caprice either!

[1] This 'not' seems somewhat contradictory, and could possibly be the result of haste on Schoenberg's part. W.R.

This was the mood in which Schoenberg approached his first literary assignment. He wrote an article about music criticism and sent it to Kraus for publication in *Die Fackel.* In a covering letter he said:

I don't know if I dare. Yesterday, still, I quite liked it; today I feel terrible. And now, of all times, your letter arrives, so that I really have no idea where I am, no idea what I should do. I think—let things take their course! So, please, read my manuscript, and if you don't like it and don't feel like returning it, then tear it up! Perhaps you'll write me a word or two about it. If you felt able to publish it I should be delighted. I need ask for no allowances to be made where my 'works' are concerned, so it's sad for me to have to tell you 'this is the first thing I have written'. And I am writing in self-defence, writing as a kind of training to defend myself better, for I feel I need to. I can't go on swallowing my bile. So far I have stood there like a mute; but now things have gone too far.

Kraus seems to have raised objections to the article, his main reason being, ostensibly, that he thought it would prove damaging to Schoenberg. His reservations prompted Schoenberg to reply as follows:

Meanwhile, what prompted the essay is over—rage at my shocking treatment by the dogs of the press; I have calmed down, and am headed towards the next onslaught. And I now see all the more clearly that my article was not designed to give a true picture of me. A snap-shot, perhaps, recording an unusual state—rage, irritation, hate. But that is not at all the average level of my feelings, even though I would not deny my temperament for a single moment. . . . I do not absolutely share your view that it would harm me to prove I could, perhaps, push a satirical pen. I should be delighted if I could; it is something I have always envied you. Lucky the man who has something to say. But luckier the man who can say it so sharply that one either believes it or cuts oneself on it. And a lot of other things, besides that!—So, as I say, I should not regard it as at all harmful. Nor do I see how it could detract from the faith my works are to inspire. Nor, if that were possible, should I feel the slightest desire to prevent it. I should think it shameful and pointless to try and cheat destiny—my talent—by pretending to be different from what I am. So I produce something like that, and it is no good; I am no good, then—no use. And by now the faith my works could gain is definitively determined. It rests in the works. No more is attainable!

Shortly afterwards, Schoenberg set down the basic ideas of his article in a longer essay. It appeared in October 1909, under the title 'Über Musikkritik', in the Viennese musical periodical *Der Merker*, which was edited by Richard Specht. A central section of this article ran as follows:

If one is to be receptive to a work of art, and gain an impression of it, one's own imagination must play a creative part. A work of art bestows only the warmth one is able to dispense on one's own account, and almost every artistic impression is, ultimately, a product of the listener's imagination. It is indeed released by the work of art, but only if one has available receiving apparatus tuned in the same way as the transmitting apparatus. To convert an artistic impression into an artistic judgment, one must be practised at interpreting one's own unconscious feelings; one must know one's own leanings, and the way in which one reacts to impressions. As for dispensing value-judgments: one must then be able to compare artistic impressions with each other; either through one's nature, which must not lack characteristic qualities, or at least through one's training (=education plus development) one must find a vantage point from which it is possible to gain a closer insight into the nature of the work concerned. One must have a sense of the past and an intuition of the future. Finally, one may indeed go wrong; but then at least one must be someone!

My friend Rudolf Ploderer, who died in 1933, commented on the passage about 'receiving apparatus', and his remarks were included, at my suggestion, in Universal Edition's 1934 volume commemorating Schoenberg's sixtieth birthday, under the title 'Divination'. He said:

At that time—1909—radio did not yet exist. Wireless telegraphy was still in its infancy, and meant little more than an interesting experiment in technical physics, as yet of no practical value. At that time, the comparison must surely have been found precious, farfetched, exaggerated. Nowadays it is something every schoolboy knows, something derived from an object familiar to everyone. It is certain that Schoenberg would hardly have taken more notice of this invention than did any other educated man of his time; yet, even then, his genius must have clearly realised its general applicability, its importance for the future. So the relationship emerged in his mind, unsoughtafter. His musical inventiveness and construction were turned towards the future; how should it have been any different, here?

From 1907 onwards Schoenberg became intensely active as a painter, as well as in music. His friends relate that his talent for painting 'suddenly' emerged about that time—though, by now, it is too late to determine exactly when. His posthumous papers contain paintings and drawings dating from between 1910 and 1940. Karl Linke called Schoenberg's earlier pictures 'inner visions expressed in painting'. Here, again, his creative activity was the result of an inner necessity, as his own words testify: 'Something is happening to me. My hand is being guided.'

There are fine reproductions of pictures by Schoenberg in the 1912 book of tributes, and, in colour, in Rufer's catalogue.

In the 1912 book there is also the famous self-portrait from 1911, in which Schoenberg has his back to the onlooker, walking away, in no particular hurry, with his two hands clasped behind his back, holding a massive stick. The book also contains two essays, by painters, on the subject of Schoenberg's pictures. Here are some excerpts:

A. PARIS GÜTERSLOH: Arnold Schoenberg, the thinker, is trying to re-create (at last) for painting the state of psychic primitivity, that prehistoric kind of former life without which its present-day existence would not appear legitimate. He alone could patiently shape these forms that offer nothing for enjoyment, since he seems protected in advance—immunised, almost—because of another highly developed art which he comprehends: his music. Men such as this, who already possess boundless security in some field, are the only true discoverers—not the rootless ones who are merely making use of a universal gesture.

VASSILY KANDINSKY: Schoenberg's pictures fall into two categories. Some are of people, or landscapes, painted straight from nature: others are heads, intuitively sensed—he calls them 'visions'. He himself describes the first kind as necessary finger-exercises; he sets no great store by them and prefers not to exhibit them. He paints the other kind to express his emotions, those which do not take on a musical form. These two types differ outwardly. Inwardly they stem from one and the same soul set vibrating, now by external nature, now by nature within him. Of course this distinction applies in only a general way, and has a strong touch of the schematic. In reality, one cannot draw this crude distinction between external and internal experience. Both kinds of experience have, so to speak, many long roots, fibres, twigs, which interpenetrate, wrap around each other and form, as the final result, a complex which is, and remains, characteristic of the artist's soul. This complex is, so to speak, the soul's digestive organ, its trans-forming, creative energy. This complex is the author of the transformative inner activity which manifests itself in a transformed external form. Through this complex's charac-teristics, unique in each and every case, the individual artist's productive technique produces works which bear, as one says, his 'imprint', and show the artist's 'handwriting'. These well-used expressions are, of course, quite superficial, since they emphasise only what is external, formal, and disregard what is internal almost completely. That is to say: here, as so often, too much respect is paid to external aspects. With artists, the external is not merely determined, it is, as in all creation, even that of the cosmos, also created by the internal.

Seen from this point of view, Schoenberg's paintings let us see the complex of his soul under the imprint of his form. In the first place, we notice at once that Schoenberg is not painting in order to paint a 'beautiful', 'attractive', etc. picture, but that, when painting, he does not in fact think of the actual picture. Without an eye to the objective result, he seeks *only* to pin down his subjective 'feeling', and for the purpose uses *only* whatever resources strike him as indispensable at that moment. Not every professional painter can flatter himself that he creates in that way! Or, to put it in another way: infinitely few professional painters have this fortunate power—amounting at times to heroism—, and this power of abnegation, which ignore all manner of pictorial diamonds and pearls, leave them unnoticed, or even throw them away if they press themselves on him of their own accord. Schoenberg goes toward his goal in a straight line—or, guided by his goal, he merely moves toward the currently necessary result. . . .

In each of Schoenberg's pictures we recognise the artist's inner desire expressing itself in the appropriate form. Schoenberg renounces the superfluous (that is to say, the harmful) in his paintings as he does, if I as a layman may say so much, in his music, and he takes the shortest path to the essential (that is to say, the necessary).

Schoenberg and Kandinsky had known each other since 1910, probably brought together by an excerpt from Schoenberg's *Treatise on Harmony* reprinted that year in the Berlin periodical *Die Musik* (10/2, page 104). Kandinsky used a quotation from it in his book *Das Geistige in der Kunst* (The Spiritual in Art) which he completed in 1910. Commenting on the quotation Kandinsky continued:

This shows Schoenberg to be absolutely aware that while freedom, a maximum of freedom, is the free and indispensable breathing air of art, it cannot be absolute. Each epoch is allotted its own measure of such freedom. And the power of the greatest genius can not leap beyond the bounds of *this* freedom. But *this* measure must be exploited to the full, and it always is exploited to the full. Let the wagon resist and rock as it will! Schoenberg, too, is trying to exploit this freedom to the full, and on his path towards things of inner necessity he has already discovered goldmines of the *new beauty*! Schoenberg's music leads us into a new realm where musical experiences are not acoustic, but *purely spiritual*. This is where the 'music of the future' begins!

Schoenberg was in close contact with the 'Blue Rider' group of artists from the time it was founded in Munich in December 1911 by Kandinsky and Franz Marc. In the group's first exhibition, opened on 18 December 1911, he was represented by three oil paintings. For the almanac *Der Blaue Reiter*, which appeared in mid-May 1912, Schoenberg wrote the essay '*Das Verhältnis zum Text*',[1] and for its musical supplement he made available the manuscript of his song *Herzgewächse*, Op. 20, for reproduction in facsimile. (Apart from this song, the musical supplement contained one song each by Berg and Webern in normal print; the almanac itself also reproduced two of Schoenberg's self-portraits.) Three letters which Schoenberg wrote to Kandinsky (Nos. 42, 63, and 64 in the selection edited by Erwin Stein, 1958) and three letters from Kandinsky, excerpts from which are reproduced in Rufer's catalogue, tell us how the relationship between the two artists developed subsequently. In his letters Kandinsky also recalls their first meeting.

Anticipating slightly, I should like to mention the first exhibition of Schoenberg's pictures. It was arranged in October 1910 at the artistic salon of Hugo Heller's bookshop (Bauernmarkt, Vienna) and included forty-one portraits and studies. At the opening ceremony the Rosé Quartet played Schoenberg's two published string quartets. Mahler attended a rehearsal, and shortly afterwards left for America; he returned to Vienna only in May 1911, as a dying man. Even as he lay on his deathbed, his mind was full of anxiety about Schoenberg's future.

Mention of the last meeting between Schoenberg and Mahler provides an opportunity to examine briefly the whole relationship between these two artists.

Their first personal meeting—in 1904, at a rehearsal of *Transfigured Night*—has been described above (page 16).

[1] 'The relationship to the text', translated in *Style and Idea*.

A few years before, Schoenberg had still been very sceptical about Mahler's works. In 1899 he had heard him conduct the Second Symphony, and in 1900 the First, both in Vienna, and, as he put it in his 1912 memorial lecture in Prague, he had remained an 'unbeliever', even though his immediate musical impression had been a powerful one. However, by 1904 he was already a 'believer', at least so far as Mahler the man was concerned. This is proved by a letter written to Mahler on 12 December 1904, after the latter had conducted a performance of the Third Symphony:

If I am to do any kind of justice to the unparalleled impression your symphony made, it is no good my speaking as one musician to another: I must speak as man to man—for I saw your soul laid bare. Stark naked. It lay before me like a wild, mysterious landscape, where there are horrifying abysses and chasms side by side with gay, charming summer meadows, idyllic retreats. I felt it as one does a natural event, with its terror and devastation and its transfiguring, calming rainbow. What matter that, when later I was told your 'programme', it hardly seemed to fit what I had experienced. Does it matter whether I am good or bad at interpreting the feelings an experience releases in me? Once I have experienced, felt, do I also have to understand correctly? And I believe I did experience your symphony. I felt in it the struggle for one's illusions; I felt the pain of the disillusioned, I saw evil forces and good, locked in battle, I saw a human being painfully stirred by the search for inward harmony; I sensed a man, a drama, *truth*, the most ruthless truth! Forgive me, I had to give vent to all this, with me there are no moderate feelings, it is 'either—or'!

The personal contact between Mahler and Schoenberg is very drastically described by Alma Mahler (in her *Gustav Mahler: Memories and Letters*, London 1946 and 1968, page 78):

When I was twenty Zemlinsky taught me in composition, and through him I got to know his pupil. . . . Schoenberg was inspired by a youthful rebelliousness against his elder, whom at the same time he revered. They used to come in the evening. After one of our devastatingly simple meals, all three went to the piano and talked shop—at first in all amity. Then Schoenberg let fall a word in youthful arrogance and Mahler corrected him with a shade of condescension—and the room was in an uproar. Schoenberg delighted in paradox of the most violent description. At least we thought so then; today I should listen with different ears. Mahler replied professorially. Schoenberg leapt to his feet and vanished with a curt good night. Zemlinsky followed, shaking his head.

As soon as the door had shut behind them, Mahler said: 'Take good care you never invite that conceited puppy to the house again'. On the stairs Schoenberg spluttered 'I shall never again cross that threshold'. But after a week or two Mahler said: 'By the way, what's become of those two?' I did not, of course, say, 'But you told me not to ask them again', but lost no time in sending them an invitation; and they, who had only been waiting for it, lost no time in coming. Nevertheless, it was a long time before there was much solace to be had from their intercourse together.   [Trans. Basil Creighton]

Among Schoenberg's letters to Mahler two were very cordial ones written during the summer of 1906, the second containing a charming reference to Mrs Mahler: 'Do please give her my very kindest regards and say that I am delighted to know she has at last got wind that I am a "dear man". Just what I have always said; what a shame hardly anyone ever believes me.'

Mahler supported Schoenberg's application for a teaching post at the Vienna Academy (cf page 58), writing the following (undated) letter to Karl Wiener, the Academy's President:

I have pleasure in informing you, in reply to your honoured enquiry, that I support in every particular the application by A. Schoenberg. He is one of those fiery spirits—of the kind bound to provoke opposition but just as certainly to add life and set things in motion—who have always had a fructifying and productive effect on other minds. And particularly when, as in the present case, this is linked with so eminent a didactic talent, the Management of any Conservatoire should seize their chance with both hands.

Schoenberg and some of his pupils attended Mahler's funeral on 21 May 1911. Their wreath bore the inscription: *Der Reiche, der uns in die tiefste Trauer versetzte: den heiligen*

Menschen Gustav Mahler nicht mehr zu besitzen, hat uns fürs Leben das unverlierbare Vorbild seines Werkes und seines Wirkens hinterlassen. ('This rich man through whom we have come to know the deepest sorrow—the loss of the saintly Gustav Mahler—has left us, for life, a model we cannot lose: his work and his works.') This idea of 'saintliness' occurs in all Schoenberg's utterances from the time immediately after Mahler's death. First, on the dedicatory page of the original version of the *Treatise on Harmony*, published in 1911, Schoenberg wrote:

This book is consecrated to the memory of Gustav Mahler. The dedication was intended, while he still lived, to give him some small pleasure. It was also meant to express reverence for his immortal compositions, and to show that these works, which academic musicians pass by with a shrug of the shoulders, indeed with contempt, are worshipped by someone who is perhaps not entirely ignorant either. Gustav Mahler was denied greater joys than my dedication was meant to provide. This martyr, this saint, had to pass on, before he had even seen his work through to the point where he could safely hand it over to his friends. To give him pleasure would have been enough for me. But now he is dead, I want my book to win me respect, so that nobody can pass by when I say, 'That was one of the truly great men!'

Schoenberg summed up his views about Mahler's personality and art in the long memorial lecture he gave in Prague in 1912 (not 1913, the date wrongly given in various publications). It has been reprinted in the collection *Gustav Mahler* (Tübingen, 1966). A Schoenberg essay about Mahler that appeared in *Der Merker* deserves special attention, as an important supplement to the Prague lecture:

Gustav Mahler was a saint. Anyone who knew him even slightly must have had that feeling. Perhaps only a few understood it. And even among those few, the only ones who honoured him were the men of good will. The others reacted to the saint as the wholly evil have always reacted to complete goodness and greatness; they martyred him. They carried things so far that this great man doubted his own work. Not once was the cup allowed to pass away from him. He had to swallow even this most bitter one: the loss, if only temporarily, of his faith in his work.

How will they seek to answer for this: that Mahler had to say 'It seems I have been in error'? How will they seek to justify themselves when they are accused of having brought one of the greatest composers of all time to the point where he was deprived of the sole, the highest recompense for a creative mind, the recompense found when the artist's faith in himself allows him to say, 'I have *not* been in error'? Let it be remembered that the creative urge continues, the greatest works are conceived, carried through, and born, but the creator who brings them forth does not feel the bliss of generation, he feels himself merely the slave of a higher ordinance under whose compulsion he ceaselessly does his work. 'As if it had been dictated to me', Mahler once said, to describe how rapidly and half-unconsciously he created, in two months, his Eighth Symphony.

What the whole world will someday believe in, he no longer believed in. He had become resigned.

Rarely has anyone been so badly treated by the world: nobody, perhaps, worse. He stood so high that even the best men often let him down, because even the best did not reach his height. Because in even the best there is yet so much impurity that they could not breathe in that uttermost region of purity that was already Mahler's abode on earth. What, then, can one expect of the less good and the wholly impure? Obituaries! They pollute the air with their obituaries, hoping to enjoy at least one more moment of self-importance: for those are the moments when dirt is in its element.

And the more exactly such a man knows how much he himself will come to be despised, and how just it will be, the more 'respected' the writers he quotes for their mistaken judgments of Mahler. As if it had not always been so: lack of respect for the work of the great has won people their contemporaries' respect. But what did posterity have to say?

Admittedly such people are not worried about posterity, otherwise they would have to do away with themselves. I do not believe there is one man who would want to go on living if he realised the shame he has piled on himself by offending against the highest there is among men. It must be terrible for such a man, thoughtlessly living from one day to the next, suddenly to become conscious of the full extent of his guilt.— Enough of him!—To Gustav Mahler's work!—Into its pure air!

Here is the faith that raises us on high. Here is someone

believing, in his immortal works, in an eternal soul. I do not know whether our soul is immortal, but I believe it. What I do know, though, is that men, the highest men, such as Beethoven and Mahler, will believe in an immortal soul until the power of this belief has endowed humanity with one.

Meanwhile, we have immortal works. And we shall know how to guard them.

This essay's significance far transcends its immediate occasion. Schoenberg's fiery words also vividly reflect a crisis in his own thought and creation, which by then had already passed its climax.

This crisis seems to have reached an acute stage in 1906, during the composition of the Chamber Symphony, Op. 9. Webern, in his 1932 lectures (*The Path to the New Music*), used the word 'catastrophe' to describe it. Schoenberg himself confesses (cf page 49) that 'he lacked the strength and confidence to approach an ideal of expression and form' which had been in his mind for years. This reference to the concepts of 'expression' and 'form' is evidence that as the composer weighed up all the various creative factors, orientation on a definite tonic or a definite basic key played a thoroughly secondary role. The most essential elements were expression and form; they decided the musical details of all the works from Schoenberg's mature period, and at all times, in his case, the sole criterion for musical detail was the imagery of his powerful, fruitful imagination, produced from deepest inner necessity. Nor, certainly, is it a coincidence that the first gradual realisation of his sound-ideal ran parallel to his first manifestations, already described, in the visual field.

The epoch-making works of this period were all completed in 1909, though most of them had been begun several months earlier. They are: the fifteen poems from Stefan George's *Das Buch der hängenden Gärten*, for voice and piano, Op. 15 (completed 28 February 1909), three piano pieces, Op. 11 (completed 7 August 1909), and five orchestral pieces, Op. 16 (completed 11 August 1909). Schoenberg's sovereign mastery of the new style can be gathered from the fact that his next work, the monodrama *Erwartung*, Op. 17, which takes about half an hour to perform, was composed in seventeen days, between 27 August and 12 September.

In *My Evolution* the composer said, about the path that led to these works:

Most critics of this new style failed to investigate how far the ancient 'eternal' laws of musical aesthetics were observed, spurned, or merely adjusted to changed circumstances. Such superficiality brought about accusations of anarchy and revolution, whereas, on the contrary, this music was distinctly a product of evolution, and no more revolutionary than any other development in the history of music.

Schoenberg often emphasised that his musical inspiration is mostly melodic in nature—that is to say, it appears in the horizontal—and that the harmonies then formed are vertical condensations of these melodic lines. This kind of inspiration also explains the 'emancipation of the dissonance'—which at that time was becoming ever more apparent—since on the horizontal plane there is, after all, no such thing as a dissonant clash. The things that come to exert the decisive influence on the musical flow, or on its comprehensibility (which is determined by logical *cohesion*), are thematic (motivic) development and formal layout. Both were products of Schoenberg's absolute familiarity with all that the great masters had achieved in the past—achievements he developed further (consciously and unconsciously).

On 14 January 1910 the Ansorge-Verein, by then renamed the Society for Art and Culture, arranged a Schoenberg evening in the Ehrbar Hall; the George Songs Op. 15 were sung by Martha Winternitz-Dorda, and the piano pieces Op. 11 were played by Etta Werndorf, both being first performances anywhere. The first part of the *Gurrelieder* was also heard at the concert, the orchestral parts being played in a six-hand arrangement made by Webern. Schoenberg's programme notes on that occasion included some statements about his new creative period that are of fundamental importance. He wrote:

I composed the *Gurrelieder* early in 1900, the George songs and piano pieces in 1908. The time between perhaps justifies their great difference in style. Since the combination of such heterogeneous works within the confines of a single concert is a striking expression of one particular person's will, it, too, perhaps needs a word of justification. With the George songs I have for the first time succeeded in approaching an ideal of expression and form which has been in my mind for years. Until now, I lacked the strength and confidence to make it a reality. But now that I have set out along this path once and for all, I am conscious of having broken through every restriction of a bygone aesthetic; and though the goal towards which I am striving appears to me a certain one, I am, nonetheless, already feeling the resistance I shall have to overcome; I feel how hotly even the least of temperaments will rise in revolt, and suspect that even those who have so far believed in me will not want to acknowledge the necessary nature of this development. So it seemed a good thing to point out, by performing the *Gurre-lieder*—which years ago were friendless, but today have friends enough—that I am being forced in this direction not because my invention or technique is inadequate, nor because I am uninformed about all the other things the prevailing aesthetics demand, but that I am obeying an inner compulsion, which is stronger than any up-bringing: that I am obeying the formative process which, being the one natural to me, is stronger than my artistic education.

Recalling this Schoenberg evening, a quarter of a century later, Erwin Stein wrote (in the 1934 commemorative volume):

At the time the listener was struck, above all, by the new sound. It was as if a new spatial dimension had been opened up. One could make out contours, which hardly seemed any longer to belong to the realm of music. In a strange light, the most delicate gradations of psychic excitement became clear. One heard new harmonies, with the luminous quality of the colour-ful garden flowers they portrayed. At one moment the sounds would float, released from any division into metre, as if time were trying to stand still; the next, sharply rhythmical figures, together with harsh chords, drew sound pictures whose dynamics approached the threshold of pain. And over it all, a singing voice, far above the accompaniment, heightened the natural intonations of speech—with its excitement, now held in, now bursting forth—to the point of melodies, radiant as none ever heard before, and more tender than one could ever have imagined. Such was Schoenberg's world of sound, as it con-fronted us in his George songs.

On the other hand, the critic Richard Batka, who was on the whole well disposed toward Schoenberg, had the following to say, immediately after the concert, as part of an article in Vienna's *Fremden-Blatt* (he discussed at length the essay Schoenberg had contributed to the programme, and went on):

When Schoenberg speaks of those who up to now believed in him, this implies the existence of people who did the opposite. There are in fact musicians who regard Schoenberg's music as a fraud, intended to take in the snobs, and anyone who has now heard his three piano pieces feels tempted to agree cordially with such an assumption. One really had the impression that anyone sightreading a difficult piano piece in a badly lit room can provide his listeners, impromptu, with delights similar to those here presented as the fruits of a development lasting years. . . . Were I to name the mood which, according to the old aesthetics, might conceivably produce music such as that in Schoenberg's piano pieces, it would be something in the nature of physical indisposition, transcribed for piano, but goodness knows what sublime thoughts Schoenberg has been getting off his chest by means of it all. Ceterum censeo: if *that* is art, then from now on, there's nothing to it. . . .

After praising the *Gurrelieder* and the five early songs at the start of the programme, Batka goes on:

An embarrassing question was surely on the tip of everyone's tongue: how could the author of these songs possibly descend to the pointless ugliness of his piano pieces, and the pseudo-ecstatic posing in his Georgics? Well, it's said that perversions often begin when normal instincts are left unsatisfied. Could not the lack of response to his earlier works have driven this artist into his unhappy, perverse 'latest period'? It would not be the only such case. The sensitive nature of an imaginative man does not survive years of obscurity and contempt unharmed. This single point is enough to explain other eccentricities of Schoenberg's, too. . . . Now he's made it. He is at the peak of his antics. It can never get worse than this. So? Perhaps we shall shortly read in the *Kleine Anzeiger*, 'Come back, Arnold, all is forgiven!'

Rufer published an interesting diary entry of Schoenberg's about the five orchestral pieces, Op. 16 (January 27, 1912):

Letter from Peters, arranging a meeting on Wednesday in Berlin, to make my acquaintance. They want titles for the orchestral pieces—for technical reasons to do with publication. I may give in, since I have thought of titles that are at least possible. Not, on the whole, sympathetic to the idea. For the wonderful thing about music is that one can tell all, so that the educated listener understands it all, and yet one has not given away one's secrets, the things one doesn't admit even to oneself. Whereas titles are a give-away. Moreover: what had to be said has been said by the music. So why add words? If words were needed, they would be there. But after all, art says more than words.—The titles I shall perhaps give do indeed give nothing away, being partly technical, partly very obscure. Here they are. I *Vorgefühle* (Premonitions) (everyone has those). II. *Vergangenheit* (The Past) (which everyone also has). III. *Akkordfärbungen* (Chord-colourings) (technical). IV *Peripeteia* (surely that's general enough?) V. The obligato (perhaps better than 'worked-out' or 'endless') recitative.—In any case, with a note that this is a technical matter to do with publication, and has nothing to do with the 'poetic' content.

In the score published in 1912 by C. F. Peters, Leipzig, the individual pieces were not preceded by titles. However, Schoenberg's diary entry is important in principle, since it is characteristic of his attitude towards 'programme-music' in general.

The third piece, for which Schoenberg thought up the 'technical' title 'Chord-colourings' is also important as the first perfect realisation of the 'tone-colour-melodies' which he had extensively discussed at the end of the *Treatise on Harmony*, and which he thought should be regarded as an independent dimension of music. The piece is dominated almost exclusively by the chord C–g sharp–b–e–a, laid out in every possible combination of registers and instruments, these changing frequently. In the score, Schoenberg made the following remarks about the quite unusual and very tricky performing problems raised by the piece:

In this piece, the conductor's task is not to encourage individual parts to stand out because they strike him as (thematically) important, nor to tone down sound mixtures because they seem uneven. Whenever one part is meant to be more apparent than the others it is scored in a suitable way, and the sounds are not meant to be toned down. His task is, on the other hand, to ensure that each instrument plays at exactly the level of dynamics indicated: with (subjective) exactness, i.e. in terms of the instrument—not subordinating itself (objectively) to the overall sound.—The changes of chord are to happen very gently; the instrument entering must not receive any perceptible emphasis, so that one only notices the change because the colour has altered.

Broadly speaking, and without going into technical detail, the remaining pieces show the application to the sounds of a large orchestra (17 woodwind, 12 brass, percussion, harp, celeste and strings) of the procedures developed in the Op. 11 piano pieces and the George songs; 'thematic work' has become considerably more complex, as befits the greatly increased possibilities, linear and colouristic, offered by the orchestra. At certain points there are thematic complexes whose technique of composition already foreshadows the twelve-tone technique, something systematically developed only much later.

Webern was the first to publish analytical remarks about the orchestral pieces (in the 1912 commemorative volume), and he particularly pointed out that, in them, none of the traditional forms any longer applied; he summed up Schoenberg's handling of form by means of a quotation from the *Treatise on Harmony*, which reads like a confession:

In composing, my decisions are guided solely by what I sense: my sense of form. This it is that tells me what I must write, everything else is ruled out. Each chord I introduce is the result of a compulsion; a compulsion exerted by my need for expression, but perhaps also the compulsion exerted by a remorseless, if unconscious, logic in the harmonic construction. I am firmly convinced that such logic is present, even here; to at least the same degree as in harmony's existing built-up areas. And I can offer proof of this: namely, that modifications of my inspiration, made because of the kind of external, formal second thoughts that all too often beset one's wide-awake conscious mind, have usually spoiled the original inspiration. To me, this proves that the idea was compulsive, that the harmonies set down there are components of the idea, and that one may not alter anything about them.

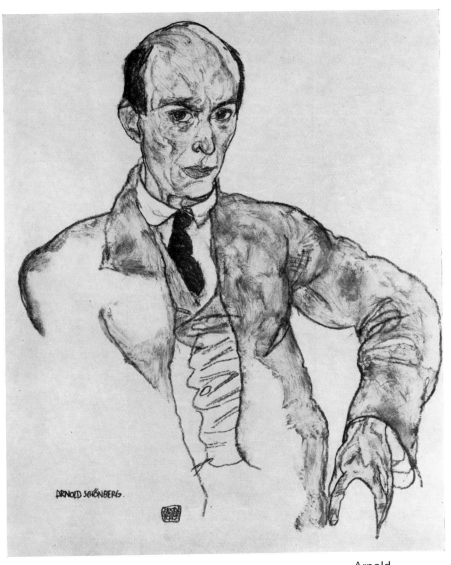

Arnold
Schoenberg.
A watercolour
by Egon Schiele

Samuel
Schoenberg, the
composer's
father

The composer's
mother,
Pauline
Schoenberg,
née Nachod

The first performance of the five orchestral pieces was on 3 September 1912, at a Promenade Concert in London conducted by Sir (then Mr) Henry J. Wood.

The monodrama, *Erwartung* (Expectation) (27 August–12 September 1909) came into being at a time when Schoenberg was particularly active as a painter. He called many of his paintings and drawings 'visions', and the same term, transferred to the realm of sound, would have to be used to describe the spiritual content and musical detail of *Erwartung*.

The idea of the monodrama was his own, and he also collaborated closely with Marie Pappenheim in settling the final form of the text. What happens on the stage—an inner monologue by the only living character, a woman who looks for her lover at night in a forest and eventually finds him dead, victim of his passion for another woman—is decidedly like the self-revelation demanded of patients during psychoanalysis. The frequent references to unconscious thought, which also appear in earlier remarks of Schoenberg's, indicate a certain resemblance between his ideas and those of his contemporary and fellow-Viennese Sigmund Freud, although the two were not personally acquainted, and Schoenberg probably knew no more about Freud's theories than did any educated man of his time. In the booklet accompanying his 1960 gramophone record of *Erwartung*, the American conductor Robert Craft has very convincingly pointed out the resemblances between the woman's ejaculatory and often incomplete remarks and the things said by patients during psychoanalysis; he has thus added a new facet to the work's visionary character mentioned above. I find this reference to psychoanalysis nearer the mark than the frequently attempted comparisons with Wagner's idea of 'salvation', and between the woman's fate and Isolde's *Liebestod*, particularly since Wagner's technique of composition has virtually nothing to do with Schoenberg's music for *Erwartung*, full-sounding though the latter is.

When *Erwartung* received its first performance in Switzerland (Zürich, October 1949) the Swiss writer on music Willi Schuh said some very pertinent things about the music's expressionist style, 'in which the resources of a large orchestra are used with a degree of differentiation that carries the methods of chamber music to an extreme', and about Schoenberg's 'radical procedure, which rejects every musical convention and all traces of any formula: signs of this are the way the course of monodrama is carried through a-thematically,[1] the superimposition of harmonic complexes, the sensibilising of rhythm, and the unprecedented psychological refinement and spiritualisation of orchestral technique. The only explanation for Schoenberg's surefootedness amid the boundless immensities of his new musical realm is that he moulded this music as if obeying the compulsive dictates of his inner visions.'

Erwartung was first performed on 6 June 1924 at the New

1 That is, the work completely avoids thematic repetition. W.R.

Alexander von Zemlinsky and Arnold Schoenberg. A caricature by E. Weiss on the occasion of the first performance of Erwartung *at the Prague Music Festival* 1924.

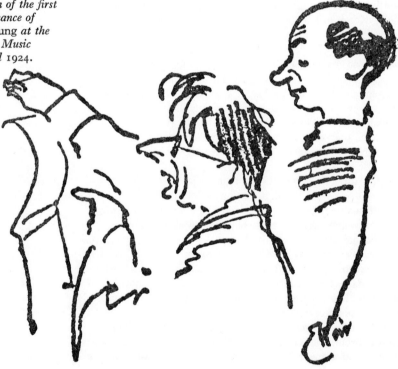

German Theatre in Prague, conducted by Zemlinsky; the part of the woman was sung by Marie Gutheil-Schoder; the producer was Louis Laber, who also created the stage sets. The première was very successful, but the rumours that subsequently arose, about 'almost insurmountable difficulties' in preparing the work, prevented its becoming more widely known. Zemlinsky published a long essay attacking this rumour, in the Viennese periodical *Pult und Taktstock* (Desk and Baton: a specialist periodical for conductors. March/April issue, 1924); he said this, among other things:

Certainly the difficulties appear extraordinary on a first perusal of the score. But in my experience the worst is over once two artists—singer and conductor, both convinced of the work's great value—completely devote themselves to studying it, until they really know it: a conductor who does not join in the orchestra's jokes at rehearsals, and a singer who has not only a beautiful voice—for the role absolutely demands beautiful *singing!*—but strong powers of dramatic characterisation. If these requirements are satisfied, then the worst is over. The orchestral part is not much harder than in many other modern works, and has, moreover, an advantage over the latter, in that, being wonderfully scored, it almost automatically sounds right. . . . In order to ease certain difficulties of intonation in the vocal part, I had a harmonium built into a sunken part of the stage, and this occasionally gave the singer her note, without in any way disturbing the audience. Thus we achieved a performance which never betrayed even a trace of all the difficulties involved.

The last work Schoenberg completed during this period in Vienna was the set of six little piano pieces, Op. 19 (composed between 18 February and 17 June 1911). The final piece is said to have been sketched out immediately after Schoenberg returned home from Mahler's funeral; it is a picture in sound, based on three chords, of an extreme tenderness, testifying to unbounded grief.

The especial brevity of these pieces (from 9 to 18 bars) is characteristic of the crisis into which Schoenberg's instrumental composition had been plunged, vis-à-vis the creation of extended forms, once he had given up the traditional links with a definite key or tonic. In the time immediately following he completed only vocal works, whose formal compass was determined, basically, by their texts. At the same time he sought unceasingly for new rules of law which would make the production of longer instrumental forms possible again, a search which finally led to the discovery of the 'method of composition with twelve tones related only to each other'.

The 'aphoristic' style so vividly documented by the piano pieces Op. 19 also left its mark in a significant way on works by Schoenberg's pupils Webern and Berg. All the instrumental works Webern composed between 1909 and 1914 (Opp. 5-11) fall into this category, as do Berg's five orchestral songs to post-card texts by Peter Altenberg (1912), and the four pieces for clarinet and piano (1913).

One can take as the literary apotheosis of the 'aphoristic' style the preface which in June 1924 Schoenberg wrote for the score of Webern's six Bagatelles for string quartet, Op. 9 (composed in 1913):[1]

1 Schoenberg's prose, which was strongly influenced by the style of Karl Kraus, is never easy to translate, and this preface, one of his tersest and most poetic pieces, presents special problems. The following attempt at a translation is not that found in the printed score.
L.B.

While the brevity of these pieces is their eloquent advocate, such brevity stands equally in need of advocacy. Think what self-denial it takes to cut a long story so short. A glance can always be spun out into a poem, a sigh into a novel. But to convey a novel through a single gesture, or felicity by a single catch of the breath: such concentration exists only when emotional self-indulgence is correspondingly absent. These pieces will be understood only by someone who has faith in music as the expression of something that can only be said musically. They can no more withstand criticism than this faith can, or any other. If faith can move mountains, disbelief can refuse to admit they are there. Against such impotence, faith is impotent. Does the performer now know how he is to play these pieces— the listener, how he is to take them? Can any barriers remain between performer and listener, when both are men of faith? But how is one to deal with the heathen? With a fiery sword, they can be kept in check, bound over: but to be kept spellbound—that is only for the faithful. May they hear what this stillness offers!

Art is the cry of distress uttered by those who experience at firsthand the fate of mankind. Who are not reconciled to it, but come to grips with it. Who do not apathetically wait upon the motor called 'hidden forces', but hurl themselves in among the moving wheels, to understand how it all works. Who do not turn their eyes away, to shield themselves from emotions, but open them wide, so as to tackle what must be tackled. Who do, however, often close their eyes, in order to perceive things incommunicable by the senses, to envision within themselves the process that only seems to be in the world outside. The world revolves within—inside them: what bursts out is merely the echo—the work of art!

This aphorism published in 1910, and the sentence 'I believe art is born, not of "I can", but of "I must"!', which opened the essay *Probleme des Kunstunterrichtes* (Problems in teaching art. *Musikalisches Taschenbuch*, II, Vienna, 1910), contain Schoenberg's view of art in its most concentrated form.

They also apply to his activities as a teacher of music, for which he had a deeper inner calling than anyone had ever had before. This assertion is overwhelmingly supported by his *Harmonielehre*[1] (*Treatise on Harmony*) published in 1911 and reprinted in a third, expanded and revised edition in 1921; the book has already been quoted at various points. In a book such as the present one, it is impossible to give a full idea of how meaningfully the whole work is constructed, and of the intellectual and spiritual distinction of its language. I should merely emphasise that although it offers a course that takes one to the uttermost limits attained by the method of tonal composition, the latter is never abandoned; Schoenberg merely adduces, in the closing pages, a few examples of chords (taken from musical works created about that time) which can hardly be explained tonally. The opening of the foreword is characteristic, conveying Schoenberg's personality as a teacher:

[1] The title describes both the book as a whole and also its contents. It is a *Treatise on Harmony*, i.e. a repository of harmonic 'lore' or 'learning'—all the accumulated facts of harmonic practice. The word 'Lehre' is often used in the latter sense during the course of the book. L.B.

What is in this book was learnt from my pupils. When teaching, it was never my aim merely to tell the pupil what I know. Rather, what *he* did not know. But even that—enough in itself to make me invent something new for each pupil—was not the main thing; I strove to show him the essence of the matter, starting from the simplest things. So, as far as I was concerned, there were never these rigid rules which so conscientiously entwine themselves around the pupil's brain. Everything was broken down into instructions, which bind the pupil no more than the teacher. If the pupil can do it better without the instructions, then let him do without them. But the teacher must have the courage to be wrong. His task is not to prove infallible, knowing everything and never going wrong, but rather inexhaustible, ever seeking and perhaps sometimes finding. Why want to be a demigod? Why not, rather, be a complete man?

In order to improve his artistic and economic position in Vienna, Schoenberg aimed about this time at a teaching post as *Privatdozent* (an outside tutor or lecturer, not contractually on the staff) 'lecturing on music-theoretical subjects, or giving instruction in matters of composition' at the Imperial and Royal Academy of Music and the Graphic Arts in Vienna. The final version of his application ('I had to work hard to make it sufficiently tame'), which he sent on 17 March 1910 to the President of the Academy, Karl von Wiener (a man well-disposed toward him), was published in the *Selected Letters* (No. 6): I would here lay particular stress only on one single sentence which occurs at the midpoint of Schoenberg's arguments: 'I am by nature inclined towards teaching, which is why I seek scope for this ability of mine'.

To further Schoenberg's cause by obtaining artistic support for an application to the institution's governing body, Wiener approached Mahler, Ferdinand Löwe, Karl Goldmark, and Felix von Weingartner, asking them, as Vienna's most currently prominent musical figures, for their views on Schoenberg's personality and abilities as a teacher. Mahler's reply has already been quoted (page 44). All I have been able to discover about Weingartner's attitude (he was at that time Director of the Court Opera) is a fragmentary text published by Carl Nemeth in the periodical *Phono* (Vienna, 1961 v/vi):

At that time Weingartner had heard only one of Schoenberg's string quartets, and had read the scores of other works. As conductor and opera director he found Schoenberg's way of composing 'the opposite of his idea of music'; all the same, he was not entirely opposed to Schoenberg's engagement, recommending merely 'that the effect of his teaching on the students should from time to time be checked by a commission'.

The conductor, Ferdinand Löwe, a former pupil of Bruckner, had recently recommended Heinrich Schenker as a teacher of theory, and now wrote:

Not knowing what Arnold Schoenberg has achieved as a private teacher, and having, moreover, so far failed to form more than a doubtful impression of him even from his works, one finds it very difficult to give a definite opinion about the composer's application to be allowed to hold a course in musical theory and musical composition at the I. and R. Academy. I would tend, even so, to express a rather affirmative reaction in the present case, above all because of the communication addressed to me, in which one of the factors emphasised is Schoenberg's great enthusiasm for teaching, and the loyalty and affection of his pupils—something which is certainly most important. Bearing all this in mind, I would be in favour of granting his request, and in the manner suggested: free courses, outside the Academy's normal curriculum.

The reply sent on 17 April by Karl Goldmark[1], from Abbazia (the holiday resort on the Adriatic, now Opatija in Yugoslavia; it was there that he spent his last years) is of general human and artistic interest:

Continuing absence from Vienna means that I have unfortunately had little opportunity to acquaint myself with Mr Schoenberg as a composer; in fact I do not know a single note he has written. But it seems to me that in the present case I do not even need to. Every report I have of him has been of a highly idealistic artist, who does, however, also follow an extreme ultra-modern line. There is an implied question here: do I regard the instruction given by a teacher with so extreme a line as dangerous—and my answer can only be a categorical 'No!' Let us assume (something still to be proven) that Mr Arnold Schoenberg would, in his lectures, train his guns on everything established, in order to reproduce his own kind. This would be regarded as harmful in the conventional sense. I, however, am most firmly convinced that, in the long run, no-one of genuine talent will let himself be forced to pursue a line contrary to his own inner self, whereas a person of a different and stormier nature, however conservative his upbringing, needs but a single hearing of some ultra-modern work to make him transfer his allegiance and break through. I think that a

[1] Goldmark was then one month away from his eightieth birthday, and had been composing for over half a century. The work by which he is now best known, the *Rustic Wedding* symphony, dates from the 1850s, and his best-known opera, *The Queen of Sheba*, occupied him between 1865 and 1875. He continued to compose until well into his seventies: his last two operas were based on Goethe's *Götz von Berlichingen* (cf page 3, produced 1902), and on Shakespeare (*The Winter's Tale*, produced 1908). He died in 1915.

'line' never results from teaching, only from a living example—
and once the latter exists, there is no removing it, be it never
so harmful. The young fall head over heels in love with what
is new, but they soon sort themselves out and swear by Mozart.
If they do not, so much the worse for them. In neither case,
however, is anyone to be held responsible, their teaching least
of all, and so certainly not Mr Arnold Schoenberg either, insofar as we are concerned not with his example but with the way
he teaches. I therefore support the granting of Mr Arnold
Schoenberg's application. I regard a pure, high-minded and
artistic outlook as an essential factor in musical education—
and *that*, surely, nobody will deny Mr Arnold Schoenberg.
And, as an ultimate safeguard, the director is always there to
keep a tactful eye on things. So, no danger whatever!

Although someone asked in Parliament 'how the government could answer for such a thing', the governing body of the
Academy approved Schoenberg's application, on the basis of
these expert opinions, and during the academic year 1910–11
he was able to hold a course in composition at the Academy,
though outside the official curriculum. However, the material
results of this teaching and also of his other Viennese projects
were so unfavourable that, prompted by certain friends of
his in Berlin, he decided to move there.

The following appeal, written without Schoenberg's
knowledge by Alban Berg in September 1911, bears witness
to the catastrophic deterioration in his economic position
during the course of that year:

Arnold Schoenberg's friends and pupils consider it their duty
to bring his extremity to the notice of the public. Shame prevents him from doing so himself; that is why we take the initiative and cry for help over his head. Our mouths are opened
by the thought of this artist coming to grief for lack of the
common necessities of life. Catastrophe has overtaken him with
unexpected speed, and help from a distant source would be
too late. For at the time of writing these lines, Schoenberg is
living, deprived of any means whatever, in a village near
Munich. (The above call will be sent to patrons of the arts with
a view to a monetary collection. You are requested to support
the planned action by appending your signature. We urgently
beg for your early reply to: Alban Berg, Vienna XIII, Trautt-
mannsdorffgasse 27.) [Trans. Cornelius Cardew]

Couched in this form, the appeal obtained about forty signatures, but in the meantime the wider collection envisaged had become unnecessary, Schoenberg's economic position having improved with his move to Berlin.

About eight months later, in Berlin, he also received an enquiry from Karl von Wiener, asking him whether he would be willing to take over a professorship of harmony and counterpoint at the Academy. Schoenberg's letter of refusal appears complete in the *Selected Letters* (S.L. 9): two sentences are reprinted here, since they reflect Schoenberg's attitude toward Vienna at that time:

My main reason is: for the present, I could not live in Vienna. I have not yet got over the things done to me there, I am not yet reconciled. . . . Perhaps, even if you should now be as irate with me as I now am with Vienna, perhaps after a while you will think of me less harshly, and perhaps after some time I shall feel a greater affection for my native city than I do now; perhaps you will then think of me and I shall then certainly wish to return.

But now I cannot.

4 From the *Gurrelieder* to *Pierrot Lunaire*

1 Before this, on
22 September and
6 October 1911, a
'committee of
Schoenberg's friends
and admirers'
announced in the
Berlin *Allgemeine
Musik-Zeitung* that he
would be holding
courses 'of the type
he has previously held
in Vienna at the
I. & R. Academy'.
Edward Clark (cf note
to page 162) acted as
secretary for the
enterprise.

Schoenberg arrived in Berlin during the late summer of 1911 and took up residence in the suburb of Zehlendorf, on the outskirts of the city. Once again he taught at the Stern Conservatoire[1], but his circumstances were happier than in 1902, because his economic position was made temporarily safe by a sizeable contribution from a rich patron. Ferruccio Busoni (1866–1924), the composer and pianist who had been living in Berlin since 1894, and his circle of friends did much to help Schoenberg in all his activities during this period. Already (in 1909) Busoni had prepared a somewhat problematic arrangement of the second of the Op. 11 piano pieces 'for concert use'. When it was published in 1910, he wrote the following magnanimous foreword:

This composition demands that its performer command every subtlety of touch and pedalling; that his delivery be intimate, improvised, 'floating'; and that he immerse himself lovingly in its content—the interpretation of which, purely in terms of keyboard texture, is counted an artistic honour by F.B.

Schoenberg's arrival in Berlin had been effectively prepared in October 1910 by a performance of *Pelléas and Mélisande* under Oskar Fried (1871–1949); this formed part of a concert in the series organised by the Berlin *Gesellschaft der Musikfreunde*, a body founded in the autumn of 1907. It was the first time one of Schoenberg's large-scale works had been heard outside Vienna. Unlike the work's first performance (cf page 20), this one was a great public success. The work was played by the Blüthner orchestra; one of their youngest viola-players was Hermann Scherchen (1891–1966), who thus became acquainted for the first time with the music of Schoenberg, on whose behalf he was later to work so enthusiastically. Recalling that performance almost half a century later, Scherchen said, 'Mahler's Seventh Symphony had been my first whiff of a new artistic feeling, one that marked the transition to Expressionism; now, in Schoenberg's *Pelléas and Mélisande*, I felt the full fiery blast of it.'

But in Berlin, too, very unfriendly voices made themselves heard right from the start. For example, in the *Kleine Journal* of 26 February 1912 the critic and writer on music, Walter

Dahms, published an 'open letter' to Schoenberg, to greet him on his arrival. It began:

Sir!

While you were still leading your existence in Vienna, and we merely saw newspaper reports about your violations of art, you could be a matter of indifference to us. For (to be honest) what business of ours are the charlatans currently active in Vienna, the city of Haydn, Mozart, and Beethoven? Vienna, where the lust for sensation is dominant, not the love of art, leaves us completely cold. Not until certain artists, lusting after sensations, tried to emerge from their obscurity by introducing your lunatic 'art' (excuse the expression!) into Berlin too, did matters become more serious. Last winter some pianist whose name entirely escapes me played your three piano pieces, Op. 11, at the *Singakademie*. He was laughed out of court— a sign that people saw the humorous side of your attempts to bring down the final curtain on music. Then Fried performed your symphonic poem *Pelléas and Mélisande* at the *Gesellschaft der Musikfreunde*. People for whom music is a lofty and serious thing got the belly-ache and fled. Alfred Kerr[1], and a few others from the Pan-Clique, applauded. This clarified the situation. The Berlin public's self-restraint was the only reason why the performance of your rubbish was allowed to continue, with no audible and tangible hostile demonstration at the end. A fiasco having been avoided thanks to public indifference, some of your local 'adherents', led by Maestro Busoni and other Pan-ites, were emboldened to fetch you here, by means of an appeal in the Pan Press. Well, we have so many jobbers and peddlers of humbug here, in all the faculties, that one more makes no difference. But now people are taking your presence here as their cue to keep performing your 'compositions' (forgive the old-fashioned term!), and the time has come to tell you the truth. . . .

After further violent attacks and threats, the letter ends

So, Mr Schoenberg, at some suitable opportunity, a few well-functioning house-keys,[2] a few well-chosen missiles, and a small collection (of money), to facilitate your hasty return to Vienna: with these wishes I remain

Yours

Walter Dahms

1 Leading Berlin theatre-critic and editor of the progressive Berlin periodical *Pan*. L.B.

2 This was the contemporary method of producing a loud whistle at concerts, the keys concerned being large metal ones for the front doors of apartment-houses (cf page 71). L.B.

After an afternoon concert of works by Schoenberg (on 4 February 1912), one of the most respected Berlin music critics, Leopold Schmidt, discussed a Schoenberg song which appeared in the printed programme, but which had had to be omitted, an announcement to that effect having been made during the concert. Schoenberg paid homage to his absent-minded reviewer in an ironic article entitled 'Sleepwalker', printed in the periodical *Pan* on 22 February 1912.

About the same concert Busoni wrote the following notes for *Pan*:

Is a renaissance of sentimentalism on the way? It looks almost like it, after a hearing (performance, study) of Arnold Schoenberg's piano pieces and songs. Suppressed tears, heaving sighs, gusts of wind through mournful trees, the rustling of autumn leaves; here and there a moment of defiance, or the reflection of early spring sunshine, which soon vanishes again. In-between times, the occasional quirkish moment. Lonely voices creep, recitative-like, through unheard-of intervals—we can only just sense that they hang together at all. Harmonic audacity so persistent as to take the edge off itself—naïvety in almost barbaric measure. And an equal amount of unaffectedness, clairvoyance, and honesty. Finally, three pieces, played on two pianos, eight hands.[1] Seated at the two keyboards, four young men with refined, characteristic heads; almost moving, to see how they place their young intellects at the service of what is still undeciphered, with devotion and efficiency. At the back of the small platform two eyes glimmer uneasily, and a baton makes short, nervous movements. One sees only Schoenberg's head and hand, communicating with his four braves, infecting them with more and more of his own fever. An unusual picture, and, together with the unusual sound, it exerts its own fascination. In any case, different from that of a sonata evening by two royal professors.

[1] From the five orchestral pieces, Op. 16. W.R.

Webern lived in Berlin-Zehlendorf from October 1911 to mid-May 1912, and his letters to his friend and fellow-pupil Alban Berg tell of Schoenberg's personal situation during this early period in Berlin. Webern tells, among other things, of the rapidly diminishing attendances at Schoenberg's lectures at the Stern Conservatoire, of the lack of private pupils, and of the resulting marked deterioration in Schoenberg's economic position. The letters also furnish some valuable data about performances of Schoenberg's works during that period.

First of all, the orchestration of the *Gurrelieder* was completed, on 7 November 1911. A letter Schoenberg wrote to Alban Berg in 1912 provides us with a detailed history of the work. Berg included it in his 'complete' guide to the work, a 100-page book with 129 music examples published by Universal Edition in 1913. Later, a much abridged version was also published.

Here are some extracts from the text of Schoenberg's letter:

I composed Parts I and II, and much of Part III, in March 1900. Then a long interval while I orchestrated operettas. March 1901 (early in the year, then), *remainder completed*! Orchestration then begun in August 1901 (again with other work getting in the way, for something has always got in the way of my composing). Continued mid-1902, in Berlin. Then a long break, because of operettas to orchestrate. At it again, at last, in 1903, and completed up to *c*. page 118.[1] Then put aside, and in the end given up completely! Resumed, July 1910 (in Vienna). Everything scored, except the final chorus, which was completed 1911 at Zehlendorf. So the whole work was completed, I believe, by April or May 1901. The final chorus, only, was still in the form of a sketch, but this already included, in full, the most important parts and the overall form. The work as originally composed contained very few indications as to scoring; I never jotted down that kind of thing, for after all one retains the sound in one's head. But, even apart from that: people are bound to notice that the part orchestrated in 1910 and 1911 differs from Parts I and II as regards the style in which it is scored. I had no intention of concealing this. On the contrary, it is self-evident that I scored differently ten years later. In preparing the full score, I altered the composition of a mere handful of passages; groups of from 8-20 bars, particularly in the section 'Klaus the Fool', and in the final chorus. The rest (even certain things I should have been glad to see different) remained as it had always been. I could not have recaptured the style, and anyone knowledgeable, if he has any experience at all, must surely be able to identify, without difficulty, the four or five corrected passages. These corrections gave me more trouble than did the original composition of the whole work.

[1] Of the score, corresponding to page 105 of the vocal score prepared by Berg. W.R.

The cycle of poems *Gurresange* (*Songs of Gurre*), written in 1868 by Jens Peter Jacobsen (1847–85), was based on the old Danish legend of Waldemar, King of Denmark, and his illicit love for the beautiful maiden Tove at the castle of Gurre. Helwig, Waldemar's jealous wife, has Tove killed. After his own death, Waldemar's ghost roams the land with the 'wild hunt', searching for Tove.

The translation of the *Songs of Gurre* by Robert Franz Arnold (a pseudonym used by the Viennese classical scholar and writer Levisohn, 1872–1938) was first published in 1899, a second edition appearing in 1921. In Schoenberg's setting there are, however, numerous divergences from the text published in 1899, some significant, some less so, and these changes suggest that the two men worked closely together. For example, in the 1899 version the end of Tove's second song ran as follows:

Höher und höher nun tragen die Stiegen	Now the stairs bear my splendid knight
Meinen herrlichen Rittersmann,	Higher and ever higher,
Bis ich mein Herz an das seine schmiegen	Until I can press my heart to his
Und ihn zu Tode küssen kann.	And kiss him to death.

Schoenberg, however, set the following text:

Und die steigenden Wogen der Treppe	And the climbing waves of the staircase
Tragen zum Hafen den fürstlichen Held,	Bear the princely hero into port,
Bis er auf alleroberster Staffel Mir in die offenen Arme fällt.	Till on the very topmost rung He falls into my open arms.

Schoenberg grouped Jacobsen's poems to form three parts, with one extended postlude. In Part I, Waldemar and Tove sing alternately of their longing, and of the fulfilment of their love; the nine songs are formally self-contained, linked by short interludes. The postlude begins after the last song, being initially for orchestra alone, and later merging into the Song of the Wood-Dove, which describes Tove's death and Waldemar's anguish. Part II consists of one single song, in which Waldemar accuses God of cruelty and senseless tyranny. Part III again contains nine songs, and begins with the spectral Wild Hunt of the dead Waldemar and his men; this then gives way to the Wild Hunt of the summer wind, in which Nature awakens to new, radiant life, and is shiningly transfigured in the 'morning dream' of the sunrise.

The sound aimed at—especially in Part III—is a monumental one, and demands the following forces; vocal soloists (soprano, mezzo-soprano or contralto, two tenors, bass, and a speaker), three four-part male-voice choirs, an eight-part mixed choir, and an orchestra of around 150, composed of 25 woodwind, 25 brass, 11 percussion instruments (among them heavy iron chains), four harps, celeste, and more than 80 strings (violins dividing into ten parts, violas and cellos dividing into eight). But it should be pointed out that the solo use of various instruments often produces chamber music effects of the most delicate kind—particularly in the sections when Tove sings. In the parts completed later, even the orchestration clearly shows Schoenberg anxious to achieve the utmost contrapuntal clarity of line.

The dominant thematic traits stem from Wagner's world of sound, but the frequent wide intervals in the vocal parts already give a hint of Schoenberg's later manner. Harmonically, there are further refinements of the phenomena of expanded or 'floating' tonality, first produced by Wagner in *Tristan*. A typical example is the prelude to Part I, which is closely connected with the first song, and has a definite E flat major as its main key; not until bar 143, at the end of the first song, is the tonic chord heard in its simple form. The way in which Schoenberg unfolds the themes of the *Gurrelieder*, the nature of his thematic work, and the formal layout of the whole work show him already far beyond Wagner's technique of development, and ahead of his own contemporaries. 'Dramatic' sections, which introduce much new material and use a bold technique of variation, as a further continuation of Wagner's leitmotif technique, are juxtaposed with 'narrative' sections, which cast a retrospective eye on previous material, as in a symphonic development. A specific and supreme example of the latter would be the close of Part I, with its narrative and reflective Song of the

Wood-Dove. Berg's main aim, in his 'guide', was to show the work's infinitely subtle motivic cohesion, and the way this forms part of the overall symphonic structure. In this context, I want to draw attention only to the work's close, with its grandiose eight-part Hymn to the Sun, based on an inversion of the opening theme (transposed from E flat major to C major), and the Wild Hunt of the Summer Wind, which directly precedes the hymn; here the text, set to specified note values, is spoken, as in a melodrama. In a letter Schoenberg said the following about this 'melodrama':

Here, the notation of pitch need be taken nowhere near so seriously as in the melodramas of *Pierrot*. There, the aim is a speech melody akin to song; here, nothing of the kind is to occur. Rhythm, and dynamics (to match the accompaniment), must be adhered to throughout. At a few points of almost melodic character the text could be spoken *somewhat* (!!) more musically. The pitches shown are to be regarded as 'variations in register'—that is to say, the passage concerned (!!! not the individual note) is to be spoken higher or lower. But not as interval proportions!

The *Gurrelieder*, together with the symphonic poem *Pelléas and Mélisande* which likewise calls for gigantic forces, represent Schoenberg's farewell to the over-ripe late-Romantic world of sound inaugurated by Liszt and Wagner and carried to its extreme by Mahler, Richard Strauss, and many of their contemporaries. To characterise the special way in which, in the *Gurrelieder*, Schoenberg treated his musical inheritance from the past, Berg quoted the following lines from the poem which Jacobsen had in his turn added as an introduction to the first edition of the cycle:

Tief ist der Sinn und	The meaning is deep, and
Wietum bekannt:	Known far and wide:
Ist der Vergangenheit	For the past's
Grosse Bedeutung doch,	Great significance is, after all,
Dass in die Zukunft sie	That in the future it
Tragen den Namen kann	Can bear the name
Des, der dem Dunkel sie	Of the one who rescued it
Wieder entrissen,	From obscurity,
Tag ihr gebracht.	And brought it to light.

The first performance of the *Gurrelieder* took place on 23 February 1913, in the large hall of Vienna's *Musikverein*; it was conducted by Franz Schreker, whose 'Philharmonic Choir' was augmented by the *Kaufmännischer Gesangverein* (the Mercantile Choral Union); the soloists were Ferdinand Gregori (speaker), Martha Winternitz-Dorda (Tove), Marya Freund (Wood-Dove), Hans Nachod (Waldemar), Alfred Boruttan (Klaus the Fool) and Nosalewicz (Peasant); the instrumental parts were looked after 'most valiantly' to quote one critic, by the *Tonkünstlerorchester*. The work was an extraordinary success with the public, the first triumph for Schoenberg in any of the major halls of his native city. This is the appropriate place to quote a graphic 'mood picture', the opening of a long article by Richard Specht in the Berlin periodical *März* (20 September 1913), under the striking title 'Der Hass gegen Schönberg' (literally, 'The hate directed against Schoenberg'):

The public for this work is an expectant assembly including not only all the musicians, all the snobs, and all those thirsty for art, but also certain agreeable folk—those interested not in the evening's business but in a sensation, a scandal even; those for whom the performance of a Schoenberg work, especially, seems always to count as a 'rumpus', which they must on no account miss, one which incidentally is no mere expression of Vienna's good-natured flippancy, the way she enjoys making a joke about anything strange, but rather of an underhand defensive reaction against the unusual, against something that, by its seriousness, forces one to come to terms with it; of hatred for people who go their own way, unconcerned and defiant, making no flattering concessions—those who find it intolerable to have to wear themselves out and put their inmost secrets on show for the hoi polloi; and, last but not least, of the shame aroused by such an example, and of envy and rage when faced by these overweening artists who dare to live so freely and contemptuously, without needing others or their approval. So it was with Mahler, so it was with Klimt, so it is with Schoenberg.

Malicious pleasure already lurks in fifty pairs of eyes; today, they are once again going to 'show him'—whether he may really make so free as to compose the way he wants to, rather than the way already laid down by the others. But the very first bars are enough to bring disappointment: this glittering and hovering, this aromatic, tender twilight mood, expressed in sounds where weary waves of the sea seem to break dreamily on a shore illuminated by the sun's last rays; where the earth, breathing peacefully, sings its song of evening; whose gently rustling monotony, with its sudden points of subdued light, resembles some priceless sound of nature—and then King Waldemar's first song, as he rides toward Tove in the land of Gurre, a song that tells us quietly of a soul where a radiant, almost gay passion has brought with it a splendour of stillness: this opening is enough to enfold everyone in its spell, that of a forgetfulness of self, whose ever more liberating and felicitous tide washes away all heaviness, all impurity. One felt immediately: here are lofty thoughts, couched in terms of pure and wondrous relationships; one felt the language—experienced through and through, absolutely necessary, blazing forth in pride and splendour—of an artist whom Wagner taught to speak, but who has no need to imitate, someone in whom there lives the ordering power which creates for a spiritual content the form latent within it.

In these splendid, romantically blossoming and dreamy love songs of Waldemar and Tove, there lives the whole of Schoenberg, who is now seeking, along such lonely paths, the fatal adventure of an uncertain future, and who once said, 'Art is born, not of "I can", but of "I must" '. Here, too, it was a matter of 'I must'—passionately and unresistingly—just as it is nowadays. Only, this inner commandment had not led him so far afield from everything inherited; his new content in the Songs of Gurre lies less in this type of glowingly intoxicated, unspeakably compellingly melody than in the magic of the personality that expresses itself with such memorable richness and magnificence. A personality that still wears a kind of costume, and, above all, one that has not yet said goodbye to all the things it feels to be 'formalistic' or 'rationalist' (though one will find little enough that is formalistic or rationalist in these *Songs of Gurre*); one which, with youthful and auspicious trust, believes in life and walks in the sun; it knows nothing as yet of haunted hours filled with panic fear at the dark mysteries of existence, of moments of waking dream, when the voices of night are heard and the secret terrors of the abyss appear as spectral visions in sound. Here, the vision of Eros[1] still sings, in its felicity and its sorrows, its eternal song of life. . . .

But there were further disappointments in store for the sensation-seekers; the exultant shouts that broke out even after Part

1 'Die grosse Liebe', literally 'the great love'. L.B.

One rose to a tumult after Part Three, as—after the spooky triple choir of the wild hunt in its wild and ghastly progress, and the demonic scherzo-burlesque of Klaus the Fool—in the most brilliant melodrama anyone ever dreamed, the Wild Hunt of the Summer Wind, was caught in a web of sound which re-created, before our very ears, the great symphony heard by anyone who lies with receptive heart amid grass hot from the July sun: a soughing, flying music with strangely distracting harmonies—the music of tree-tops rustling in the breeze, of whispering meadows, of sparkling, murmuring streams, the singing and humming of ripe golden fields, where the wind settles as if to blow through delicate organ-pipes. And then, when the strong and surging choral hymn to the sunrise was over, and the work's opening harmonies returned, even down to the G flat major that had appeared there briefly, like a premonition (here sounding like a metaphysical fulfilment, in an overwhelming F sharp major episode)—returned with such a transfigured, splendid radiance—then the jubilation knew no bounds. Many faces were wet with tears, as the composer received a grateful ovation, which sounded warmer and more insistent than a 'success' usually does; it sounded as if amends were being made. A number of young people, complete strangers, came up to me, their cheeks glowing with shame, and confessed that they had brought along house-keys, in order to supplement Schoenberg's music by additions of a kind they had thought appropriate; now they had been so completely converted to him that nothing could break their allegiance. Their shame and regret were the finest triumph that could have been desired by this artist who painfully wrestles, and who unflinchingly takes upon him all the sorrows of the conquistador.

The 'leading' Viennese music critic of the time, Julius Korngold, devoted seven columns to the *Gurrelieder*, an effusion containing many criticisms, but of a generally benevolent tone, ending with the sentences quoted below, which need a little explanation. Jacobsen's 'frame' for his poems was a story, set in the house of an old military counsellor with a beautiful daughter, Julie; she has five young admirers, who spend the rest of their time writing poems. One evening, all the young men are assembled at the old man's house, waiting for a very rare cactus to blossom: after nine years' intensive care, it has at last put out a bud, which is likely to open that very night. To pass the time till the great event, and to oblige the master of the house and his beautiful daughter, the young men read their latest poems, one after another, refreshed by generous helpings of fruit and tea. The third of them is Paul, who first fortifies himself with three glasses of water, and then reads the Songs of Gurre, which he has just completed. His listeners' only reaction is a tactful 'No criticism—on to the next' from the old counsellor. Korngold's seven-column article in the *Neue Freie Presse* of 1 March 1913, ended with the words: When a prickly, determined and mutinous artist like Schoenberg offers us an accessible work like the Songs of Gurre, we may wait hopefully for his next; like the expectant assembly in Jacobsen's tale, we may rejoice in the fact of 'a flowering cactus.'

Schoenberg's old friend David Josef Bach ended an affectionate report in the left-wing *Arbeiter-Zeitung* (28 February 1913), as follows:

The audience's emotion erupted into an ovation lasting a quarter of an hour. This was genuine rejoicing, even if one or other member of the public may have introduced a jarring note of snobbery. What does it matter? Schoenberg has thirsted for recognition long enough; one may allow him to swallow a drop of harmless poison along with the honey of success.

A drop of less harmless poison had to be swallowed soon enough. On 31 March 1913, five weeks after his triumph with the *Gurrelieder*, Schoenberg conducted a concert promoted by the 'Academic Union for Literature and Art'. The programme contained works by Webern (Orchestral pieces, Op. 6), Zemlinsky (Songs with orchestra), Schoenberg (Chamber Symphony Op. 9), Alban Berg (second and fourth of the Songs, Op. 4, to words sent on picture-postcards by Peter Altenberg), and Mahler (*Kindertotenlieder*). Demonstrations and counterdemonstrations by members of the public had already begun after the Webern and Schoenberg works, but during the first Berg song there was such an uproar that the concert had to be abandoned. A precise account of the scandalous scenes at this concert, based on a report in a Viennese daily paper, was printed in the 1924 commemorative volume and reprinted in my 1963 biography of Berg. I merely want to mention here that there was a legal hearing arising out of the fights that broke out in the concert hall. Egon Wellesz reports a well-known operetta composer, called as a witness, as telling the judge 'I laughed too; is one supposed not to laugh, if something's genuinely funny?' According to another witness, a doctor, the effect on a large section of the audience of the music in question had been 'enervating, and so damaging to the nervous system that many of them manifested, even externally, the symptoms of severe depression'. Hermann Scherchen reported a further sequel. He had travelled to Vienna especially for the concert. 'On the journey back, I met Schoenberg in the dining-car. The master, whose face was usually so peaceful, wore a downright war-like expression. He looked at me, his eyes blazing with anger, and asked, "What do you think of the scandal?"—and then, without waiting for my reply, he added, "I should have had a revolver with me!" '

Having looked ahead to the triumphs and scandals of eighteen months later, let us return to Schoenberg's creative work in Berlin. The next piece that should be mentioned is the song *Herzgewächse*, completed in December 1911 (after a poem by Maeterlinck) and shortly afterwards published in facsimile in the Blue Rider year book. It is for high soprano, celeste, harp and a harmonium whose part contains many indications as to registration, suggesting an orchestral sound that was probably in the composer's mind at the outset. The vocal part must surely be Schoenberg's hardest, from a technical point of view. At the opening it moves on and below the treble stave (going down to G sharp); it ascends, with wide leaps, in the middle section, and shortly before the end it holds, for $1\frac{1}{3}$ bars of $\frac{3}{4}$, the F an octave above the stave (on the first syllable of the phrase 'mystisches Gebet'), then descending into the lower register again. In a letter to Berg (17 December 1911) Webern called the song the 'summit of music'. It is very rarely heard in the concert hall, but a gramophone record of it was made several years ago (Columbia ML 5099).

Three months later, Webern wrote to Berg about a recent commission for a new Schoenberg work, one which came 'all the more opportunely' since 'he had himself had something of the sort in mind for a long time'. The commission was from Albertine Zehme, a Viennese actress married to a Leipzig lawyer, and a specialist in the performance of melodramas. I have been unable to discover who drew Schoenberg's attention to the collection of poems *Pierrot Lunaire*—fifty 'Rondels', originally published in French in 1884, by the Belgian poet Albert Giraud, and later translated into German by Otto Erich Hartleben (1864–1905) whose very free translation, considerably deepening the content of the cycle, appeared in 1892. The 1962 recording of the work (Wergo WER 60001) has an accompanying booklet by Helmut Kirchmeyer entitled 'The historical symbolism of *Pierrot Lunaire*' (*Die zeitgeschichtliche Symbolik des Pierrot Lunaire*), and this contains an extensive, well-documented survey of the work's history.

Schoenberg's Opus 21, dedicated 'to its original interpreter, Frau Albertine Zehme, in cordial friendship', bears the title 'Thrice seven poems from Albert Giraud's *Pierrot Lunaire* (German translation by Otto Erich Hartleben). For a speaking voice, piano, flute (doubling piccolo), clarinet (doubling bass clarinet), violin (doubling viola), and cello. (Melodramas)'. Schoenberg himself chose the poems and decided their order (which is not that of the original); their grouping into three seven-poem sections was also his idea. Sometimes he stipulated a pause between two songs, to separate them clearly; elsewhere, when two songs were closely akin in spirit, they run consecutively, with brief interludes; the only extended interlude is in Part II, between Nos. 13 and 14. Only in the final piece are all eight instruments used; seven of the pieces use five instruments, and in one piece (No. 7), the speaker is accompanied only by the flute. Some remarkable musical variants arose from the composer's strict adherence to the prosodic scheme of the Rondel, which has thirteen lines, the first, seventh, and thirteenth being identical, as are the second and eighth.

It is hardly possible to describe the work's prevailing atmosphere in any generally valid way; Schoenberg once said that his original conception had as its basis 'a light, ironic and satirical tone', but even this is not maintained throughout.

The part that comes nearest to doing so is the first, in which the seven pieces are headed *Mondestrunken—Colombine—Der Dandy—Eine blasse Wäscherin—Valse de Chopin—Madonna —Der kranke Mond* (Moondrunk—Columbine—The dandy —A pallid laundry-maid—Chopin waltz—Madonna—The sick moon); here the moon also plays an important part as the originator (even if a passive one) of all the bizarre visions in the poems. In Part II, the bizarre is often carried to the point where it becomes truly demonic (*Nacht—Gebet an Pierrot—Raub—Rote Messe—Galgenlied—Enthauptung—Die Kreuze*: Night—Prayer to Pierrot—Robbery—Red Mass— Gallows Song—Beheading—The Crosses). Part III looks back, often with grotesque humour, on the fantastic dream-world experienced under the moon's influence, and in the final piece the onlooker is reminded of this world by an 'ancient scent from legendary times' (*Heimweh—Gemeinheit —Parodie—Der Mondfleck—Serenade—Heimfahrt—O Alter Duft*: Homesickness—Dirty Work—Parody—The Moonspot —Serenade—Homeward Journey—O Ancient Scent).

In the instrumental score of *Pierrot Lunaire* Schoenberg created a veritable marvel of contrapuntal and colouristic subtleties; any analysis of its technique of composition could only be fragmentary, and would take up many pages of text, with numerous musical examples. Here I want to refer to only two of the pieces, which show how the content of the poems directly stimulated the composer to create subtle musical forms. No. 18 (The Moonspot) tells how Pierrot, out for a walk, discovers a bright spot on the back of his coat, caused by the light of the moon. This is something he could only have discovered by looking in a mirror, and the piece is full of musical figures inverted and mirrored in the boldest possible way. In the final piece (O Ancient Scent) the poet himself speaks—among other things—of 'joys I long have scorned'. At this point, without the music's settling into any definite key, there are allusions to Schoenberg's early creative period, when his music was still dominated by tonal relationships which, though traditional, gradually grew in boldness until the utmost limits were reached. In each piece of the cycle one could point out something analogous in some way or other.

Although in the final years of his life Schoenberg still insisted (for instance, in a letter to the conductor Hans Rosbaud dated 15 February 1949) on the overriding importance of *Pierrot Lunaire*'s instrumental parts, which contain everything of musical and thematic importance, it is nevertheless true to say that the absolutely new and epoch-making feature of the work is its treatment of the voice. In his preface to the score the composer discussed this as follows:

The melody notated in the speaker's part is *not* meant to be sung (the occasional exceptions are clearly marked). The performer's task is to transform it into a *speech melody*, while paying due regard to the written pitch of each note. This is done as follows:

1. The rhythm is observed with absolute exactness, as if the performer were singing; that is to say, he takes no more liberties than he would be entitled to take with a sung melody.
2. He is well aware of the distinction between *singing tone* and *speaking tone*: singing tone maintains the pitch without modification; speaking tone does, certainly, announce it, only to quit it again immediately, in either a downward or an upward direction.

In a note for the 1962 Wergo recording of the work, which he conducted, Pierre Boulez calls these sentences 'enigmatic', and advances the idea that Schoenberg failed to take adequately into account the connection between speaking voice and singing voice, particularly the variable compass of the different registers. In my view, Boulez has failed to bear in mind the fact that Schoenberg anticipated the singer's using a *glissando* between the notes indicated in the score—the *glissando* that constitutes one of the particular charms of speech-melody, and which Berg once compared to 'bel canto', as a kind of 'bel parlare'.

Schoenberg composed *Pierrot Lunaire* between 12 March and 30 May 1912, except for piece No. 14 (*Kreuze*), which was not completed until 9 July. Rufer's exact list of dates of composition shows that fourteen pieces—two-thirds of the whole—took one day each to compose, and that the order in which they were written was by no means that in which they were finally grouped.

Rehearsals began in September 1912, at Albertine Zehme's house in Berlin-Zehlendorf. Hermann Scherchen had originally been suggested to play the violin part; he declined the offer, feeling he would not be adequate technically, but obtained permission to attend all the rehearsals. The ensemble consisted of the violinist Jakob Maliniak, one of Scherchen's colleagues in the band that played at night in the Café Kutschera (Berlin-Charlottenburg, Wilmersdorferstrasse), two Court musicians, H. W. de Fries (flute) and Karl Essberger (clarinet), the Dutch cellist Hans Kindler (who later became a conductor), and the pianist Eduard Steuermann (1892–1964), then a student in Berlin (piano with Busoni, composition with Schoenberg); later, he was one of the ablest musicians of the Schoenberg circle in Vienna, and subsequently (from 1936 onward) in the U.S.A. Although Scherchen and Maliniak played at the café until three a.m., they always appeared punctually at the rehearsals, and one meeting with Schoenberg was enough to make the deepest possible impression on Scherchen, who decades later said: 'My first glimpse of him was only through a glass door in a groundfloor room, where he and Frau Zehme were doing some preliminary work before a rehearsal; I could hear him speaking some of the text, in a voice of thunder. His voice and expressive gestures betrayed the ecstasy of a man transported quite beyond himself'.

The first performance of *Pierrot Lunaire* took place, after forty rehearsals, on 16 October 1912, in the Choralion-Saal in Berlin's Bellevuestrasse; it had been preceded, on the 9th, by a final run-through with invited audience. Dressed in a Pierrot's costume, Albertine Zehme spoke her text in front of a black Spanish wall behind which sat the instrumentalists, with Schoenberg conducting. In the programme book, the texts of the poems were preceded by the following quotation from Novalis:

One can imagine tales where there would be no coherence, and yet associations—like dreams; poems that are simply euphonious and full of beautiful words, but with no meaning or coherence whatever—at most, a few comprehensible strophes—like fragments of utterly various things. Such true poesy can have, at most, an allegorical meaning, as a whole, and an indirect effect, like music.

Pierrot Lunaire's direct effect—on the public—was basically positive; indeed, there was so much applause that pieces had to be repeated. On the other hand, reactions by the critics and experts were very hostile, except for a few voices from Schoenberg's Berlin circle of adherents. The only example I need quote is the anxious prayer offered up by the German composer Otto Taubmann in Berlin's 'Financial Times', the *Börsenkurier*, in November 1912; 'If that is the music of the future, then I have a prayer to my Maker: please never make me endure another performance.'

Stravinsky, too, had been at one of the rehearsals, as he mentioned briefly in his 1935 memoirs. When in 1957 Robert Craft asked him what his impressions had been, he replied:

It is difficult to recollect one's impressions at a distance of forty-five years; but this I remember very clearly: the instrumental substance of *Pierrot Lunaire* impressed me immensely. And by saying 'instrumental' I mean not simply the instrumentation of this music but the whole contrapuntal and polyphonic structure of this brilliant instrumental masterpiece.

In his book *Ivory, Apes, and Peacocks* (New York, 1915) the American writer James Huneker (1860–1921), who was music critic of the *New York Times*, called *Pierrot Lunaire* 'the decomposition of the art', and called Schoenberg himself 'the cruelest of all composers for he mingles with his music sharp daggers at white heat, with which he pares away tiny slices of his victim's flesh. Anon he twists the knife in the fresh wound and you receive another horrible thrill'.

Immediately after the first performance, the *Pierrot* ensemble went on tour and performed the work in eleven cities in Germany and Austria, including Munich, Vienna and Prague. Half the performances were conducted by Schoenberg, the others by Scherchen, who had shown his exceptional gift for conducting when he deputised for the composer at some of the rehearsals. On the tour there were disturbances among the audience in a number of cities; indeed, it 'went without saying' that in Vienna the successful

Gurrelieder would be played off against the problematic *Pierrot*. But, to redress the balance and be fair to the city, it should be said (anticipating considerably), that Vienna was to be the scene of the work's first public performance by music students (see page 170). In 1929 Franz Schmidt, then head of the state conservatoire of music in Vienna, arranged a Schoenberg evening by his pupils, with himself conducting, and one of the works was *Pierrot Lunaire*, performed with an understanding and a beauty of sound that left nothing to be desired.

If that event can be taken as a very welcome symptom of the way in which this work established itself after such initial mistrust, we can only deprecate its adaptation as a ballet by the American choreographer Glen Tetley (1962). As early as 1922, Schoenberg expressed very definite disapproval of such plans, unless he was able to take entire artistic responsibility.

In his book *Richard Strauss und die Neue Musik* (Berlin, 1924) the Berlin music critic Walter Schrenk provided an excellent 'historical assessment' of *Pierrot Lunaire*:

This melodrama is numbered among the unique, unrepeatable creative works which, both positively and negatively, point the way for, and mark the destiny of, the art of music. Seen in this lofty historical perspective, it takes its place in the line of works such as Mozart's *Don Giovanni*, Beethoven's *Missa Solemnis* or late quartets, Wagner's *Tristan*, Mahler's *Song of the Earth*, and Richard Strauss's *Elektra*. This is not a matter of drawing comparisons: when I place *Pierrot Lunaire* alongside the works just mentioned, it is only to point out that, like them, it was, in a sense, created at a crucial moment for music.

In June 1912—that is to say, shortly before Schoenberg completed *Pierrot*—an article about him appeared in the Berlin periodical *Die Musik*. This—if one disregards the 1912 commemorative volume—was the first literary assessment of him on any large scale. It is not mentioned by any of his previous biographers. The article was entitled *Arnold Schönberg. Wesenhafte Richtlinien in der neueren Musik* (Arnold Schoenberg. Essential guide-lines in the more recent music), and its author, Arno Nadel, belonged to the Busoni circle. His view of the composer, which is all the more sympathetic for its modesty and restrained language, is shown by the following quotation:

Schoenberg elevates inner compulsion to the highest artistic virtue, and wherever he sets foot he is in command of himself. In command and determinedly individual, but always the artist. Anyone naïvely approaching his compositions, his most decided ones, will, according to his moral temper, either find himself faced by an insoluble riddle, or regard the man who created them as an invalid or a liar. It takes almost a degree of immodesty to claim to have grasped the meaning of a piece by Schoenberg. Nor, moreover, can one yet establish whether in such an act of intuitive understanding our mind reinforces our emotions. What I mean is this: it is an open question whether, in a case such as that, we follow our mind more, or our sensations. In the case of two pieces which, though short, are splendidly characteristic of Schoenberg's art, my experience was that I did in fact hear in them what is organic. When I heard the song 'Nie, ward ich, Herrin, müd' [Op. 8, No. 4], and the second of the Op. 11 piano pieces, my experience was as of a distant, very distant, sun, rising with a strange light, and a strange still warmth. The utterly farfetched diction struck me as entirely necessary, or at least thoroughly genuine. And in praising these pieces I am trying to say that I also became aware, in them, of what is objective, that is to say, of something that holds good even outside the bounds of our old-fashioned taste. For Schoenberg's art has strictness and form. He is, however, hard to follow—very hard—because we are suddenly called upon to alter our entire sensory system. His music stands in the same sort of relationship to ours—but in the opposite direction—as does medieval organum to our choral music. . . .

A few months after this essay, Schoenberg was also accorded a 'biographical' assessment in Vienna, in the October 1912 volume of the shortlived Viennese periodical *Modernes Musikleben*; it was No. 6 in a series of 'biographical sketches of modern musicians'. In a rather dry article the editor, Dr H. R. Fleischmann, limited himself for the most part to an enumeration of Schoenberg's works up to *Pierrot Lunaire*; these were discussed with vaguely complimentary generalisations and references to the bold way in which they had been conceived and carried through. The article ended with the following paean to the *Treatise on Harmony*:

Here, with strictest objectivity, and with the freshness, direct-ness, and truthfulness of a man drawing on experience, Schoen-berg has set down thoughts whose succinctness of content and rare linguistic perfection give the book the imprint of a work of art; its importance is indeed attested by the *universal recogni-tion* hitherto accorded *from all sides* to the Treatise on Harmony.

As evidence that recognition was not yet quite 'universal', one may take the first encyclopedia-entry about Schoenberg; this appeared in the eighth edition (1916) of Hugo Riemann's famous *Musiklexikon*. However, the list of works shows it to have been drafted as early as 1914. The article contained passages such as this:

Schoenberg; a composer who by the extravagant nature of his most recent works provokes protests, but to whom, despite his mania for doing the unprecedented, one can not deny talent, and who in his earlier works also shows a normal face (in the line of Liszt, Wagner, and Strauss).... His *Treatise on Harmony*, published in 1911, is a strange mixture: out-of-date theories and prejudices, derived from Simon Sechter's system, along-side a hyper-modern negation of all theory. The author's naïve confession that he has 'never read a history of music' provides the key to this unprecedentedly dilettantish effort. The 'artistic craftsmanship' taught by Schoenberg is something that still forms no part of the average musician's world, thank goodness.

In the later editions of Riemann's *Musiklexikon*, revised by Alfred Einstein and Willibald Gurlitt, these unprecedented jibes have been eliminated, thank goodness.

Continuing our examination of Schoenberg's works, we come next to the 'drama with music' *Die glückliche Hand*,[1] Op. 18, completed in November 1913; the composer described the title as 'symbolic, so far as the main point is concerned'. This symbolism, which plays a decisive role, especially in the work's 'higher strata', has been discussed very exten-sively and thoroughly by Karl H. Wörner, in a large-scale study published by the *Schweizerische Musikzeitung* in 1964. He draws attention in no uncertain manner to the clear connections between the plot of *Die glückliche Hand* and Strindberg's stage works from about the turn of the present century—*To Damascus*, *Dance of Death*, and *A Dream-Play*.

[1] The nearest English idiom would be the gardening expression 'green fingers'. Hans Keller has suggested 'The Knack'. Thirty-five years after the work's composition, in describing a minor incident with a manu-script, Schoenberg punningly translated the title as 'The hand of fate'; the catalogue adopts this as the 'authorised' translation. L.B.

Schoenberg had already begun work on *Die glückliche Hand* at the time when he composed *Erwartung*; this is proved by a short note he made on 11 October 1908, consisting of three brief musical ideas, alongside which appear the words 'Taten, Beschwichtigung, Schein-Glück'[1]. This time Schoenberg devised his own text, unaided, and in this first of his own libretti the literary results of his labours are no less attractive and illuminating than the musical work.

As in *Erwartung*, the drama in fact takes place within the soul of a single character—there a woman, here a man. However, *Die glückliche Hand*, unlike *Erwartung*, makes use of projections to show the thoughts and events that shatter the protagonist's soul. The man's painful self-examination is made manifest in the form of a spectral choir—six women and six men—who employ a diction consisting mainly of the type of speech-melody systematised shortly before in *Pierrot Lunaire*, though at a number of points they also sing. The other characters—a beautiful woman, an elegant gentleman, and a group of metal-workers—act purely in mime. The lighting, with its changes of colour and intensity, plays an essential role, almost as important as that of the music; the score indicates every lighting nuance, and at one point— after the scene with the workers—Schoenberg indicates parallel crescendi for the lighting and the (musical) storm.

Before the 'plot' begins, the man is shown as if in a kind of vision. He lies on the ground, in almost complete darkness, face downwards. A vicious-looking mythical beast sits on his back, 'into which it appears to have buried its teeth'. The man is watched, through small spy-holes, by the six women and six men, whose faces are lit by a green light; they speak, and sing, very softly, and with the deepest pity:

Quiet, ah be silent, restless one!—You[2] are aware; you were aware before; and are you blind, for all that? Can you not find peace at last? So often! And ever and again? You know it is the same, ever and again. It ends the same, ever and again. Do you have to hurl yourself into it, ever and again? Will you not, at last, believe? Believe in the truth: in the dream; ever and again you hanker after the unrealisable; ever and again you abandon yourself to the siren call of your senses, which scour the universe, which are unearthly, but long for earthly happi-

1 'Deeds, Appeasement, Illusion of Happiness'— though 'Glück' can mean fortune (in either sense), happiness, or luck, hence the manifold meanings of the work's title. Cf also the Male-Voice Choruses Op. 35 (page 172).
L.B.

2 The familiar 'du' is used throughout.
L.B.

ness![1] Earthly happiness! Poor man!—Earthly happiness!—
You, who have within you things that are more than earthly,
long for the earthly! And cannot endure! Poor man!

The man rises, and sings, with deep passion, 'Yes, ah
yes!' At this moment, the stage becomes light, and in the two
ensuing scenes the plot proper unfolds. First, it shows the
man's love for the woman, who is, however, spirited away by
the 'gentleman'.[2] Then we are shown the man as fighter and
as creator, arousing resentment on the part of the workers.
He tries once more to win the woman's love, but is rejected,
and sinks to the ground on the same spot as at the beginning.

The six men and six women again appear at the spy-holes,
but now their faces are in a grey-blue light, and there is a
tone of 'severity and accusation' about their words:

Did you have to experience, again, what you have so often
experienced? Did you have to? Can you not deny yourself?
Not, at last, be content? Is there no peace in you? Not even
now? You seek to grip what can only slip from you if you grasp
it; but it is within you and about you, wherever you may be.
Do you not feel what is in you? Not hear what is in you? You
grasp only what your hands can grasp! Do you feel only what
you touch—your wounds only through your flesh, your pain
only through your body? And for all that, you seek!—And
torment yourself!—And know no peace!

As a certain amount of red is mixed into the grey-blue light
on the faces, and before complete darkness falls, the final
words of the drama are heard: 'Poor man!'

This brief outline of the plot should suffice to make clear
the basic idea of the drama: the tragedy of the creative man,
gifted with 'green fingers', who has to pay for the happiness
of creation by renouncing worldly fortune and happiness—
and, significantly enough, Schoenberg wrote this drama and
set it to music at the very time when his worldly humiliation
was at its most profound. His music, in which the part of
The Man is sung by a baritone, uses the same orchestra as
in *Erwartung*—about ninety players; but the overall sound is
more transparent, and the line-drawing for the most part
harsher; at two points in the score, 'shrill, contemptuous

[1] *Glück*—see
previous note.

[2] The German
Herr also means
'Lord', and
contains a
stronger element
of domination,
of being the
master, than
does the English
'gentleman'.
L.B.

laughter' is called for, set to a bitonal chord. As far as possible the course of the music is matched by a visual scheme running in parallel, particularly as regards the colour effects that are aimed at.

Not surprisingly (in view of the links between the dramatic and visual sides of *Die glückliche Hand*) Schoenberg was approached, not long after completing the work, with a plan to make it into a film—a silent film, of course, with accompanying music. One of his letters, from late in 1913 or early in 1914 (it appears in the *Selected Letters*) leads one to suppose that the intermediary in the affair was Emil Hertzka, the head of Universal Edition. Schoenberg was strongly in favour of the idea, on the understanding that the substance of his music would in no way be altered, and that he could play a major part in preparing the performance. He was even prepared to entrust the orchestra score to a mechanical organ, and to do without an orchestra. At the time, he regarded the development of such organs very hopefully, and wrote (*S.L.* 18): 'I expect great things of these instruments with their magnificent bass stops and the innumerable precisely defined timbres.' He made very detailed suggestions about many visual details; but his total conception of the nature of the film was far more important still. He expressed it as follows: 'I want: *the utmost unreality*! The whole thing should have the effect (not of a dream), but of chords. Of music. It must never suggest symbols, or meaning, or thoughts, but simply the play of colours and forms.'

Before the start of filming, an artist would have had to design the main sets; his first choice was Oskar Kokoschka, or as second choice Vassily Kandinsky, or, failing either of them, Alfred Roller. The film project was never realised, but in view of the present never-ending growth in technical resources it would still be a desirable thing, particularly since *Die glückliche Hand* must surely be the least often performed of all Schoenberg's major works.

The first performance was on 14 October 1924, at the Vienna *Volksoper*, conducted by Fritz Stiedry, and produced by Josef Turnau. The solutions were Alfred Jerger (The Man), Hedy Pfundmayr (The Woman) and Josef Hustinger (The Gentleman).

Alban Berg,
Vienna 1909

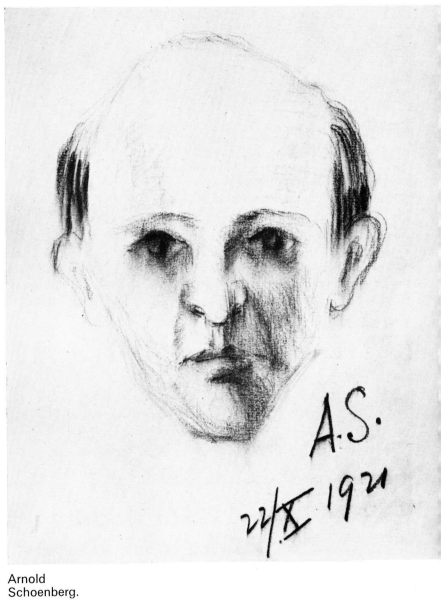

Arnold
Schoenberg.
Self-portrait
in crayon

Between 1912 and 1914 Schoenberg, in addition to his activities as composer and teacher, spent a good deal of time on guest appearances as a conductor, which not only showed how his artistic reputation was growing, but also helped considerably in improving his economic position. After completing the tour with *Pierrot Lunaire,* he conducted performances of *Pelléas and Mélisande* in Amsterdam (12 November) and Saint Petersburg (12 December). The most important events in 1913 were the two Viennese concerts already mentioned—the first performance of the *Gurrelieder,* under Schreker, on 23 February, and the notorious concert he himself conducted on 31 March. In 1914 he conducted the Five Orchestral Pieces, Op. 16 in London and Amsterdam, and the *Gurrelieder* in Leipzig, to mention only three concerts. There were other important performances in Prague (the Six Orchestral Songs, Op. 8 conducted by Zemlinsky), Leipzig (Chamber Symphony, Op. 9 under Nikisch) and Berlin (two performances of the Chamber Symphony under Scherchen). At the second Berlin performance of the Chamber Symphony there was a major disturbance; Scherchen's mother (he later told me) was at the concert and was most upset. Finally she was impelled to intervene, in a touching manner. She sidled diffidently up to the man who was producing the loudest whistles, touched him gently on the shoulder, and said, 'But why are you whistling, Sir? And after the lad's worked so hard!'

Another Schoenberg work was performed on 19 November 1913, as part of the celebrations marking the twentieth anniversary of the 'Monuments of Music in Austria' (*Denkmäler der Tonkunst in Österreich*), whose editor was Guido Adler; Franz Schalk conducted the Vienna Philharmonic Orchestra, with Casals as soloist, in the G minor cello concerto by Georg Matthias Monn (1717–50), one of the works published in vol. 39 (1912) of the *Denkmäler,* with a continuo-realisation by Schoenberg.

In 1912 and 1913 the proceeds of the Gustav Mahler Foundation—about 3000 Kronen each year—were awarded to Schoenberg. The jury consisted of Busoni, Bruno Walter, and Richard Strauss. The first two made an unqualified recommendation to continue the award for a second year, but

D

1 The most casual
and unskilled labour
conceivable, which
was, and still is, the
last resort of the South
German unemployed.
L.B

Strauss wrote to Alma Mahler, 'I agree with you that the interest from the foundation should be given to Arnold Schoenberg. I believe he would do better to shovel snow[1] than to scribble on music paper, but, all the same, give him the grant. . . . One can never tell what posterity is going to think.' By an indiscretion, Schoenberg heard what was in this letter, and one of his own letters (*S.L.* 25) contains a violent tirade against Strauss as man and artist.

In the spring of 1913 there was a tentative exchange between Schoenberg and the Austrian composer Josef Matthias Hauer (1883–1959), the founder of an entirely personal twelve-tone system, which will later be discussed at length (pages 136-8). For the moment, all that need be said is that Hauer was then thirty, and that early in 1913 he wrote from Wiener Neustadt to Schoenberg in Berlin, asking for an interview, probably intending to show Schoenberg the music he had so far written (he had reached Op. 3 at the time), and to obtain his opinion. On 23 June Schoenberg apologised for taking so long to reply, pleading overwork and fatigue; he advised Hauer first to consult one of the Viennese Schoen-berg-pupils—Webern, Berg, or Karl Linke—and to let him know what they had thought; a meeting could then be arranged, if the person consulted thought it might prove useful. In his letter Hauer appears to have mentioned that his compositions had been praised by various people—hence, presumably, the closing sentence of Schoenberg's letter: 'It takes courage to compose, and once one has something to say, one must think as little of those who praise as of those who criticise.'

Just before this, in December 1912 and January 1913, there had been an exchange of letters between Schoenberg and the poet Richard Dehmel (1863–1920), who since 1901 had been living at Blankenese, near Hamburg. The letters have not been discussed earlier on, because in them Schoenberg developed a number of ideas whose full creative elaboration occurred only later. The letters, seven in all, were published by Joachim Birke, who also added brief comments, in the third volume (1958) of the periodical *Die Musikforschung*.

Dehmel's first letter to Schoenberg (12 December 1912) followed closely on a personal meeting between the two artists, mentioned by Schoenberg in his letter of 13 December. He had used poems by Dehmel for some of his songs (in Opp. 2, 3, and 6); the poem on which *Transfigured Night* was based is summarised on page 8. Dehmel's first letter refers to a performance of the work; writing after the concert, he told the composer how enchanted he had been by the music, and ended with the following quatrain, which does not appear in the printed editions of his works:

	(*literal translation*)
Ein Wörtlein Dank—o schöner Schall;	A word of thanks—o beauteous sound;
des Schöpferwortes Widerhall.	The echo of the creative word.
Uns allen ahnt kein höher Glück;	We all can sense no loftier joy;
Nun tönt die Welt zu Gott zurück.	The world now answers God in sound.

Schoenberg replied by return of post, and in a most cordial letter of thanks (*S.L.* 11) he asked Dehmel whether he would be willing to write the text for an oratorio he had long planned to compose. The words 'the prayer of presentday man' had occurred to him as the initial idea for the work, whose content he imagined as follows:

Modern man, having passed through materialism, socialism, and anarchy and, despite having been an atheist, still having in him some residue of ancient faith (in the form of superstition), wrestles with God (see also Strindberg's *Jacob Wrestling*) and finally succeeds in finding God and becoming religious. Learning to pray!

In the same letter, Schoenberg went on to tell Dehmel many details of his idea for an oratorio, mentioning also that he was thinking of basing an oratorio text on Strindberg's auto-biographical fragment 'Jacob Wrestling' (written in 1897-8, as a sequel to his 'Inferno'), and that he meant, with the same end in view, to adapt the closing chapter (The Assumption) of Balzac's novel *Séraphita* (one of his favourite books, on which he based a plan for an opera, according to information given in 1958 by Josef Rufer).

Dehmel's reply began: 'Your letter gave me pleasure of a lofty kind—the loftiest, probably, that an artist can know; indeed, creative stimulus given to other spirits is the sole proof of our own spiritual creativity.' Dehmel could not, however, meet Schoenberg's request for an oratorio text, since he was unwilling to make his creative promptings depend on anyone else's will, experience having taught him that under such circumstances his soul 'did not give of its inmost'. He did, however, enclose his poem *Schöpfungsfeier/ Oratorium natale*, and expressed the hope that it might be of some use to Schoenberg.

In his letter of 28 December, Schoenberg showed that he fully understood Dehmel's attitude, and mentioned that he was going to base a piece of music on *Schöpfungsfeier*—but not an oratorio; he had in mind the middle movement or finale of a symphony. Dehmel's letter of 29 December explains *Schöpfungsfeier* in more detail, and also mentions drafts of a 'heroic drama' with biblical figures. In his next letter (12 January 1913) Schoenberg was obliged to explain that during the months to come he would be unable to get down to composing, since he was too involved in 'activities'— a reference to the conducting commitments he had accepted for the immediately ensuing period, but above all to the Viennese first performance of the *Gurrelieder*.

Only one other letter from Schoenberg to Dehmel has come to light, the one in which he congratulated the poet on his fiftieth birthday. He dwelt at length on the stimulus he and everyone else had found in Dehmel's art, saying, among other things: 'What it taught us was the ability to listen to what goes on inside us, and to be a man of *our own* time for all that. Or rather, just because of that, since in reality time was within us rather than outside us. But it also taught us the opposite: how to be a man of *all* times, simply by being a man.'

The last work on which Schoenberg worked in Berlin (where he completed most of it) was the set of four songs for voice and orchestra, Op. 22. These songs are based on: the poem *Seraphita* by Ernest Dowson, in Stefan George's German translation; and three poems by Rilke—two (*Alle welche dich suchen*—All who seek Thee, and *Mach mich zum Wächter*

Arnold Schoenberg. A caricature by Lindluff, 1913

deiner Weiten—Make me the guardian of Thine immensities) from the *Stundenbuch* (Book of Hours), and one (*Vorgefühl*—Premonition) from the *Buch der Bilder* (Book of Images). The first three songs were composed in Berlin between October 1913 and January 1915, the fourth in Vienna in July 1916. The songs vary in length from eighty-five bars (No. 1) to twenty-five (No. 2).

In a lecture which Schoenberg drafted for Radio Frankfurt in February 1932 (he did not speak it himself), he told how, at the time he composed these songs, he had almost overcome the main difficulties caused by his renunciation of all links with traditional tonal relationships, but said that in setting to music such poems, which are of unusual expressive power, he had had only his inner sense of form to guide him. It had led him far beyond anything achieved before. This applies, above all, to the general atmosphere and sound, which are achieved by a different body of instruments in each song. For example, No. 1 calls for 24 violins, 12 celli, 9 double-basses, 6 clarinets, trumpet, 3 trombones, bass tuba, timpani, cymbals, xylophone, gong; No. 2, for 4 flutes, cor anglais, 3 clarinets, 2 bass clarinets, double-bassoon, harp, 3 solo celli. The vocal part covers a range from G below the treble stave to top C♯, and yet the demands made on the singer's diction and interpretative powers are still greater—considerably greater—than those made on her technique.

When in 1917 Universal Edition published the songs, Schoenberg contributed an extensive foreword, giving full reasons for his way of laying out the 'simplified study- and conducting-score', here used for the first time. This kind of score has as many staves as are necessary (from two to six), and the underlying principle is that of notating each musical occurrence as simply as possible, while still making it possible to follow exactly the course of each individual part. Schoenberg compared this notation to the way in which he initially set his orchestral works down on paper; all the sounds actually heard are notated on a few staves, the rhythm being indicated exactly, and full details of scoring are added. This 'short score' (Particell) is then to be used both in preparing the full score (used only for copying out the parts) and as a basis for the 'simplified study- and conducting-score', which contains only as many staves as are needed, with parts that share the same rhythm notated on the same stave wherever possible. Harmonic formations, too, are if possible to be made clear by chordal notation. The result strongly resembles a piano score for two or more hands, except that the instrumentation is also shown.

Immediately after the score of Schoenberg's Op. 22 appeared, the editors of *Der Merker* sent it to Siegfried Ochs, Arthur Nikisch, Felix von Weingartner, Max von Schillings, Bruno Walter and Wilhelm Furtwängler, the foremost German conductors of the day, and asked their views on Schoenberg's reforms. The replies were published on 15 July 1918. As far as concert use of the score was concerned, they were entirely negative, mostly for 'technical' reasons. Schillings thought the innovation valid for study purposes. Weingartner ended his rejection with the sarcastic remark: 'For the rest, I found Schönberg's way of writing his score wholly in keeping with his way of writing music.'

The next work Schoenberg published after the Op. 22 songs was the set of five Piano Pieces, Op. 23 (Hansen, Copenhagen, 1923). During the intervening years, there were vitally important developments in the composer's creative career.

5 First World War

After the outbreak of the First World War, Schoenberg's economic position in Berlin became increasingly difficult. The letters which about that time Berg wrote to Webern (who had already joined the army) show the touching efforts made by Schoenberg's Viennese pupils to provide him with an adequate income. Berg tried, above all, to ensure that Schoenberg should receive further sums from the Mahler Foundation; this led to some violent clashes with Alma Mahler, who finally agreed to back Schoenberg, even arranging for him to have a summer holiday near Semmering in July 1915, at the country house of a lady friend of hers.

He had already spent a number of short periods in Vienna. On 26 April 1915, in the large hall of the *Musikverein*, he had conducted the augmented *Tonkünstlerorchester*, the Philharmonic Choir, the Mercantile Choral Union, and a quartet of distinguished soloists in Beethoven's Choral Symphony, preceded by the Egmont Overture. Berg, who spoke enthusiastically of this concert, gave me a copy of a criticism that appeared on 1 May 1915, in the *Ostdeutsche Rundschau*, an organ of the yellow press published daily in Vienna; in tone, the article anticipates the days of rampant Nazism. Here is part of it:

The way this promotion turned out well and truly lifted the veil of alleged distinction which a group of musical politicians, artistic tradesmen of various kinds and anarchistic tendencies, with a common and very characteristic basic outlook, had cleverly spread over this man, for their own good or someone else's, and, so it seems, intend to go on spreading. Surely even the most convinced opponents of this fellow, who for a number of years has been the constant cause of the most repellent phenomena in Vienna's musical life, cannot have expected so complete a fiasco (not only in point of technique but also in every musical respect) as this crazy attempt at conducting. His movements on the rostrum were a picture of utter helplessness. He did not betray even a trace of an attempt at a conception that would strive after the work's content, let alone of penetration into the lofty spirit of this eternal monument to Germany's cultural greatness. Mr Schoenberg is lacking even in physical gifts—simple manual fluency, orientation in the orchestra— to such a degree that, had it been anyone but this white-headed boy, who is defended to the point of shamelessness by tribal prejudice, the voices of the critics would, to say the least, have been raised, as one man, in a thunderous 'Completely untalented!' It was a crafty idea to hand over Beethoven's Ninth Symphony to Mr Schoenberg for him to practise conducting on in public, but it has been utterly put to shame: the grain of Mephistophelean malice it contains will give rise to no poison tree, for Mr Schoenberg lacks the true hellish juice. But we now see clearly how the string-pullers in this comedy are minded—people of whom we shall take due note in future.

The fact that, even so, the performance was something of a public success is disclosed as follows, with true 'east-German' casuistry:

At the end, a crack-brained, God-forsaken group planted them-selves before the podium and, with the help of certain well-known louts of the concert hall, carried on in an excess of applause; Talmudic casuistry deduced from this that the epi-sode had pleased the public.

On 20 May 1915, Schoenberg had to report for an army medical examination in Vienna, and was found fit to serve. On 15 December he enrolled as a one-year-volunteer in the 4th Imperial-Royal Hoch- und Deutschmeister Infantry Regiment, stationed in Vienna. Since he had left grammar school prematurely, before taking his leaving examination, he had had to obtain a special dispensation giving him the right to volunteer for a year; this had been granted him in 1912 by the Hungarian defence ministry, the only body competent to do so, since his family were subject to Hungarian law. (They were legally domiciled in Pressburg (Poszony), now the Czech border town of Bratislava.)

After his basic training Schoenberg was drafted to the reserve-officer training course at Bruck-on-the-Leitha. At the time he was subject to attacks of asthma, and his state of health was also unsatisfactory in other ways, so that his friends and pupils in Vienna tried hard to get him sent on indefinite leave. Application had to be made in Budapest, since the Hungarian ministry was responsible. In the spring of 1916 an application was sent to the defence ministry from Vienna, but was refused, and on 12 May 1916 the secretary of the Viennese *Tonkünstlerverein* wrote, asking for help and advice, to Bartok, who at the time held an official teaching post, and who thought highly of Schoenberg's works. The request was repeated at greater length on 23 May. The two letters were published by Professor Denijs Dille, the head of the Budapest Bartok archives, in a 1964 issue of the *Öster- reichische Musikzeitung*, as part of an essay 'Bartok and Vienna', in the course of which he hazarded a guess that Bartok played an important part in bringing about the second application's favourable outcome. On 20 October 1916 Schoenberg was released from military duties till further notice. The following day he wrote to the composer Julius Bittner, president of the Viennese *Tonkünstlerverein*:

Now that I have time at last, I hasten to thank you most sincerely for all the trouble you have taken on my behalf. Do not think, because I have not done it earlier, that I did not think of doing so. Quite the contrary. I was, however, truly in no condition to. Truly, I had to count my time in minutes. And then I was irritated, or tired, or numb in a cheerfully animal sort of way. Now, slowly, I shall turn back into a man again, and my first step in that direction is to thank you from the bottom of my heart for your unblemished comradeship.

Immediately he was discharged, Schoenberg began work on the music of *Jacob's Ladder* (cf pages 98 ff.) About this time, however, he was also intensely concerned to give encouragement to the young, as is shown by the following passage from a hitherto unpublished letter written, from his address in the Gloriettegasse, Wien XIII, to a young musician at Krümau in Southern Bohemia:

When you need advice, ask me. Then, if it's urgent, I shall write at once. Today's word of advice: look at a lot of music! Not just modern music, though. Like every good musician, know your Beethoven, Mozart, Wagner, Brahms, Bach, etc.— *know them well!!!* You see, that is the most important thing for you, and for anyone who wants to be called a musician. How are you to understand presentday things fully, unless you have grasped and digested the things they are based on? Schopen- hauer writes somewhere that anyone wanting to read his works must first have read this, that and the other. So, you see, it's the same with the most recent music. One must know a mass of things; when one no longer knows where one is, then one begins to understand! Of course, each person has *one* favourite author—often the one he happens just to have read (and that is a very sympathetic trait); but one only does justice to an author when one loves him the most, despite knowing and loving the others. But, finally, the main thing is: to make music a great deal, and to hear a great deal of music. Is there nothing of the kind near where you are? How are things in the church?

In September 1917 Schoenberg, who was classed as Grade C, was called up for lighter military duties, which he performed very conscientiously and with remorseless consistency, until his final discharge, on medical grounds, the following month. In an article 'Arnold Schoenberg as a soldier in the First World War' published in Germany in the June 1966 issue of *Melos* (Schott, Mainz), the Viennese singing-teacher Viktor Fuchs told of some very amusing meetings with Schoenberg while the composer was in the infantry. The following story told by Hanns Eisler (1898–1962) in the 1924 commemorative volume is equally amusing and characteristic.

When he was in the army, Schoenberg always disliked being asked about anything to do with music. He wanted simply to be a soldier, and nothing else. He reacted particularly violently to the question, 'Are you that controversial composer?' Now, it so happened that he was drafted to a different company, and as soon as his name was called, the inevitable question came. After some hesitation, Schoenberg replied: 'I have to admit that I am: but it's like this—somebody had to be, and nobody else wanted to, so I took it on myself.' However, his questioner was undeterred, and went on to declare that it was a great honour for anyone to serve in the same company as Schoenberg; he received the following answer. 'It's not so bad, all that great honour. There are four hundred men in the company, so no one will be landed with much!'

This seems the place to review Schoenberg's production as from the outbreak of war. In his much-quoted letter of 3 June 1937, to the American composer and musical theorist Nicolas

Slonimsky, about the invention of his 'method of twelve-tone composition', Schoenberg told of his 'first step', in December 1914 or early 1915, when he sketched a symphony, whose finale was later used as material for the oratorio *Jacob's Ladder*. The scherzo of this symphony was based on a theme consisting of all twelve tones of the chromatic scale. The composer said of it, 'But this was only one of the themes. I was still far away from the idea to use such a basic theme as a unifying means for a whole work.'

Josef Rufer's researches among Schoenberg's posthumous papers, plus letters from Berg to Webern (13 and 22 June, 1915), tell us that on 15 January 1915 Schoenberg completed the text of a monologue, 'Dance-of-Death of the Principles' (*Totentanz der Prinzipien*), which was to be the basis of the above-mentioned scherzo, and three days later, on 18 January, he began to write the text of the oratorio *Jacob's Ladder* (*Die Jakobsleiter*), which for the moment was intended to be the symphony's fourth movement. Both texts were included in the volume published in 1926 by Universal Edition—it also included the libretto of *Die glückliche Hand* and the poem *Requiem* (see pages 142-3). The text of *Jacob's Ladder* had already been published separately in 1917.

The manuscript of *Totentanz der Prinzipien* is headed *III. Satz* (third movement); there is no way of telling whether this refers to the entire text, which runs to five printed pages, or merely to certain orchestral pieces indicated in the text (prelude and interlude). Schoenberg was accustomed to the idea of combining elements of symphony and melodrama, as is shown by an entry in what Rufer calls the Third Sketchbook, hinting at the inclusion of a melodrama entitled *Wendepunkt* (Turning-point) in the Second Chamber Symphony. A note prefacing the main text of *Totentanz der Prinzipien* suggests that Schoenberg imagined its being staged: 'Orchestral prelude, brief sketch of an event, in a hard, dry tone; then a funeral, speech at the grave-side, all very short; brief pause, followed by heavy bells behind the scenes. During the ensuing scene these become ever louder and more frequent, and the sound gradually turns into a furious pealing.'

The speaker's opening words are spoken against this

pealing of bells; when they stop, the monologue proper begins
—a passionate and combative address, seeking to trace the
fundamentals of human existence. Life is examined and discussed from every possible angle: with mocking cheerfulness,
with ironic pathos, with precocious didacticism, with wild
despair. It is the eternal struggle against the merciless commandment, 'Thou shalt!'; for the monologue's 'hero', the
reply 'I must!' is the sole decisive criterion, but he is not yet
ready to say it.

The monologue's spiritual content is closely related to
that of Schoenberg's poems for the first two of the Four
Pieces for mixed choir, Op. 27, composed in late September
and mid-October 1926 respectively. (The other two pieces
are based on poems by Chinese authors, from Hans Bethge's
collection *Die chinesische Flöte*, which also provided Mahler
with poems for *The Song of the Earth*.) Here are the two
Schoenberg poems:

Ineluctable (*Unentrinnbar*)
Valiant are those who accomplish deeds beyond their courage.
All they possess is the power to conceive of their mission, and
a character that will not let them decline it.
Should a God have been so ungracious as to grant them a
sense of their situation, then they are not to be envied.
And for that they are envied!

Not 'Thou shalt', but 'You must' (*Du sollst nicht, du musst*)
Thou shalt make unto thyself no image.
For an image restricts,
limits, grasps,
what is to remain unlimited and inconceivable.
An image demands a name—
Which you can take only from the small;
You are not to honour the small!
You must believe in the spirit!
Directly, unemotionally,
and selflessly.
You must, chosen one, you must, if you are to remain the
chosen one!

The image of the 'Chosen One' is elaborated in *Jacob's
Ladder*. In *Totentanz der Prinzipien*, after a 'long pause', the

dispute is broken off with the words, Enough! This is intolerable! Then, after an indication that the orchestra has vanished entirely, the text concludes with the following words:

All is lost! [Thirteen chimes are heard.] Thirteen. Not, indeed, twelve, but at least a limit to this emptiness! Contrition remains; but it explains nothing, for it does not say what led to it. It does not lack repentance, but lacks a visible image. It leaves the spiritual eye blind, and one's will is not of a mind to render sacrifice to it. It cannot prompt one to give up anything at all. Everything that could lead to it exerts greater attraction; for contrition lacks any image. [Interlude] A hollow hope: as if one had just awoken, still remembering carefree or neutral dreams —it is not really hope at all, merely that hopelessness is forgotten for a few moments; truly, no more than forgotten. All the same, one is refreshed and reinvigorated; man is glad to live, and glad to believe. Deception or forgetfulness is enough; to be blind! The darkness disperses—but the sun has no power.

Two dates show when Schoenberg began and finished work on the composition of the poem *Jacob's Ladder*: the first draft of the text is dated 18 January 1915, and a clean copy of the whole text was found among his papers, dated 26 May 1917. This latter was probably used by Universal Edition in preparing the printed edition, which followed later in the year. Another important date is 22 May 1921, when the complete poem was read at a matinée of the Society for Private Musical Performances (cf chapter 6), by the actor Wilhelm Klitsch, a member of Vienna's *Deutsches Volkstheater*. Berg wrote enthusiastically about the matinée to his friend and fellow-pupil Erwin Stein, and he must have been deeply involved, together with Schoenberg, in rehearsing the reading. Among his papers was a copy of the printed edition, in which he had entered numerous comments on the text, evidently written in great haste—which suggests that these pencilled notes are based on remarks made by Schoenberg either before or during the rehearsals with the actor: certain 'performing indications' make the second supposition the more likely of the two. The following brief discussion of the poem has been considerably influenced by these notes of Berg's.

The poem's clear division into two sections—with a long symphonic interlude as a musical bridge—arises from the basic difference in the condition of the individuals and groups of people who participate in the 'plot' of the oratorio. In Part I they are still 'under way', in Part II they are souls of the dead, who are either accepted into higher spheres or sent back to earth in new incarnations. The two sections are linked in spirit by the figure of the Archangel Gabriel, whose commands and explanations in Part I ensure that the humans concerned keep on the move, while his two long speeches in Part II indicate the new goals that are to be aimed at. The basic idea underlying the whole is the glorification of the power of prayer, which Schoenberg emphasises in Gabriel's final speech by a quotation from Balzac's *Séraphita*: 'Whoever prays, has become one with God.'

The text begins with Gabriel's much-quoted words: 'Whether to right or to left, forward or backward, uphill or downhill—you must go on, without asking what lies before or behind you.' The demand, to do so 'without asking,' prompts the various choral groups to try and discover to what purpose they are moving onward—'whither?', and 'for how long'? The three main groups—the discontented, those in doubt (the disillusioned and the heathen), and the jubilant —arrive at a common conclusion—'There is neither beginning nor end!'—though each group interprets it in a quite different way. The need for prayer is not recognised and with their attitude, 'One takes what comes, and bears what comes,' the undifferentiated mass have pronounced their own sentence, and recede for the moment into the background, to reappear at the end of Part II.

Gabriel now summons individuals who believe that 'their deeds have brought them nearer'. The first is 'one of the called'; he has sought after beauty, making all meaning subordinate to it, and so has become a pure and self-satisfied formalist. Gabriel denounces him as a worshipper of idols, who has called upon himself the blindness of the heathen. The next to appear is a 'rebel', who in a passionate tirade names as the cause of all earthly distress the condition into which man is plunged by the conflict between the God of the instincts and the God of the commandments. Gabriel points out to him the senselessness of this 'either-or' attitude, which prevents the state of calm wonder at God's greatness. Next we hear of 'one wrestling'; he has a dim recollection, from an earlier incarnation, of long-standing guilt, which he has overcome by renunciation—in the text, Schoenberg acknowledges that the idea of 'painlessness through renunciation' is taken from Schopenhauer—but he laments the fact that he can not tell right from wrong, so that he is also unable to avoid fresh guilt.

As a contrast to these three, Gabriel now introduces 'the Chosen One', in a solemn speech: 'Approach, you who, on the middle level, are a likeness, endowed with the true splendour; who resemble One far higher Being, just as the distant overtone resembles the fundamental, whilst others, deeper, themselves nearly fundamentals, are farther removed from him, as a glittering rock crystal is further from a diamond than is pure carbon!' The 'Chosen One', who now 'approaches', has Schoenberg's own features. A note made ten pages later by Berg expressly confirms this, but even without such proof, the Chosen One's speech is enough to make it clear that he is identical with Schoenberg; for instance, in his sense of kinship with the whole of humanity, which is his 'theme', he himself being a 'variation'; equally characteristically, there is his longing for clarity, which drives him on toward an unknown goal along a path where he takes with him his 'form', leaving behind him his work, which he calls his 'word'.

Gabriel, in his reply, addresses not the Chosen One but the people around him, explaining the nature of the man as follows: 'He must bring forth, so long as he is impure; bring forth, from within himself! When it has passed, it no longer moves him.'

The remainder of Part I is concerned with developments on a higher plane, after a considerable lapse of time; a monk appears before Gabriel, accusing himself of presumption, because he has believed himself to be a just man, whereas in fact all he has achieved is due to God's grace. He always believed that God demanded the sacrifices which, out of his vainglorious urge to be His good servant, he has imposed on himself. Now he is afraid his sacrifices have all been to no purpose; he has no knowledge of the happiness he has renounced, and, coward that he is, he has avoided exposing himself to its temptation.

Gabriel reassures him, pointing out that what he now knows places him on a level higher than the one he had reached as 'one of the called'; he sends him back to earth in a new incarnation—to bear witness and to suffer, to be a prophet and martyr. (When Gabriel speaks of the sins the monk will commit, even in his new incarnation, he uses the words 'for sins are punishments that cleanse'—a train of thought that goes back to Strindberg. At the time, Schoenberg was a great reader of Strindberg's autobiographical writings and 'blue-books'; moreover, Strindberg, like Balzac, constantly turned his mind back toward Swedenborg.)

Since, as mentioned, matters have now reached a higher level of development, we now hear a 'dying soul' (according to Swedenborg, this is the final stage before that of 'angel'), who looks back on her sufferings during all the thousands of years her incarnations have lasted, and describes the bliss of dreaming. As the soul is extinguished, her description becomes a wordless vocalisation. A distant choir of high women's voices announces that the dead one has attained the condition of a pure soul. While the others speak of the need to continue their wanderings, Gabriel at last indicates what the new direction is: 'Now you no longer complain; you begin to grasp what you must soon forget again. Returning, leave complaint behind you. When you no longer complain, you will be near. Then your ego will have been dissolved.'

These words end the first part of the oratorio, at bar 603. Schoenberg had begun to compose the music on 19 June 1917. In his sketchbook, this bar is followed by the words, 'called up to the army! 19.9.1917'.

In the May 1961 issue of the *Österreichische Musikzeitung*, Winfried Zillig published a comprehensive survey of the entire musical material for *Jacob's Ladder*, remarking, incidentally, that the passage about the 'dissolution of the ego' has tragically ironic overtones, in view of Schoenberg's forthcoming military service. Later in the essay, Zillig says:

Here, surely, is the underlying and tragic reason why the work remained a torso. The impetus of his inspiration had been checked, the flow from the sub- and unconscious had been violently cut off. And Schoenberg, of all people, always had to write each of his major works in intense spells, since his stylistic development was proceeding so rapidly that each new work found him at a new station along his way, one which only too often ruled out the preceding one.

The second part of the poem begins with a long speech by Gabriel, who prepares the souls for the transformations they are about to undergo; it ends with the words: 'Now take leave of your demons, genii, stars, gods and angels, each according to his degree of remoteness from the model, which remains here to represent him before the Highest. Take with you a recollection of it all: the obscure sense of your immortal soul.'

Gabriel speaks to the souls of those who in Part I were still under way; new souls, at a higher stage of evolution, appear singly, and later in groups. In the same order, they speak with their demons, genii, stars and angels, and are advised by them. The Chosen One observes all those around him, who are revealing their baser inclinations, and asks his God, 'And I must stand so near to these people that I almost believe I am one of them?' The God ends his reply with the admonition: 'Equally near to, and far from, all of them, you are surrounded by them as if by walls, from which you will only escape when your eyes, lifted in ecstasy, lose sight of them.'

Now follows the Chosen One's passionate confession; as to its autobiographical nature we have Berg's explicit testimony.

But I know that I shall see them, these walls, and nothing but them, and shall run my head against them, shall hardly be able to avert my gaze from them, shall destroy myself in profitless battles, losing super-earthly joy and brightness and faith, love and hope, and you my God will again not hear me; I shall again have to believe I stand alone; thrown back solely on myself, deserted and betrayed; and shall have to feel, as a compulsion, that I am led; and yet shall not feel myself supported; shall have to say what I should never have dared to think, do what I should never have dared answer for. What I do is, then, done almost unconsciously—so does it take me any further on? I have absolutely no idea where I stand—high or low.

'A God' speaks several times, in forceful terms, explaining to the Chosen One the nature of his calling, and saying finally, of the lower souls:

They are no further from you than are their betters. The destiny and the paths of souls are unequal; whoever carries out his task, improves his standing. And yet the soul's greatest achievement, beside which all the rest appears relatively slight, is to bear the earthly burden. All of them bear it, as you do. And yet you carry all the others as well.

By so accepting others' burdens the Chosen One atones for a major part of his guilt, so that the God can send him forth on the path to elevation, with the exhortation,

In you is assembled whatever is the essence of all creatures. So you, as the vanguard of the spirit, which at some time draws the parts to itself, are a picture, in miniature, of the future, according to whose nature you develop. In your own advance, you lift them up too. However you despise them, you suffer for them. You suffer with them; have pity on them!

Gabriel's final long speech, which covers four pages in the collected volume of texts, takes up this idea of pity, and culminates in a glorification of prayer:

The Eternal One, your God, is no jealous God, who takes revenge, but a God who takes account of your imperfect nature, who is aware of your inadequacy, who knows that you must fail and that your path is a long one. He hears you, grants your prayer according to your path, you are eternally in His hand, led despite your free will, protected and sheltered, bound to Him despite the evil pleasure you take in sinning, loved by Him —if you are able to pray. Learn to pray: knock, and it shall be opened unto you!'

After this speech the closing scene of the oratorio unfolds with ever-increasing power. Musically it was to have been an even more extended and still more compelling variation of the close of the first part. From the platform, and from the deep and the heights, the prayers of all the creatures were to have been heard, finally uniting in a single powerful chorus. In 1921 Schoenberg noted down his idea of how this ending was to sound: 'The choir and the soloists join in: at first mainly on the platform, then more and more from far off—offstage choirs located next to the offstage orchestras—so that, at the close, music is streaming into the great hall from all sides.'

The authoritative source of information about the progress of Schoenberg's work after bar 603 of *Jacob's Ladder* is the 'large sketch book', which Rufer calls No. IV. It is the most important additional source, supplementing the short score, which breaks off at bar 686, in the middle of the great symphonic interlude, having indicated, on only a few staves, virtually the entire composition up to that point, though with only a few indications as to scoring. Apart from a brief attempt on 30 November 1917, which he then discarded, Schoenberg resumed work on 7 December 1917; at this point the sketch-book contains a remark indicating that he had again been discharged from the army (*wieder enthoben*). Composition of Part I had gone quickly and continuously, taking exactly three months; work on the remainder proceeded only very hesitantly; the entries in the sketchbook cover a period from January 1918 to July 1922, and refer to fifteen separate and unconnected passages from the text of Part II. This way of working shows us that Schoenberg initially had in his mind a clear vision of the musical structure of the entire work, but that, once his steady stream of inspiration stopped, this disappeared.

Zillig gives a very plausible explanation of why things turned out as they did; the years concerned were those during which the 'method of composition with twelve tones related only to each other' was finally developed by Schoenberg, who first mentioned it to Josef Rufer in the summer of 1922. Zillig remarks:

The twelve-tone system having been discovered, once and for all, work on *Jacob's Ladder* clearly became impossible. Schoenberg had to express himself by means of the resources he had newly discovered; the rapid succession of twelve-tone works, and the progressive consolidation of the new system from one work to the next, are the decisive proof of this. And although *Jacob's Ladder* contains constant premonitions of this new system, in this of all pieces his search had kept leading him along other paths, which were no longer negotiable.

The letter dated 20 July 1922 (*S.L.* 42), which marked the resumption (after eight years) of Schoenberg's contact with Kandinsky, shows what his work on *Jacob's Ladder* meant to him during the difficult years from 1915 onward:

. . . perhaps the worst was after all the overturning of everything one has believed in. That was probably the most grievous thing of all.

When one's been used, where one's work was concerned, to clearing away all obstacles often by means of one immense intellectual effort and in those eight years found oneself constantly faced with new obstacles against which all thinking, all power of invention, all energy, all ideas, proved helpless, for a man for whom ideas have been everything it means nothing less than the total collapse of things, unless he has come to find support, in ever increasing measure, in a belief in something higher, beyond. You would, I think, see what I mean best from my libretto *Jacob's Ladder* (an oratorio): what I mean is—even though without any organisational fetters—religion. This was my one and only support during those years —here let this be said for the first time.

Between October and December 1944 Schoenberg resumed work on *Jacob's Ladder*, and prepared a short score of the first 44 bars, with new indications for scoring. There is also a note, from the same period, giving the following orchestration: four flutes, oboes, clarinets, bassoons, and horns (plus a tenor horn); three trumpets and trombones, tuba, percussion and strings. Evidently Schoenberg had very much reduced the instrumental forces foreseen in 1917: 10 piccolos, 10 flutes, 10 oboes, 10 cor anglais, 18 clarinets, 6 bass-clarinets, 10 bassoons, 10 contra-bassoons, 12 horns, 10 trumpets, 8 trombones, 4 to 6 bass tubas, 8 harps, celeste, percussion, 50 violins, 30 violas, 30 cellos and 30 double-basses. As well as this main orchestra on the platform, he planned also to use four offstage orchestras. The vocal forces demanded by Schoenberg were thirteen soloists, a twelve-part double choir of 720 singers on the platform, as well as two unseen choirs above and below the platform. As early as June 1921, once Schoenberg had begun seriously to go into the possibilities of a performance, even drafting a rehearsal plan, he had begun to envisage much smaller forces.

In 1926 Schoenberg sketched in outline a system of pipes

to regulate the distribution into the hall of the sound from the offstage orchestras. There is also a note from 1944 about replacing the pipes by microphones and loudspeakers. Both ideas foreshadow the stereophony now in general use—an example of the way in which, even in his thinking on technical points, Schoenberg was far ahead of his time.

There is evidence of this extraordinary clairvoyance in matters technical, not only in the remark about the 'receiver and transmitter tuned alike' (cf page 39), but in a fairly long article about mechanical music-instruments dating from 1926; this appeared in *Pult und Taktstock* (Desk and Baton), a specialist periodical for conductors published by Universal Edition, Vienna, and ended with the words: 'It is sentimental to wail about mechanisation, and unthinkingly to believe that spirit, so far as it is present, is driven out by mechanism; only very small spirits suffer at every turn if they are not given enough room. Wailing room.'

There were few signs of any unusual technical difficulties at the first performance of Part I of *Jacob's Ladder*, which took place on 16 June 1961, at a special concert during the 35th International Festival of the International Society for Contemporary Music, in the large hall of Vienna's *Musik-verein*. The performers were seven leading singers, the choirs of the Cologne and Hamburg radios, and the Cologne Radio Symphony Orchestra, conducted by Rafael Kubelik. The performance was preceded by a reading of the entire text, with fifteen actors and the Zürich Speaking Choir, produced by Gustav Rudolf Sellner.

The score used for the performance had been prepared at the request of the composer's widow, Mrs Gertrud Schoenberg, by one of his pupils, Winfried Zillig (1905–63), after another former pupil, Karl Rankl, had declined the task which the master had hoped he would take on (he said so in a letter, *S.L.* 245, to Rankl dated 27 June 1951, i.e. a mere fortnight before his death). In 1961 Zillig published a 'work report', with many musical examples, and referred to Schoenberg's letter to Rankl, particularly to the passage:

What I want to ask you is if you would, in principle, be willing to do such a score. In the manuscript there are plenty of often very full indications of my orchestral intentions. It would then be a matter of supplying, with the necessary discretion, such interpretations and elaborations as would make it possible to perform this part effectively.

In view of this, Zillig's task, as far as he could see, was clear:

Obviously, not a single note was to be added to Schoenberg's musical text. Nor, indeed, was it necessary in a single bar of the score; for even when Schoenberg's short score contains the remark 'Still to be elaborated'—i.e. in bar 142—the existing music for a-cappella chorus, expressing the way the 'indifferent' fade out of the light, is not only complete, but it expresses perfectly this weary process of fading. Again, although Schoenberg would obviously have loved to complete the interlude, the way in which it breaks off makes it seem not in fact to break off at all, but sounds like a genuine ending, floating off into the beyond. Having begun purely instrumentally, with four offstage orchestras, the interlude culminates with the entry of the voices—the women's choir, and the high and highest sopranos—this entry being thematically identical with the high-soprano music for the dying soul. (It would, surely, have been worked out identically, too.) All this strikes me as enough in itself to be a convincingly effective symbol (anticipating the end of the whole work) for the union of the soul with God, that being the goal of all human aspiration.

The only problem in carrying out Schoenberg's wishes, and in making performable the part of *Jacob's Ladder* whose composition he had completed, was one of orchestration.

In his orchestration, Zillig adhered to the reduced main orchestra indicated by Schoenberg in his 1944 note (cf page 105), adding only a celeste and two harps; in each of the offstage orchestras, whose members could be taken from the main orchestra, an additional harmonium was used. Except for any possible special effects of orchestration that might have occurred to the composer in the course of completing the score, the sound of Zillig's version at the performance was absolutely authentic.

On 22 May 1950 Schoenberg remarked to Hermann Scherchen that *Jacob's Ladder* rather matched *Erwartung* and *Die glückliche Hand* in style—an important remark, if one wishes to assess the style in which the work is composed, though in many passages Schoenberg in fact looked further back, to a style earlier than that of the two stage works from the so-called 'atonal' period. In the aforementioned article, Zillig remarked very pertinently on this odd phenomenon:

Dissecting *Jacob's Ladder* in terms of its musical content, and relating it to Schoenberg's total output, one is astonished to find, after the uncompromising boldness of the 'atonal' epoch, that it contains much pointing rather to the Schoenberg of the First Chamber Symphony or even earlier. The melodic ductus is far simpler than in the immediately preceding works; there, the line had been constantly broken down in a 'pointillist' way, whereas here one suddenly finds a return to the long melodic arch. There are even tonal reminiscences at times, and they are often conscious ones—for instance, at one point Schoenberg takes a long, complicated melodic structure, and leaves out certain notes, so producing a pure D-flat-major line. The harmony, too, often looks back and uses forms simpler than those introduced in, for instance, the 5 Orchestral Pieces Op. 16, or *Die glückliche Hand.* Long chains of augmented triads constantly occur. The six notes of the main idea, which constantly return, give rise to repetitions sometimes reminiscent of the symmetrical correspondences found in classical forms. Contrapuntal forms are here realised strictly, and in the old manner—they had, indeed, already been present in *Pierrot Lunaire* but had there appeared as if in a distorting mirror. 'Speech-song' is also used here—something Schoenberg had brought to a pitch of fascinating perfection in *Pierrot*—but the manner of its use is basically different, above all in the choruses. In *Pierrot* Schoenberg gives express instructions that the speaking voice is on no account to be governed by the absolute pitch indicated by the notation of its part, these pitches being meant merely to represent certain relationships within the compass of the speaking voice (something that varies from person to person); this is, moreover, confirmed by the fact that, almost throughout, the instrumental accompaniment goes its own independent way. Throughout *Jacob's Ladder*, on the other hand, the orchestra's melodic and harmonic complexes are written in unison with those of the speaking chorus, and one is therefore obliged to conclude that in this case the speech-melody has to adhere to a specific absolute pitch, thus approximating far more nearly to song than in the previous works where Schoenberg had used speech-melodies. This interpretation—a 'tonal' one, as it were—of the speech-melodies in *Jacob's Ladder* is also supported by the fact that, if they are so treated, the work's 'religious and oratorio-like' expressiveness is heightened.

The music's 'religious and oratorio-like expressiveness' has stood out strongly at every performance of the work. In one of his last letters (13 June 1951, to Josef Rufer, *S.L.* 244) Schoenberg expressly emphasised the religious and philosophical significance of *Moses and Aaron*, as regards both its subject matter and the way this is treated; a comparable point applies to the earlier *Jacob's Ladder*, as regards the work's themes and the way they are developed. In a long article significantly subtitled *Musik zwischen Theologie und Weltanschauung* (Music between theology and philosophy of life), published in the *Schweizerische Musikzeitung* (1965, Nos. 5/6), the German musicologist Karl H. Wörner comprehensively surveyed, in all their richness and variety, the religious and philosophical elements demonstrably present in the oratorio. Wörner has investigated how the text of *Jacob's Ladder* is related to the Bible, to Theosophy (hierarchic ladder as the path to God), to Anthroposophy (comparison with Rudolf Steiner's four mystery dramas: *Portal of Initiation, Soul's Probation, Guardian of the Threshold*, and *Soul's Awakening*), to the doctrines of Swedenborg elaborated in works of Balzac, to Swedenborg's own mysticism (particularly to his doctrine of correspondences), and to Chassidism. Wörner finally mentions, as a hypothesis, the identity of 'The Chosen One' with Schoenberg, and Berg's notes, quoted above, support him.

The idea that these notes were directly based on Schoenberg's own remarks is confirmed by an essay about *Jacob's Ladder* written in 1937 by the poet Berthold Viertel. The essay appeared in a symposium on Schoenberg edited by Merle Armitage (New York, 1937), and dedicated to the memory of Berg. There is a close connection between Berg's notes and the opening of the essay, which describes the oratorio's text as a literary creation representing 'the theme and its variations'. This idea, like Berg's, can only have been inspired by some actual remarks of Schoenberg's. Again, the central passage in the essay, discussing prayer as the fundamental problem, proves the absolute authenticity of Viertel's observations, as does the general explanation he offers:

Praying becomes a fundamental problem to him, and not only his individual problem—but a general one. The problem of humanity. He must understand it universally, as action and fulfilment of the human soul—and in all its possibilities. He thinks it through in all its forms. He may have done so for years. Until, one day, the religious thinker, Schoenberg, had a vision which became the inspiration of the artist.

However, the most impressive evidence for the decisive importance of prayer in Schoenberg's life and creative work is provided by his very last work, on which he was still working a few days before he died. He was engaged in writing the texts for sixteen 'Modern Psalms'—the last of which remained incomplete; they date from between 29 September 1950 and 3 July 1951, and were published (in both facsimile and transcription) in 1956 (Schott, edited by Mrs Gertrud Schoenberg and Rudolf Kolisch), together with Schoenberg's music for the first psalm, which breaks off at the second appearance of the words 'Trotzdem bete ich' (For all that, I pray). We see, then, that the master's creative thoughts were centred, until the very end, on the theme treated in *Jacob's Ladder*.

While working on *Jacob's Ladder*—he completed the text in May 1917 and composed Part I between 19 June and 17 September of that year—Schoenberg was also deeply involved with new educational projects. At that time he drafted the prospectus of a Composition Seminar, published on 1 September. Here are some of its principal passages:

One learns perfectly only those things for which one has an aptitude. Then, no particular pedagogic discipline is needed: a model, provoking emulation, suffices; one learns whatever one was created for, without knowing how; one learns as much as one's inborn aptitudes allow.
  This carefree way of learning has to be helped out by pedagogic means only because the number of things to be learned

is ever on the increase, and the amount of time available correspondingly smaller.

Now, though it is astonishing how many people can in fact reach a 'prescribed standard' in matters for which they have little aptitude, there is no denying that the results are but mediocre. This is particularly apparent in the artistic field. At one time, the difference between the very best amateur and the artist might lie not in their respective performances, but merely in the fact that the amateur did not earn his daily bread through art; nowadays, there are all too many artists whose performance is amateurish, the only difference being that their sole concern is with breadwinning. The able amateur has, however, become relatively rare.

One main cause is teaching. It asks too much and too little of artist and amateur alike; too little, since in bringing him to the prescribed standard it gives him more than he needs, and so relieves him of the need to find, within himself, the superabundant energy through which his natural gifts can spread themselves and take on fullness; too much, since by the same token it gives him less than he needs, so paralysing whatever energies he has, and preventing his becoming even the specialist his aptitude fits him to be.

In art there is but one true teacher: inclination. And he has but one usable assistant: imitation.

In order to pass on to the learner the fruits of these conclusions, reached after twenty years' experience of teaching, I have decided to found a *Composition Seminar*, at the Schwarzwald School, No. 9, Wallnerstrasse, Wien I, and to formulate the conditions of admission in such a way that anyone, *rich or poor, artist or amateur, advanced student or beginner*, can take part.

Schoenberg set particular store by these conditions of admission. He also wanted to link the seminar with 'a reform of a social nature', which he described as follows, in an interview printed in the *Neue Wiener Journal* (18 September 1917):

This is a reform I have already proposed—in 1912, when I was summoned to teach at the Academy of Music (a summons I eventually had to decline). I was told that the 'state' could not indulge in any such reform; I can only retort, 'If not the state, then who?' After all, my reform is as follows: the person receiving instruction is the one who decides the fee payable. To the extent that I conceive of this becoming an official procedure, I imagine the teaching fee as determined on the basis of tax assessment. Such a course is obviously not open to me as a private individual. And so I say: let each person pay as much as his circumstances allow.

In the same interview Schoenberg spoke as follows about the teaching system he wished to adopt, and did in fact adopt in the seminar:

I want to avoid teaching and learning 'by the book'. It is no good for the pupil and the teacher to 'go through the next chapter'. With a rigid curriculum, the pupil mostly hears only things that leave him utterly uninterested. For this reason, I have adopted a completely new, free system as the basis for my course, which I call a 'composition seminar':
One particular period in the day is entirely set aside for my pupils—all of them at once. Each pupil comes when he wants to learn, when he is eager to know this or that. A subject is not settled before each lesson, but is freely chosen by the pupil. So one never just goes down the list—harmony, counterpoint, instrumentation . . .; it is all done by entirely free choice. In more detail, the course runs as follows: I meet my pupils in the classroom, with as little formality as possible. One of them asks me about some point or other, and I reply, to suit the scope of his question, or perhaps going rather beyond it, according to whether or not I think this a good thing for the person who asked the question. I may not even answer at all, if at that moment I am not attracted by the subject touched on; I may perhaps occasionally go so far as to send home all the pupils who have turned up, because I do not feel like teaching that day, so should be unlikely to have much, or anything, to offer them as teacher.

Schoenberg's further period of military service (19 September to 7 December 1917) meant that he could not begin the seminar until early in 1918; in April of that year he moved to a new apartment at Mödling-bei-Wien, and also moved the seminar there. He continued it until 1920. Among his pupils at that time were Josef Rufer, Erwin Ratz, Karl Rankl, and, from 1919 onward, Hanns Eisler. What Schoenberg's teaching meant, even to the non-creative, can be gathered from the following remarks by a lady who was once his pupil:

The hours I spent at Schoenberg's classes were among my most priceless musical experiences. Schoenberg preferred to analyse Brahms and Mozart. Once, Brahms's Fourth Symphony was discussed, and a Mozart piano sonata. The subtlety with which he followed Brahms's thematic lines, right down to their subtlest ramifications, the way he demonstrated the balanced equilibrium in Mozart's a-symmetrical Rococo—these lessons will remain engraved on my mind. It was as if a beam of light had suddenly shone through a hovering cloud of darkness. Schoenberg knew how to 'explain' things, to make them truly 'clear'. At moments such as that, one felt his genius and his affinity with the genius of others. He always exerted a fascination, but at such times it grew beyond all measure, and no one could resist it.

In June 1918 Schoenberg arranged a most unusual experiment in musical education; he coached an ensemble of fifteen outstanding musicians in ten public rehearsals of his 1906 Chamber Symphony, Op. 9, after which the listeners were sent away without having been given a 'real' concert performance of the work. There is an objective report on this whole undertaking, in the form of a newspaper article covering many columns, by the highly educated music critic Heinrich von Kralik (1887–1959), published on 4 July 1918 under the title 'A musical summer course'. Since, to my knowledge, this essay is not mentioned in any of the previous literature about Schoenberg, I am here reprinting those parts of the text which refer to the critic's experiences at the rehearsals, omitting those sections in which Kralik, by no means an adherent of Schoenberg, dealt in a gently and benevolently ironic way with the situation of the artist in Viennese musical life. Kralik began his report as follows:

It was not meant exactly for beginners, but certainly for those who still have something to learn. For active minds, not content with comfortable, hedonistic enjoyment of art, but lacking, as yet, any initiation into the dark secrets of the most recent developments; those thirsty to find out, at last, what they are supposed to hear in it all, and how. An experimental course of instruction, with the aim of making the listener's aural faculties (physical and intellectual) more sensitive to the new acoustic assumptions and sounds contained in the most extreme secessionist music. That, roughly, was the intention behind the ten public rehearsals of Arnold Schoenberg's Chamber Symphony.

Kralik next describes at some length the general alienation that Schoenberg's compositions aroused when heard, above all because of their novel treatment of the material of music, a treatment that ran counter to every tradition; an alienation which made it impossible for the terrified listener to grasp what the composer was really trying to say in his music. Kralik then says of the rehearsals:

In them, the aim was to mellow the recalcitrant aural faculty. Practical schooling—a kind of propaganda through action—was the only means left (and certainly the right one), after well-intentioned theorising and benevolent exhortation had failed to do the trick. Schoenberg's *Treatise on Harmony*, a respectable volume, full of excellent ideas, very stimulating, is incapable of remodelling one's ear, lavish though it is with its wise sayings. The only thing that can help is a methodical hardening course. Something that, heard for the ninth time, was still an acoustic monstrosity, emerges, when heard for the tenth time, as something already familiar, and may even be on the point of revealing all manner of mysterious beauties—next time . . .

Is Arnold Schoenberg's path the right one? His renunciation of everything sickly-sweet, conventional, all polite phrase-making—that is tempting; his harshness, masculinity, his sparkling intellectual machinery, that is tempting. But there are intolerable, grotesque figures that get in the way; a hydra blocks the road, spewing dissonances and painful discord from its manifold maws. Along with Schoenberg and fifteen valiant musicians, a no less valiant adventurous flock of listeners tackled the vile beast. One cacophonous passage after another was tackled, and the muscular power of one's aural apparatus was steeled by the struggle with its sharp points, its hard surfaces, and its asperities. And, even before the day of the tenth and final rehearsal, the players were played in, the listeners listened-in. The worst had been overcome. The terrifying apparitions looked less full of menace, their appearance had taken on a new mildness, their way of living a new accessibility. One began to feel thoroughly at home and cheerful in their company. . . .

So a tense, complicated business has been turned into a simple, normal procedure; one hears, as if it were something quite self-evident, Schoenberg's Chamber Symphony, Op. 9. In form, a blend of single movement and work in several movements. In content, the typically characterised first and second subject of a sonata form movement, the droll, fantastic play of the scherzo, a long-drawn-out cantabile tune, melancholy and elegiac, in the *Quasi adagio*, and a final section referring, like a recapitulation, to the opening. Powerful thunderclouds of development gather and come pelting down; there are sweet and charming episodes where the instruments are reconciled in sounds of felicitous charm. The natural history of the harmonies, whose malevolent appearance causes so much worry, so many headaches, is the theory of fourth-chords, a varied tribe whose members include every imaginable kind of individual. There were many bad moments before, in the end, agreement was reached with these stimulatingly wild young scions of the theory of fourths.

The help given by fifteen valiant instrumentalists was crucial, and must be gratefully acknowledged; they rehearsed, without embarrassment or vanity, and went on rehearsing until things finally worked. The first violinist, a quite outstanding musician, obviously knew from the start that all would end well. Hence, even, the mischievous smile that constantly played around his animated pair of eyes, a smile the mistrustful could at first almost have taken as expressing sly mockery. It was the smile of someone who is in the know. And, in great things as in small, the doubter found himself disabused, so that he finally joined in, like Saul converted, when at the final rehearsal Arnold Schoenberg was greeted with warm and cordial applause.

Kralik's unvarnished report is of great and general relevance, not only to this particular experience with ten public rehearsals of the Chamber Symphony, but also to the reception of new music—truly 'new' music being the kind which tends at first hearing (and often on repeated hearings) to have a distinct shock effect on listeners unused to it. To overcome this shock effect, as I know from repeated experience, one needs a protracted spell of hard listening, spurred on by good will. The 'external' acoustical difficulties can mostly be overcome in this way. But new music cannot acquire real power to convince until the listener becomes certain that the work concerned was created from inner necessity. This criterion alone (and it is a very difficult one to realise) makes it possible to distinguish between legitimate masterpieces and the shoddy stuff produced by certain competitors who are out merely to create a sensation. In both categories, one may find masterly command of the technique of composition; the sole essential is the ineluctable compulsion, rooted in the individual ego, that leads to musical expression in the particular form found so 'shocking'. The aim of the present book is to bear witness, so far as is possible, to the fact that Schoenberg's entire career, as man and artist, was ruled by a compulsion of that kind.

Schoenberg
with his
daughter,
Gertrud
Greissle, and his
grandson
Arnold ('Bubi')
at Traunkirchen,
1923

Arnold
Schoenberg in
the late 1920s

6 The Society for
Private Musical Performances

Immediately after the end of the First World War, Schoenberg summarised his ideas for reforming musical life, in a contribution to a symposium published in 1919 by Adolf Loos, under the title *Guide-Lines for a Ministry of the Arts*. Schoenberg's essay had eight paragraphs, of which the first and last dealt with his proposals (cf pp. 111–12) for determining teaching fees on the basis of tax-assessment; paragraphs 3 and 4 were devoted to reforms in the laws of inheritance and copyright (Schoenberg's suggestion for the foundation of a Society of Authors, to publish their own works, is very much along the lines once propounded by Schumann, in a letter of 18 May 1837, to his friend Anton von Zuccalmaglio). Paragraph 7 outlines the way in which a planned 'Arts Council' (which never came into being) was to be formed; the remaining paragraphs (2, 5, and 6) are reproduced here in their entirety; the first two are self-explanatory, the third requires a brief explanation.

Concert life must gradually cease to be a commercial business. Given the right organisation, that will avoid all middlemen, arrangers and the like, and address itself directly to the public, it should easily be possible to do everything needed for the furtherance of art, even without state assistance.

The basic fault in public concert-life is competition (*concertare* = 'to compete').

One gives concerts for two reasons. The first, pure reason: one or more people make music, recite, sing; others, anxious to share this experience, are permitted to listen. The second, petty, impure reason: art wins prizes.[1] Many people want to win prizes, and the highest goes to the winner. So now he has to win, whereas once he merely had to sing.

Thus competition, the need to win, brings pettiness into the business of art.

Once the correct relationship is re-established, through direct contact with the public (which will then no longer be the high-handed judge, deciding between hunger and laurels) —the relationship "There is a performance: those who want to listen are allowed to"—it will be possible to find a way of paying artists appropriately, while still holding adequate rehearsals.

Musicians' social position must be improved. The oboist or horn-player who has to play a solo in the evening is an artist who in his own field needs a higher degree of infallibility than do

[1] *Kunst bringt Gunst*— literally, 'art brings favour'. L.B.

most top civil servants in theirs. His studies demand industry, perseverance, seriousness, they last so long, and require so much talent, that he should be numbered among the truly elect on the social ladder.

Paragraph 6 contains Schoenberg's reactions to proposals by Adolf Loos, who suggested that the Viennese state theatres should serve to give the most perfect possible performances of stage works. Each work was to be produced with such care, and such expensive production and casting, that thirty performances in a season would justify the work and expense involved. Each of the state theatres would perform some ten works annually. The system of ticket distribution would provide for only one visit by each theatregoer to each of the year's various productions. At the end of the season, the works included in one year's repertoire would be taken off and not given again for a long time, so as to make way for new productions. Literary experiments (first performances) would not be the business of the state theatres; they would be entrusted to the theatres under private management. Touring theatres would be set up to cover the provinces.

Schoenberg agreed with these proposals of Loos,

With certain reservations arising out of musical necessities, namely:
1. One does not know music after hearing it once. The music-lover, and especially the artist who has to perform music, must hear it often. Performances of a small number of works will, then, be particularly insufficient if, as Loos proposes, these works are not to be repeated for some years.
2. If this theatre had the best resources at its disposal, with perhaps a second or a third theatre meeting the above-mentioned artistic demand, but with only more limited resources, this would be a pity, in the sense that one would not hear outstanding performances of masterpieces often enough.

In the final sentence of this paragraph Schoenberg said:

On the other hand I strongly approve the idea of touring theatres, for which a repertoire of two or three works could well suffice. At the same time I would put in a plea for the formation of touring orchestras and professional choirs, with the same end in view.

Six years later, the Cologne publisher F. J. Marcan reprinted this Schoenberg essay in his collection *Von Neuer
Musik*, and the author added the following 'preface':

I wrote this little essay immediately after the war had been lost,
when the possession of five rational senses was threatened
right and left by Bolshevism; when the whole world looked only
to suicide for help, and only to its fantasy for a new, better
reality, building in the air bomb-proof castles meant to protect
the brain from the assaults of hunger; at a time when it could
cost a man his head to refrain from saying the things that would
satisfy the parties!

No reasonable spinner of fantasies can hope to see his dreams
come any truer than by having his article reprinted; for that
reason, it is hereby permitted.

At about the same time as Schoenberg composed his contribution to Loos's symposium, he took the first steps toward
realising another original project of an educational nature,
which during the ensuing years made great demands on him:
this, the society for Private Musical Performances, occupies
an important place in the history of new music. He founded it
in November 1918, initially for the benefit only of his small
circle of pupils and close friends. The secrecy surrounding
the Society's activities gave rise, incidentally, to misconceptions on the public's part, particularly about the extent to
which Schoenberg's own music was played there, and it
came to be jocularly known as the Viennese Schoenberg-
Society. Its first concert was on 29 December 1918 and the
following works were performed: two piano sonatas by
Scriabin (Nos. 4 and 7, played by Eduard Steuermann);
Debussy's four *Proses Lyriques* (sung by Felicie Mihacsek,
a soprano from the Vienna State Opera, with Ernst Bachrich
at the piano); and Mahler's Seventh Symphony, arranged for
piano duet and played by the two pianists in the concert.
After being active on a private basis for a few weeks the
Society, whose statutes Schoenberg himself had drafted,
turned to the public, with a prospectus written by Berg.
The opening paragraphs of this show clearly the aims and
methods of the society:

The purpose of this Society, founded in November 1918, is to provide Arnold Schoenberg with the possibility of personally carrying out his intention of giving artists and art-lovers a real and accurate knowledge of modern music.

One circumstance which contributes to a large extent to the relationship of the public to modern music, is that any impression they receive of it is inevitably one of un-clarity. The public is unclear about the purpose, the direction, the intention, the world of expression, the method of expression, the value, the nature and the aim of the works. The performances are for the most part unclear. And in particular the public's consciousness of its needs and desires is unclear. The consequence is that the works are valued, respected, praised and welcomed, or disregarded, censured and rejected, all on account of one single effect, which proceeds equally from all of them: *on account of un-clarity*.

In the long run, this cannot satisfy anybody worthy of attention—no serious author, and none of the better members of an audience. The desire to achieve clarity at last, and thus take into account such needs and desires as are justified, this was one of the reasons that moved Arnold Schoenberg to found the society.

Three things are necessary for the achievement of this aim.

1. Clear, well-prepared performances.
2. Frequent repetitions.
3. The performances must be withdrawn from the corrupting influence of publicity; that is, they must not be inspired by a spirit of competition, and must be independent of applause and expressions of disapproval.

This points to the important difference that is apparent when we compare the task of this society with that of normal presentday concert life, which the society intends to keep definitely at a distance.[1]

Next, the prospectus explains its three basic points at some length. Particular stress is laid on the Society's scrupulous preparation (for instance, the Mahler symphony heard at the opening concert had been given twelve rehearsals, mostly of four hours each). Another point emphasised is the participation of young artists, who placed themselves at the Society's disposal out of interest, and not for the sake of vain, profit-seeking virtuosity: 'The only success that an artist can achieve here is the one that ought to be the most important

[1] This and the following extracts from the prospectus are given in C. Cardew's translation.

success in having made the work, and thus the author, comprehensible to his hearers.' This aim—to make the works comprehensible—was also the reason for repeating them frequently. The exclusion of any public reporting was meant to emphasise the private character of the concerts, which were concerned solely with 'the effect made by the actual music'.

The prospectus contains a whole section devoted to explaining the point of the arrangements of orchestral works—mostly for piano or two pianos, four to eight hands—heard at the concerts. The audience were deprived of the works' original sound, but this shortcoming was turned to good account, 'since it disarms the common objection, that this music is effective only on account of its more or less rich and effective instrumentation, and lacks those properties hitherto characteristic for good music: melodies, harmonic richness, polyphony, perfection of form, architecture, etc.'

The closing section of the prospectus deals with the material organisation of the Society. The members pledged themselves to buy season tickets for the weekly promotions. The concerts took place on Mondays, in the ceremonial hall of the Schwarzwald Schools, Wallnerstrasse 9, Vienna 1, and later in the ceremonial hall of the Society of Engineers and Architects, Eschenbachgasse 9, in the same district; on Sunday mornings in the small hall (Brahms-Saal) of the *Musikverein*, or the small hall (Schubert-Saal) of the Konzerthaus. There were four price ranges for the seats. For the first, the members were left to decide how much they would pay; for the remaining categories, the following sums were fixed (expressed in Kronen, the chronically depreciating Austrian currency of the time): basic charge 24 Kr., 16 Kr. or 8 Kr.; weekly instalments 3–, 2–, 1. Schoenberg, as the Society's president, had absolute directorial powers: he was assisted by a secretary first Paul Amadeus Pisk, later Josef Rufer, Rudolf Wenzel, and Felix Greissle), a treasurer (Dr Arthur Prager), an archivist (Dr Josef Polnauer), an assistant dealing with the Society's correspondence, and the various musical assistants among them Webern, Berg alternating with Eduard Steuermann, Erwin Stein, and Dr Benno Sachs).

The first edition of the prospectus (which appeared a number of times, the later issues being abridged) is dated

16 February 1919. The next day, Berg wrote to his fellow-pupil Erwin Stein that he was the author, and mentioned that the Society at that time had about 320 members.

The rapid depreciation of the Austrian currency forced the Society to suspend its activities at the end of 1921; the only way to give an idea of just how much it did, even disregarding its indirect effects, is a statistical survey of its performances. The statistics so far published stop short at the end of October 1921. Thanks to the friendly co-operation of Dr Leopold Nowak, the director of the Music Department of the Austrian National Library, who provided me with many photocopies of Schoenberg's hand-written programme-notes (these now belong to the Library), I have been able to extend the statistics to cover the whole of 1921. Up to that point, the Society had given 117 concerts, including 154 contemporary works; of these, 54 were played once only, the remaining 100 being repeated (41 once, 29 twice, 16 three times, 9 four times, 4 five times, and 1 seven times). So the total number of programme items was 353. Apart from the Society's evenings there were a number of special events: two 'propaganda concerts', an evening in honour of Ravel, several performances of *Pierrot Lunaire*, two concerts of classical works (Mozart, Beethoven and Brahms), the reading of *Jacob's Ladder* (cf page 98), and an Evening of Waltzes—of which more later. Among the composers most performed were: Reger (24 works), Debussy (16 works), Bartok and Schoenberg (12 works). It should be added that not until the early spring of 1920 did Schoenberg allow one of his own works to be given at a concert of the Society. In the final concert, on 5 December 1921, *Pierrot Lunaire* was given.

In the Society's final prospectus, which appeared in November 1921, 93 further works were announced as due for performance in 1922: there was also reference to stage performances of ballets by Berg, Bartok, Webern, Debussy and Wellesz, also of Schoenberg's *Die glückliche Hand*. (The Berg and Webern ballets were never composed; the first performance of *Die glückliche Hand* did not take place until 1924.)

The Society's activities reached a peak of intensity at the end of May 1921. This is shown by the following extracts from a letter sent by Berg to Erwin Stein on 2 June 1921:

Since over the last few weeks Schoenberg has been exclusively preoccupied, in thought and deed, with the Society, your absence has not been felt as it would otherwise have been. I must admit that there were times when carrying out his hundreds of wishes and thousands of enquiries and ideas turned into an indescribable chase—all the more so, since Greissle was mostly busy teaching in Mödling, so that I could hardly reach him, and Webern did not have all that much chance to influence the workings of this somewhat complex machinery—and, finally, the young people, as ever, let us down when it came to doing anything; often so ostentatiously that, on the whole, I wondered at Schoenberg's patience in that direction. In all other respects his whims often took on indescribable dimensions; and I should have gone on feeling the effects far longer, were it not that in the last few days he has been a good deal more approachable, and has finally gone off today in the best of spirits. . . .

Now, in order: *Jacob's Ladder* was marvellous. Klitsch really produced something quite unprecedented, and showed himself capable of things I should never have expected from him. It was splendid, and you missed a great deal! Very badly attended, and Schoenberg very depressed about it.—N.B. This was in fact the critical time: four events in nine days: *Jacob's Ladder*/23 May, concert by the Society—the Waltz Evening (repeated on 27 May)/30 May, concert by the Society. Everyone did an enormous amount of work to make it possible. During this period I worked fourteen hours a day, or more, for the Society. On top of that, the indescribable heat! I am amazed, what with all the irritations involved, that my health stood up to it . . .

Evening of waltzes (in the Schwarzwald School): a great success. But the work! ! ! Five five-hour rehearsals. The job of scoring that kind of monster waltz in three or four days! And of writing out the parts! The wilderness of administrative groundwork! On the night, we—Schoenberg and Mrs, Webern and Trude, myself and Mrs, Steuermann, Rankl, Kolisch and Steinbauer—sold souvenir handbills in the tower room; these also served as tickets of admission, through the side door of the hall. Anyone who didn't buy one had to run the gauntlet round the entire building, to buy a ticket (at the box office) admitting him through the back door. About 160 members and thirty to forty guests were there. First Schoenberg made a speech explaining the point of the concert—to raise funds for a chamber orchestra—and he also acted as auctioneer. Both in a fabulously witty, whimsical way, which certainly also played its part in making the whole thing the success it was. All the waltzes sounded fabulously well, even my 'Wine, Women and Song'! Schoenberg's arrangement naturally towered way above mine. Admittedly, I should never have dared do a lot of the things he did. For instance, Steuermann had been seen to smile when Schoenberg said that everyone must take his part home and look at it—so Schoenberg gave him a madly difficult piano part, which did indeed sound splendid. After my waltz there was already frantic applause, which Schoenberg allowed, in order to promote a good mood. Webern's waltz, third on the programme, had to be played twice, the second time with Webern conducting and Schoenberg playing the cello. The performances went brilliantly; even my harmonium playing was up to standard. The auction fetched, for my waltz—first up, starting at 500 Kronen—5000 Kronen; Schoenberg's *Lagunenwalzer*, 14,000 Kr; for Webern's *Schatzwalzer* the bidding went up to 7000 Kr, then Schoenberg, who throughout kept bidding to force the prices up, bid 9000— and was left holding the baby, which was not at all his idea; finally, Schoenberg's *Rosen aus dem Süden* fetched 17,000 Kr. After that, a big party thrown by the Society's Direction in the Hotel de France, where Schoenberg stayed the night, and later, till four in the morning, at Mrs Pappenheim's. I had already staggered away, half dead, about one o'clock . . .

The 'best of spirits', in which Schoenberg went 'to the country' on 2 June, soon evaporated. He had chosen to spend his holiday at Mattsee, near Salzburg. Several of his pupils were also to join him there, and they were going to plan further activities of the Society. He also wanted to dictate the book (which he had long been planning, and which he never completed) on 'musical cohesion', and to get on with composing *Jacob's Ladder*. But after only a few days he received a hint from the local council that Jews were unwelcome in the locality. This experience, which naturally caused him to leave at once, for a long time made him deeply bitter, as is shown by a remark he made in a letter to Kandinsky dated 4 June 1923 (*S.L.* 64):

Must not a Kandinsky have an inkling of what really happened when I had to break off my first working summer for five years, leave the place I had sought out for peace to work in, and afterwards couldn't regain the peace of mind to work? Because the Germans will not put up with Jews!

Kandinsky had invited Schoenberg to teach, along with himself and other artists, at the *Bauhaus* in Weimar; in this passionate and deeply gripping letter, which takes up six pages of Stein's edition, Schoenberg turned down the invitation, having heard that antisemitic tendencies were in evidence at the *Bauhaus*.

In a later letter from Berg to Stein (21 July), we hear that Schoenberg has settled down at Traunkirchen in the Salzkammergut (where he spent several more summers during the ensuing years); Berg also tells of the founding of the Kolisch Quartet, and of chamber-orchestral arrangements which are to be made for use during the Society's coming season.

Looking back on the activities of the Schoenberg Society, one realises that, apart from its direct educational effect on those who took part in its concerts, it had two other, more farreaching effects: the need to make arrangements for small ensembles provided creative stimulus and gave rise to ideas in the technical field of instrumentation; and the Society's aims provided a model when, later, other organisations were founded to encourage new music. In this connection one should mention: the Donaueschingen Performances of Chamber Music, for the furtherance of contemporary music (1921), the International Society for Contemporary Music (1922), the International Composers' Guild of New York (1922), and the New York League of Composers (1923). A Society for Private Musical performances was also formed in Prague early in 1922, under the aegis of Zemlinsky, electing Schoenberg as its honorary President. In letters to Zemlinsky, Schoenberg gave the Prague Society useful advice, the fruit of his experiences in Vienna. In a letter sent to the secretary of the Prague society on 14 January 1923 it appears that Schoenberg had handed over to Erwin Stein the post of director of the Vienna Society and 'counsellor' to the Prague Society; the Viennese Society's activities by then seem to have been limited to performances of *Pierrot Lunaire* (which had already been prepared in 1921); during the next few years the

Viennese ensemble took this performance on several tours, conducted by either Schoenberg or Stein.

Although from the autumn of 1918 onward Schoenberg's working energies had to meet great calls from the Viennese Society, and from his activities as a teacher, he also appeared during these years as composer and conductor (though only from 1920 onwards, as regards appearances outside Germany). But except for two 'new piano pieces' (from the set of five, Op. 23, composed between 1920 and 1923), performed by the Society, all the works heard dated from the time before 1917— the year when Schoenberg had begun composing *Jacob's Ladder*, and also the year when an ever-increasing sharpness of contour began to attend his efforts to work out the exact 'method of composing with twelve tones related only to each other'.

During these years there were numerous performances, which finally established Schoenberg as a world figure. There was, above all, the performance of the *Gurrelieder* in the Vienna Opera House, as part of the Vienna Music Festival, on 13 June 1920, a performance which Schoenberg himself conducted, and which was a genuine triumph. Two days afterwards, he wrote an extravagant letter of thanks to the orchestra:

. . . For it is every composer's dream to be performed by this orchestra. In my case, this dream only came true rather late, and I was bitter. But do I need to tell you—or did you sense it for yourselves?—that by the end of the first quarter of an hour in which I had the pleasure of rehearsing with you, my only feeling was the enthusiasm which I am now trying, to the best of my feeble ability, to express?

Pelléas and Mélisande had already been performed at a concert in the Festival, conducted by Zemlinsky, and had achieved the success denied it in 1908, when its first performance had taken place in Vienna.

M. D. Calvocoressi reported on a London performance of the five orchestral pieces, Op. 16, in November 1921, and his remarks were typical insofar as they demonstrated the degree of understanding that even such difficult works as this were gradually coming to command. He recalled his initial impression from 1912—that the pieces contained something worth thinking about, but something to which he could find no means of access. At his recent rehearing of them, everything had fallen into place; the smallest detail had obviously been related to the motive and productive power of the whole. Whereas previously he had been able to make out only a jumble of parts, and of clashes, now he heard a powerful musical voice proclaiming its mission.

Schoenberg's participation in the great Mahler Festival in Amsterdam in May 1920 (two months after he had conducted there the orchestral arrangement of *Transfigured Night*, and two of the orchestral pieces, Op. 16) proved especially important for him. He was elected President of the International Mahler League, founded in Amsterdam, and was invited to go to Holland in the autumn and spend a considerable time there as the League's organiser, as lecturer, and as conductor. He took up this invitation in the autumn of 1920 and the winter of 1921. In an April 1921 issue of *Musikblätter des Anbruch* (a 'fortnightly paper devoted to modern music', published in Vienna by Universal Edition from 1919 onwards) C. R. Mengelberg told how Schoenberg was received:

That season, people in Amsterdam had the chance to get to know all the essential works in Schoenberg's creative output. First of all, they were given a further hearing of *Transfigured Night* and the orchestral pieces, Op. 16, and these were also repeated at a popular concert. On 6 and 8 January (in Amsterdam and The Hague respectively) the Concertgebouw Orchestra gave a complete concert of music by Schoenberg, with *Pelléas and Mélisande* and the Op. 8 songs, in which the singer was Hans Nachod. Of his chamber works, the D minor quartet, Op. 7, was played by the Budapest String Quartet, whilst members of the Concertgebouw Orchestra performed the Chamber Symphony. On 19 and 20 March Schoenberg rounded off his activities in Holland with two grandiose performances of the *Gurrelieder*. Scrupulously prepared through weeks of rehearsal, the work received a quite outstanding performance, and one that was received with an enthusiasm rarely encountered here.

Finally, two performances of *Pierrot Lunaire* should be mentioned: one in December 1921 in Frankfurt-on-Main, the first in which the vocal part was performed by a man; and one in January 1922 in Paris, conducted by Darius Milhaud, and with the text translated back into the original French and spoken by Marya Freund. Milhaud reports that the public and critics were 'full of praise'.

7 The Great Tradition

Riemann on J. S. Bach:	Alban Berg on Schoenberg:
He belongs as much to the immediately preceding period of polyphonic music and the contrapuntal imitative style	*He belongs as much to the immediately preceding period of the harmonic style*
as to the period of harmonic music	*as to the period (which makes its reappearance with him) of polyphonic music and the contrapuntal imitative style,*
and to the system, here set out in its entire scope for the first time,	*and to the system, here set out in its entire scope for the first time,*
of modern keys (replacing the church modes)	*of twelve-tone rows (replacing the major and minor keys).*
The span of his career falls in a period of transition, that is to say, in a time when the old style had still not been exhausted, while the new one was still in its earliest stages of development, and showed the signs of immaturity. His genius unites the characteristics of both stylistic genres.	*The span of his career falls in a period of transition, that is to say, in a time when the old style had still not been exhausted, while the new one was still in its earliest stages of development, and showed the signs of immaturity. His genius unites the characteristics of both stylistic genres.*

Schoenberg's historical importance in the development of music has often been compared to that of J. S. Bach, but never more drastically than by Alban Berg, who in January 1930 published in the Berlin periodical *Die Musik* a brief study, entitled 'Credo'; in the article's opening paragraph he adapted the words written about Bach by the famous German musical theorist, Hugo Riemann (1849–1919), in the eighth edition (1916) of his Encyclopaedia of Music (*Musiklexikon*),[1] so that they would apply to Schoenberg.

As the quotation above shows, Berg established an exact parallel, using Riemann's own words, between Bach's position in a transitional period and Schoenberg's.

When in 1930 Berg mentions 'twelve-tone rows', he is

1 Cf page 81.

referring to the 'method of composing with twelve tones related only to each other'; although Schoenberg had brought this to a late stage of development as early as 1921 he had not yet himself made it public. His first reference to the possibility of 'twelve-tone music' was in a footnote to the third edition (1921) of his *Treatise on Harmony* (pages 487-8 of the German edition), in which he attacked the so-called 'atonalists':

That, however, I must reject, for I am a musician and have nothing to do with anything 'atonal'. 'Atonal' could only mean something entirely out of keeping with the nature of the tone. The expression 'tonal' has itself been wrongly used, exclusively instead of inclusively. It can mean only this: everything that results from a series of tones, whether its cohesion results from a direct relationship to a single tonic or from links of a more complex nature, forms tonality. Clearly this, the sole correct definition, is no basis for an antinomy of a rational kind, such as could produce anything in keeping with the word 'atonality'. Where could one introduce the negation here? Is not everything derived from a series of tones bound to characterise its tonality? A piece of music will always have to be tonal at least in so far as, from one tone to the next, there is bound to be a relationship by which all the tones, successive or simultaneous, produce a progression that can be grasped as such. Then, tonality may perhaps be neither tangible nor demonstrable, these relationships may be obscure or hard to understand, or even impossible to understand. But it will no more be possible to call any relationship between tones atonal than it would be legitimate to call a relationship between colours aspectral or acomplementary. The latter antinomy just does not exist. Moreover, no one has looked into the question whether the way these new sounds group themselves may not in fact be the tonality of a twelve-tone row.

It was in the summer of 1921, during a stroll in the country at Traunkirchen, that Schoenberg first talked—to his pupil Josef Rufer—about the twelve-tone music he had been developing. He declared, 'I have made a discovery thanks to which the supremacy of German music is ensured for the next hundred years.'

In the letter written in English to Nicholas Slonimsky on

3 June 1937 (cf pp. 95–6) he described the path that had led him to this discovery:

After that [1915] I was always occupied with the aim to base the structure of my music *consciously* on a unifying idea, which produced not only all the other ideas but regulated also their accompaniment and the chords, the 'harmonies'. There were many attempts to achieve that. But very little of it was finished or published.

As an example of such attempts I may mention the piano pieces Op. 23. Here I arrived at a technique which I called (for myself) 'composing with tones', a very vague term, but it meant something to me. Namely: in contrast to the ordinary way of using a motive, I used it already almost in the manner of a 'basic set of twelve tones'. I built other motives and themes from it, and also accompaniments and other chords—but the theme did not consist of twelve tones. Another example of this kind of aim for unity is my *Serenade*. In this work you can find many examples of this kind. But the best one is the 'Variationen', the third movement. The theme consists of a succession of fourteen tones, but only eleven different ones, and these fourteen tones are permanently used in the whole movement. With lesser strictness still I use the tones of the first two measures in 'Tanzszene'.

The fourth movement, 'Sonett' is a real 'composition with twelve tones'. The technique is here relatively primitive, because it was one of the first works written strictly in harmony with this method, though it was not the very first one—there were some movements of the *Suite for Piano* which I composed in the fall of 1921. Here I became suddenly conscious of the real meaning of my aim: unity and regularity, which unconsciously had led me all this way.

As you see, it was neither a straight way nor was it caused by mannerism, as it often happens with revolutions in art. I personally hate to be called a revolutionist, which I am not. What I did was neither revolution nor anarchy. I possessed from my very first start a thoroughly developed sense of form and a strong aversion for exaggeration. There is no falling into order, because there was never disorder. There is no falling at all, but on the contrary, there is an ascending to higher and better order.

The first the world at large heard of Schoenberg's discovery was through Erwin Stein's essay 'Neue Formprinzipien', which appeared in the 1924 commemorative volume and was later reprinted in the collection *Von neuer Musik* (Cologne, 1924). Not until 1941 did Schoenberg himself provide an outline—a comprehensive one, illustrated by many musical examples—of the fundamentals of his method; on 26 March of that year he delivered a lecture at the University of California, Los Angeles (this was published in the original (1950) edition of *Style and Idea*, though a somewhat expanded version of it had already appeared in 1949, in vol. 4 of the Parisian periodical *Polyphonie*). Schoenberg's lecture is for the most part a detailed explanation of his first twelve-tone works, already mentioned in his letter to Slonimsky, and of succeeding works, down to the Variations for Orchestra, Op. 31, which date from 1927-8.

According to Schoenberg, we should call 'twelve-tone music' those pieces of music which are in every respect—melodically and harmonically—built exclusively from one row, the so-called 'basic set', which contains all twelve tones of the chromatic scale in a fixed order that remains unaltered throughout the entire piece. The following forms are derived from the basic set and are used in the same way, as basic points of reference: the inversion of the basic set (produced like a reflection in a horizontal mirror), the retrograde, in which the tones of the basic set are read from the end backwards (this amounts to a reflection in a vertical mirror), and the retrograde inversion; moreover, the transpositions of the basic set and of its three derivates can also be used, that is, any one of the twelve tones of the chromatic scale can be taken as starting-point for the four rows. So the composer has a total of 48 twelve-tone rows at his disposal for any piece. This is the 'unity' of the musical space within which the piece is created.

Schoenberg was emphatic about the double function of the basic set. In the first place, it is somewhat analogous to the scales used in traditional tonal music, since it, too, very often influences the melodic and harmonic configurations of musical works. But its second function can be directly grasped: that of motive, or, at times, of theme. 'This explains why such a basic set has to be invented anew for every piece. It has to be the first creative thought!' Such was Schoenberg's view of this function of the row. (Adorno once analogously described the invention of the basic set as a 'pre-forming' of the musical material.)

Schoenberg most determinedly opposed the widespread idea that composition would be made easier by the use of his twelve-tone method, since once the basic set was invented everything else would develop, in a sense, 'automatically'. In his lecture, he had this to say in reply:

The introduction of my method of composing with twelve tones does not facilitate composing; on the contrary, it makes it more difficult. Modernistically-minded beginners often think they should try it before having acquired the necessary technical equipment. This is a great mistake. The restrictions imposed on a composer by the obligation to use only one set in a composition are so severe that they can only be overcome by an imagination which has survived a tremendous number of adventures. . . .

In the first works in which I employed this method, I was not yet convinced that the exclusive use of one set would not result in monotony. Would it allow the creation of a sufficient number of characteristically differentiated themes, phrases, motives, sentences, and other forms? At this time, I used complicated devices to assure variety. But soon I discovered that my fear was unfounded; I could even base a whole opera, *Moses and Aaron*, solely on one set; and I found that, on the contrary, the more familiar I became with this set the more easily I could draw themes from it. Thus, the truth of my first prediction had received splendid proof. One has to follow the basic set; but, nevertheless, one composes as freely as before.

Two other widespread misconceptions were attacked in Schoenberg's lecture—the idea of a 'twelve-tone system', and of 'twelve-tone style'. Any rigid systematisation of the composition process is ruled out precisely because of the complete creative freedom allowed and confirmed by the use of the twelve-tone method in Schoenberg's sense. As a further consequence, the use of this method can never tie composers down to a unified style determined by the presence of twelve-tone rows. If there is any characteristic of style at all which could generally be taken as typical of Schoenbergian twelve-tone music, it could result only from the 'emancipation of the dissonance'—something postulated much earlier and practised with extreme consistency by the twelve-tone method. Having said this, we have still said nothing about the artistic value of the music produced with the aid of the method; the only features determining the artistic value are the ones valid in all other music: power and originality of invention, wealth of ideas, and the artistic certainty and comprehensibility with which these are articulated, linked, and presented.

Finally, the reader is still owed a definition of the much-used term 'twelve-tone technique': this technique may be understood to include all the devices made use of in the production of twelve-tone music. The twelve-tone technique has developed in very different ways with different composers, so it is indispensable to analyse in detail the largest possible number of twelve-tone works of the most varied origin, if one wishes to gain a deeper insight into this technique. In general, the compositions created according to Schoenberg's twelve-tone method do not require the listener to perceive the row-structure when the work is performed. There is, naturally, an exception in cases where the basic set is identical with the melodic line of a theme. This hidden nature of serial structure once prompted Schoenberg to make the significant joke, 'My twelve-tone technique is a pure family affair!'

Schoenberg's twelve-tone method can be compared, in many respects, with certain ideational models in modern physics and mathematics. The introduction of rows is analogous, so far as the 'microstructure' of the musical material is concerned, to the approach to the microstructure of matter produced in physics by the quantum theory and modern atomic theory. The first person to draw a comparison with the new mathematics was Louis Danz, in his essay 'Schoenberg the Inevitable', one of the contributions to Merle Armitage's 1937 New York symposium. Danz says at one point: 'From now on music will no longer be what it was, but has become what it will be. This change can be likened to the change from the Euclidean geometry to the higher mathematics of a Minkowski, an Einstein.'

Between January and March 1932, Webern gave a series of eight lectures at a private house in Vienna; his account of the path that led to twelve-tone composition was based on deep personal experience and amounted almost to a confession. The lectures have been published, together with other important utterances of Webern's, under the title *The Path to the New Music* (English edition, Theodore Presser Co. and Universal Edition, London, 1963). They were edited by myself. At the end of the final lecture Webern said:

. . . As we gradually gave up tonality an idea occurred to us: 'We don't want to repeat, there must constantly be something new!' Obviously this doesn't work, it destroys comprehensibility. At least it's impossible to write long stretches of music in that way. Only after the formulation of the twelve-tone law did it again become possible to write longer pieces.

We want to say 'in a quite new way' what has been said before. But now I can invent more freely; everything has a deeper unity. Only now is it possible to compose in free fantasy, adhering to nothing except the row. To put it quite paradoxically, only through these unprecedented fetters has complete freedom become possible!

Here I can only stammer. Everything is still in a state of flux. . . . It is for a later period to discover the closer unifying laws that are already present in the works themselves. When this true conception of art is achieved, then there will no longer be any possible distinction between science and inspired creation. The further one presses forward, the greater becomes the identity of everything, and finally we have the impression of being faced by a work not of man but of Nature. . . .

Now I must say this: what you see here—retrograde, canon, etc.—constantly the same thing—isn't to be regarded as a 'tour de force'; that would be ludicrous. I was to create as many connections as possible, and you must allow that there are indeed many connections here!

Finally I must point out to you that this is so not only in music. We find an analogy in language. I was delighted to find that such connections also often occur in Shakespeare, in alliteration and assonance. He even turns a phrase backwards. Karl Kraus' handling of language is also based on this; unity also has to be created there, since it enhances comprehensibility.

And I leave you with an old Latin saying:

```
S A T O R
A R E P O
T E N E T
O P E R A
R O T A S
```

One possible translation of the Latin saying 'Sator Arepo tenet opera rotas' is 'Arepo the sower keeps the work circling'. The magic square in which Webern arranged the saying clearly shows the basic principle of twelve-tone technique— the equal status of basic set, inversion, retrograde, and retrograde inversion.

As soon as Schoenberg made known the twelve-tone method, Webern and Berg adopted it, as did many of their pupils. Its independent further development was carried on, above all, by Ernst Krenek and his American pupil George Perle. From a teaching point of view, important work was done by Hanns Jelinek in Vienna, Herbert Eimert in Cologne, and René Leibowitz in Paris. There is a philosophical discussion of Schoenberg's twelve-tone music in Theodor W. Adorno's book *Philosophie der neuen Musik* (Tübingen, 1949). As Schoenberg's principles became known throughout the world, many composers were stimulated to produce independent work in the field of twelve-tone music. The extension of the principle of rows (serial principle) to other dimensions of music led to the creation of 'serial' music, which is currently still a subject for lively discussion; it takes its stand, above all, on Webern's last compositions, but the conclusions drawn by the 'serialists' from the structure of these compositions are by no means wholly convincing.

Schoenberg was not the first who had tried to organise music's material in a new way based on all twelve tones of the chromatic scale; one should mention two Russians—Scriabin (1872–1915) and Jefim Golyshev (b. 1895), but, above all, the Austrian Josef Matthias Hauer (1883–1959), since he was for a time in contact with Schoenberg, and later made a great point of claiming absolute priority in the field of twelve-tone music. It was Hauer's custom—probably from 1937 onward—to end all his letters, not only with his signature, but with the words, for which he had a rubber stamp made, 'The spiritual author and (despite many imitators!) still the sole expert in, and practitioner of, twelve-tone music'.

The personal contacts between Schoenberg and Hauer have been objectively summarised, with excellent documentation in the form of every letter Schoenberg ever sent to Hauer, in a study of Hauer by Walter Szmolyan (vol. 6 in the series 'Austrian composers of the twentieth century', joint publication by Elisabeth Lafite and the Austrian Federal Publishing House, 1965). Here I would simply point out the fundamental distinction between Schoenberg's twelve-tone compositions and Hauer's—a distinction which renders pointless all considerations of who was first: about 1918 Hauer, who had been writing twelve-tone music since as early as 1908, succeeded in organising into a clearly surveyable system of forty-four groups—which he called 'tropes'—all 479,001,600 possible combinations of twelve tones within an octave (this does not take into account the transpositions starting on the different tones of the chromatic scale, which would multiply another twelvefold the total of possible twelve-tone rows). This system of tropes forms the basis of Hauer's entire creative output, which is very remarkable and often contains very individual sounds. He himself spoke of this in his essay *Vom Melos zur Pauke*, which he dedicated to Schoenberg, publishing it in 1925:

Through years of practice I am as much at home among these turns of phrase (tropes), as are others finding their way among keys and modulations. Indeed it comes down to the same thing, basically, only it is incomparably more complicated. However, in the course of time I have come to know with quite special exactness what mood each of these turns of phrase contains, and that has been a help to me in constructing my forms.

This quotation makes it clear that Hauer made the compositional use of his theory of tropes depend on a process of aural acclimatisation to the sound world of each individual trope, and on the clear distinctions between all these worlds. In 1930 I had a chance to convince myself of this in a conversation with Hauer, which he conducted from the piano. Because of the aural acclimatisation to the world of the tropes demanded by Hauer, his twelve-tone music must remain a special case, limited to his own person, so long as other composers do not have the same aural relationship to the tropes, and express them in important works. So far as I know this has not yet happened. Schoenberg made play with this fundamental difference between his twelve-tone music and

Hauer's, in a letter to Rudolf Kolisch dated 27 July 1932 (*S.L.* 143): 'My works are twelve-tone *compositions*; not *twelve-tone* compositions'.

Reverting to Schoenberg's report in his letter to Slonimsky, something should be said here about the three works in which he gradually developed his twelve-tone method. As is shown by his own brief remarks in the letter, and the extensive analyses in Erwin Stein's essay 'New formal principles' (reprinted in his book *Orpheus in New Guises*), this development took place in a preparatory way in the five piano pieces composed between July 1920 and the spring of 1923, and was fully realised in some of the movements of the *Serenade* Op. 24 (composed between September 1921 and April 1923), and of the *Piano Suite*, Op. 25 (July 1921–March 1923).

The preparatory stage is made particularly clear by Stein's remarks about the third and fifth pieces from Op. 23. Discussing Op. 23, No. 3, Stein relates that it was *à propos* this piece, not long after its composition, that Schoenberg first told him about the new formal principles. Stein says of the piece:

The opening five-note theme almost looks like a fugue subject. With some experience in matters contrapuntal one can see at once that the theme knows a trick or two. . . . Its second entry, too—on the fifth—resembles a 'comes' (the 'answer' in a fugue). Ensuing events, to be sure, are different. It is impossible to describe the countless combinations of the basic shape or 'fugue subject'. All parts and harmonies derive from it. This does not mean, however, that the one motive repeats itself just horizontally and chordally, with its inversions, retrograde versions and transpositions. True, it often occurs with thematic significance, but elsewhere the various forms of the basic shape overlap both horizontally and vertically to such an extent that completely free melodies and harmonies seem to arise whose relations to the basic shape are not easily recognisable. Almost every note is a constituent part at once of several forms of the basic shape, and is capable of more than one interpretation. In the first two bars alone, the basic shape occurs five times within thirteen notes, thrice thematically and twice chordally.

And of the fifth piece, the waltz, Stein says:

Its basic shape consists of all twelve notes in this fixed order: c sharp–a–b–g–a flat–g flat–b flat–d–e–e flat–c–f. This note row revolves constantly throughout the movement, starting ever anew as soon as its previous run is over. To begin with, it appears as a waltz melody, vertically, and shaped *rhythmically* into three motifs. The accompaniment gives the same succession of notes, starting, however, with another note, and partly collecting them into chords. Further on, the notes are vertically distributed between the different parts in such a way that they sound successively (or a few simultaneously), regardless of whether, say, one note is thus assigned to the principal part, the next to a subordinate part, and the third and fourth to chords. It will be seen that the melody retains the greatest freedom of movement, if only the accompaniment meanwhile supplies the missing notes. Thematically, then, the row is not binding, though several of its parts are developed as principal motifs. Conforming with its lighter character, the piece shows more rhythmic repetitions and symmetric structures than its immediate forerunners.

The piece, completed on 7 February 1923, thus obeys the 'twelve-tone law' in all its strictness, and also shows that Schoenberg had completely succeeded in meeting the demands that had led him to invent his twelve-tone method: the wish to produce the most exact cohesion, and flexibility of structure, without resorting to a tonic.

In his next two works, the *Serenade*, Op. 24 and the *Piano Suite*, Op. 25, Schoenberg forcefully proved that a wide variety of traditional forms could be moulded in an absolutely convincing way by means of the new method. The *Serenade* is scored for clarinet, bass clarinet, mandoline, guitar, violin, viola, cello, and a baritone singer (who takes part only in the fourth section—Sonnet). The movements are headed: March, Minuet, Variations, Sonnet by Petrarch, Dance Scene, Song (without words), Finale. In each movement, various serial procedures are used with varying degrees of freedom; complete strictness is the order of the day only in the sonnet, in which the vocal part is so laid out that every note of it results from the recurring basic set (e–d–e flat–b–c–d flat–a flat–g flat–a–f–g–b flat); this makes twelve complete appearances, and a thirteenth one that stops short at the tenth tone (all this corresponds to the poem's fourteen eleven-syllable lines); the same row is also the basis of all the elements that make up the movement's instrumental parts. Schoenberg himself called this technique 'relatively primitive'; but the way in which, throughout the work as a whole, technical and formal problems are solved can be regarded as highly artistic, particularly the way in which at the start of the finale, the work's introductory marchlike motive is linked with references to material from the other movements. In the *Piano Suite*, Op. 25 there is a comparable command of devices of composition, enhanced by the fact that all six movements (Prelude, Gavotte, Musette, Intermezzo, Minuet, Gigue) are derived from a single twelve-tone row (e–f–g–d flat–g flat–e flat–a flat–d–b–c–a–b flat), the traditional rhythms of the old dance forms being also duly observed. Another compositional subtlety is that the retrograde of the last four tones of the row runs b flat–a–c–b, i.e. the familiar B–A–C–H motive.

Another creative enterprise at this time was the orchestration of two Bach chorale preludes (*Schmücke dich, o liebe Seele*, and *Komm, Gott, Schöpfer, heiliger Geist*), which Schoenberg made early in 1922. Both pieces were first performed in New York in April 1923, conducted by Josef Stransky. In a long and important letter, divided into eight headings, dated 31 July 1930, Schoenberg told his friend the conductor Fritz Stiedry about the ideas that had prompted him to score these two organ works (for an orchestra including harp, celeste, triangle, etc.). The letter ends:

VII.   Our aural requirements do not aim at any 'full flavour' that comes of varied colour; rather, colours help to clarify the movement of the parts, and, in a contrapuntal texture, that is very important! Whether the Bach organ was capable of it, we do not know. Presentday organists are *not*: that I do know (and it is one of my starting-points).

VIII.   Comprehending music as we do nowadays, we require the *motivic* flow to be made clear horizontally as well as vertically. That is to say, it is not enough if we can rest assured that the contrapuntal structure (which is postulated as self-evident) has an immanent effect; we want to perceive said counterpoint, in the form of motivic relationships. Homophony taught us to follow these in an upper part, and the intermediate stage of 'homophony in several parts' (Mendelssohn, Wagner, Brahms) taught us to follow several parts in that way; nowadays, our ear and our powers of comprehension are not satisfied unless we also apply these criteria to Bach. The merely 'agreeable' effect produced by the conjunction of artfully written parts is no longer found sufficient. We want transparency, in order to see right through. All this is impossible without phrasing.

But the use of phrasing must not be dominated by mood and emotion, as in the age of pathos. Phrasing has

1. To apportion correct relative weights within the line.
2. At times to reveal the motivic work, at others to obscure it.
3. To ensure that each part exercises consideration, in terms of dynamics, for all the parts, and for the sound as a whole (transparency).

And many other things too. So here, I believe, the right to transcribe turns into a duty.

In 1928 Schoenberg arranged, for full orchestra, another Bach organ work, the Prelude and Fugue in E flat major from Part 3 of the *Clavierübung*.

On 15 November 1923 Schoenberg finished writing his poem *Requiem*, which he included in his 1926 collection, *Texte*; the poem is a document of deep personal and artistic significance. In view of the date of its completion, one may assume that the work owes its origin to Schoenberg's painful sense of loss after the death of his wife, Mathilde, on 22 October 1923. The first manuscript draft is indeed prefaced by a remark in Schoenberg's handwriting, '1920 or 1921?', but this note may be the result of an error, or perhaps refers to some earlier experience. Schoenberg's dominant mood at the time is shown by two sentences from a letter he wrote to Alma Mahler, who had invited him to a large gathering at her house:

You will certainly understand, if I regard as a crime even the occasional harmless laughter that deprives a dead one of part of the mourning to which she is entitled. After all, one hardly mourns as long as the dead one deserves—the one for whom all is now over, and who now only has what we give her.

Certain musical notes in the manuscript indicate that Schoenberg originally meant to set to music the *Requiem's* twelve stanzas (there were originally to have been eleven), but that he later abandoned this plan. Here are the beginning of the first part (which covers altogether two and a half pages), and the end of the poem:

I

Pain, rage yourself to a standstill;
Grief, lament till you are weary!
Compassion, open the inner eye:
Here lies life that has run its course,
that suffered while rejoicing,
and rejoiced while suffering:
And passed away! . . .

VI

A final glance, and yet one more—and—
Too late—then no more were possible.

VII

Do the wanderers ever meet again?
In the realm of the direction-less?
Of the timeless?
And yet, on earth, time passes!
And all the directions lead far from one another!
So how is one to find anyone?

VIII

But: my ears hear nothing any more.
The eyes do not see.
Yes: to sense! to hope! to imagine! . . .
The only reality is mourning.

IX

Should one wish to die?
What is mourning, to the soul,
When one is dead?
Is it still aware of the loved one?
Perhaps it stands so far above it all
That even that is lost.
What has been gained in return?

X

Hopeless: perhaps we pass
each other by for ever,
and never meet again.

XI

To the Lord, a thousand years are as a day.
Such a day, whenever they lose each other,
He gives to lovers,
to see each other again,
to find each other, ever and again.

XII

Be strong!
Reject all comfort:
it wants only to rob you
of what is worth preserving.
Reflect:
What was loved had to go from you, uncomforted.
It, too, did not know whither.
It, too, knew nothing of all the things
you are asking about.
Be worthy of it.
Go forth on your way, bravely,
as it went forth.
If one can die—
and that is difficult—
then one can also live.

In an article entitled 'Certainty', included in a symposium, *Schöpferische Konfessionen* (Creative Confessions: Erich Reiss-Verlag, Berlin, late 1921), Schoenberg made some very revealing remarks about his way of working. The middle section of his 'confession' ran as follows:

When, after not having composed for a time, I think eagerly of future works, I always see my future direction so clearly that today, at least, I can be certain of its not turning out as I had imagined. That I am weaving, perhaps turning right round, turning in a mad circle, is a reasonable guess; that I fail to see where I stand, where I have stood—that can only be the result of my blindness. One thing alone soon makes itself clear; that I find the new just as foreign and incomprehensible as I did the old, in its time and for a time; that so long as this state of affairs continues, older things will strike me as more comprehensible, till finally the latest new thing will seem more familiar, and I no longer understand how in earlier days I could have written anything of a different kind. Yes, when one observes well, these things gradually begin to become unclear. One begins to grasp that one is fated, not merely to fail to guess the future (one merely embodies it), but also to forget the past (which one has already embodied). One begins to feel one is doing one's duty most faithfully, when one omits to do what was once sacred to one (much as one would like to do it), and betrays the things toward which the future seemed to be tempting one; one begins, on the quiet, to rejoice, open-eyed, at one's blindness. This is, however, very rare, and very furtive, since one could do harm to a delicate and secret thing: for a few moments one has seen both the stretch that is already behind one, and the stretch that is still ahead of one—both simultaneously: and one has been satisfied. I can say no more about my creative work.

During the ensuing years, this 'creative work' was to become ever more widely known, as the next few pages show.

At the international festival of chamber music in Salzburg in 1922 (which led in the course of the same year to the foundation of the International Society for Contemporary Music) Schoenberg had a great triumph with his second string quartet, the final work in a 'Viennese matinee'; the performers were the Amar-Hindemith Quartet, and the Viennese soprano Felicie Mihacsek.

In January 1923 Schoenberg was invited by the Danish Philharmonic Society to conduct a concert of his own works in Copenhagen. Since several of his works (*Pelléas and Mélisande, Transfigured Night*, and *Pierrot Lunaire*) had already been performed there, on the initiative of the conductor and composer Paul von Klenau, his appearance in person aroused lively interest. The programme included two performances of the Chamber Symphony, and of four songs from Op. 6 (sung by Marya Freund), as well as the Song of the Wood-Dove from the *Gurrelieder*, which Schoenberg had specially arranged for chamber orchestra with this concert in mind. At the final (public) rehearsal he also gave a lecture on the homophonic and polyphonic principle in music.

In June 1923 there was a Week of Austrian Music in Berlin, with Mahler's Eighth Symphony and Schoenberg's *Gurrelieder* as the major works. This was the first time the *Gurrelieder* had been heard in Berlin, and there were performances on three successive days, conducted by Schoenberg's pupil Heinrich Jalowetz. There was also an 'evening of novelties', with first performances of works by Berg, Bittner, Webern and Zemlinsky, and the Staatsoper gave the opera *Der Schatzgräber* by Franz Schreker, who had been director of the Berlin Conservatoire of Music since 1920. The leading Berlin music critic of the time, Adolf Weissmann, reported at length on this 'festival' in the June-July issue of *Musikblätter des Anbruch*; he drew the following interesting comparison:

Nowadays, at a time of political weakness, the Viennese musical atmosphere is perhaps very decisive. One sees people, even outside Austria, looking eagerly toward Vienna, that most amiably, pastorally tinged region of the German-speaking territories, where an unpolitical 'laisser-aller' favours music's subtler vibrations. In Berlin one scents (not always fairly) cool Prussian-ness. In any case, music here is under the stern eye of politics and business, and a malevolent nationalism aims to out-thunder, particularly, the subtlest art. Since, on the other hand, the more extreme values find their passionate defenders, tensions result, constituting the special attraction of Berlin's musical atmosphere. This is not to say that Vienna is all idle amiability. I know there are feuds and battles in Vienna, too. But, in the last event, it all fades before a different sun, a different landscape, and natural musicianship. So one should try some time to transplant this Austrian-ness to Berlin, to our Philharmonic—not *in toto*, but in a representative dosage. All young Viennese music begins with Mahler. The fiery breath of this conductor, who was at the same time a great man, has inspired all those who were young then. The Week of Austrian Music is an affirmation of faith by the post-Mahlerians.

In his favourable criticism of the *Gurrelieder* Weissmann contrasts early and later Schoenberg, not entirely without malice:

Sprung from the soul of an ardent Wagnerian, they do indeed show that things are changing, do indeed manifest his own character from the very outset, and yet they are too deeply anchored in his artistic past to lose their colour and inflammatory power. All in all, they carry the great body of listeners with them, until eventually—above all in Part Three—they have the musician entirely under their spell.

Schoenberg found an important 'bastion' in Frankfurt-on-Main, where his long-standing artistic associate Hermann Scherchen had settled as conductor of the concerts given at the principal Museum. When in June 1923 Scherchen performed the eight-part chorus *Friede auf Erden* (*Peace on Earth*, Op. 13, a work originally meant to be sung unaccompanied, but provided in 1911 with an *ad libitum* accompaniment) Schoenberg wrote him a letter of thanks (dated 23 June *S.L.* 68), containing the following highly equivocal passage:

Please give your choir my warmest thanks for the very kind words they sent me after the rehearsal. Tell them that my chorus *Peace on Earth* is an illusion for mixed choir, an illusion, as I know today, having believed, in 1907, when I composed it, that this pure harmony among human beings was conceivable, and more than that: would not have thought it possible to exist without perpetual insistence on the required elevation of tone. Since then I have perforce learnt to yield, and have learnt that Peace on Earth is possible only if there is the most intense vigilance as to harmony; in a word; not without accompaniment. If human beings are ever to reach the stage of singing Peace at sight, without rehearsal, each individual will first have to be immune to the temptation to sink!

The chorus was performed as part of a New Music week for chamber music organised in Frankfurt by Scherchen; Schoenberg's *Book of the Hanging Gardens* was performed as well. When the Swiss music-lover and patron of the arts, Werner Reinhart, wrote to Schoenberg telling him of the powerful impression made on him by the Frankfurt performance of *Peace on Earth*, the composer replied (on 9 July, *S.L.* 73) with obvious pride:

I may say that for the present it matters more to me if people understand my older works, such as this chorus *Peace on Earth*. They are the natural forerunners of my later works, and only those who understand and comprehend them will be able to hear the latter with any understanding beyond the fashionable minimum. And only such people will realise that the melodic character of these later works is the natural consequence of what I tried to do earlier. So I am truly delighted by your friendly words. *I do not attach so much importance to being a musical bogyman as to being a natural continuer of properly understood good old tradition!*

The last sentence is crucial, and recalls another remark of Schoenberg's: 'I am a conservative who was forced to become a revolutionary'. But the preceding sentences are very important, too: they point to the one certain way in which a complete understanding of Schoenberg's whole musical output can be acquired.

In 1924 the two stage works composed over a decade earlier finally received their first performances: *Erwartung* at the New German Theatre in Prague (6 June, conducted by Zemlinsky, by Louis Laber, sung by Marie Gutheil-Schoder) and *Die Glückliche Hand* at the Vienna Volksoper (14 October, conducted by Fritz Stiedry, produced by Josef Turnau. The Man was sung by the baritone Alfred Jerger, from the Vienna State Opera).

The Prague public and press received *Erwartung* very well. The most important literary echo of the première was a long study by Paul Bekker, prompted by the work and published in the September 1924 commemorative volume. Here are a few sentences, the first ever to emphasise an element which is of general importance for the whole phenomenon of Schoenberg as artist: the critical significance of his work.

Outwardly, *Erwartung* appears to be a vocal scena, with orchestra, presented on the stage, but one feels this to be, as it were, merely the particular way in which an artistic vision chanced to make itself palpable—a vision for which this was the clearest mode of presentation. One would hardly suppose that Schoenberg set out to write something like an opera, or even to point out new paths for the theatre. If stimulating effects of that kind should also materialise, they would be side-effects—as, indeed, any powerful phenomenon radiates in a variety of directions. But the essential thing is not the details of the work but the work as a whole, which must indeed be taken as a totality defying all categories, and, being such a totality, it appears before us as an image of the essence of our music. In it there is as much of the past as of the future—the one in proportion to Schoenberg's talent, the other in proportion to the way he applies his talent. It is the most concentrated summing-up of all that the post-Wagnerian age has done, and of what it is still trying to do; it is like a critical essay, written in sounds instead of in words and concepts, and pointing beyond all considerations of the rational mind, thanks to its powers of intuition, of creative vision.—And surely this peculiar natural blend of criticism and creativeness is altogether one of Arnold Schoenberg's hallmarks. In so far as such comparisons are admissible, one could compare the phenomenon of Schoenberg with the phenomenon of a man such as Lessing, though of course with the qualification that in Schoenberg's case the outward separation of the two fields is absent (if one excludes his teaching activities), and that both essential elements, the critical and the productive, are inseparably linked to each other, and translated into musical creation.

Die Glückliche Hand was not very well received in Vienna, especially by the critics. The following sarcastic note from the pen of Erwin Stein shows this (*Musikblätter des Anbruch*, November/December 1924):

It was eleven years before someone found the courage to perform the work. And even today it has not found a generation mature enough to take it. The public did indeed show suitable awe, and enthusiastically called on the composer to take repeated curtain-calls. Men of goodwill sense something of the spirit alive within this music and these stage events. However, the Viennese Press—with a few exceptions—was a fiasco with *Die glückliche Hand*.

Two other Schoenberg works were first performed in 1924: the Serenade Op. 24 (July 20, at the music festival in Donaueschingen, conducted by the composer; there had already been a private hearing of the work on 2 May, before an invited audience at the home of Dr Norbert Schwarzmann, No. 17 Krugerstrasse, Vienna)—and the wind quintet, Op. 26 (composed between May 1923 and August 1924); this was performed, conducted by Felix Greissle, during the 'Viennese

The composer's
son, Georg
Schoenberg

Schoenberg's
first wife,
Mathilde,
née von
Zemlinsky

Arnold
Schoenberg.
Self-portrait

Anton Webern,
Vienna 1932

festival of music and drama', promoted by the City of Vienna at the suggestion of Dr David Bach, and held between 14 September and 15 October. During the festival Schoenberg's orchestrations of the two Bach chorale preludes also received their first performance in Vienna, at a concert by the Workers' Symphony Orchestra.

There was a connection between this 'accumulation' of performances in Vienna and the composer's fiftieth birthday on 13 September 1924, which was also marked by a special celebration organised by the City of Vienna. There was a ceremony in the Town Hall as part of the festival exhibition 'Serious music in Vienna from Bruckner down to the most recent times', under the auspices of the city's official art galleries. Paul Stefan described the ceremony in the October edition of *Anbruch*:

The chorus of the Staatsoper, confidently conducted by Schoenberg's pupil and son-in-law Felix Greissle, sang his 'unperformable' chorus *Peace on Earth* to an assembly of friends, old and new, and admirers; after a very fine speech of thanks by Dr Bach, the mayor declared that Vienna could be proud of having a citizen such as Schoenberg. If only someone had said that twenty years ago, or even ten! And the society of music critics, even the Philharmonic Orchestra, had sent representatives to the ceremony, and one of the Opera's directors added his signature to those of the Committee of Invitation. Is this not matter for rejoicing? Let the city's younger composers, too, take comfort: you only have to be fifty, and things actually start to improve. . . .

The Leipzig *Zeitschrift für Musik* provided a grotesque pendant to this acclamation:

On 13 September Arnold Schoenberg was fifty; that is to say, he celebrated a major epoch in his career during the same month as Anton Bruckner. What a contrast! The one, a child of God and prophet of God, the other a denier of God, a man who, lacking 'grace', proceeded to build from within himself a quite new empire; the one a Parsifal, the other a Klingsor. One could sum up all the extremest contrasts of the present time, and of our music, with these two names: here Schoenberg, here Bruckner!

Hermann Scherchen and Hindemith planned a splendid birthday celebration in Frankfurt on Main between 15 and 18 September. There were four concerts with songs and piano pieces, as well as all the chamber music Schoenberg had composed up to that time. Here is a passage from Schoenberg's reply to Scherchen's invitation (12 August; *S.L.* 84):

Now let me thank you once again most warmly and ask you to tell Hindemith too that I am *extremely pleased with him.* By doing this he is making a splendid sign of a proper attitude to his elders, a sign such as can be made only by a man with a genuine and justifiable sense of his own worth; only by one who has no need to fear for his own fame when another is being honoured and who recognises that precisely such an honour does honour also to him if he associates himself with it.

The commemorative volume published by Universal Edition as a special issue of *Musikblätter des Anbruch* has already been mentioned a number of times; apart from the contributions already quoted, mention should also be made of an uncompromising article by Adolf Loos, later included in his book *Arnold Schoenberg and his Contemporaries.* This ended with the lapidary sentence: 'Perhaps centuries must pass before people begin to wonder what it was that so bewildered Arnold Schoenberg's contemporaries.' The volume was rounded off by Berg's long essay, 'Why is Schoenberg's music so hard to understand?' This is reprinted complete in my biography of Berg. The essay discusses the first ten bars of the Op. 7 string quartet composed in 1905 (cf pages 21-2) and so offers essential information about Schoenberg's whole way of composing. Schoenberg himself contributed a good-humoured foreword to the volume; he first mentioned the musical and theoretical works he had in mind for the coming years, and went on:

If all this has still not convinced my incorrigible friends of something less well-disposed people assume at the outset: that I have reached my limit, that, as a true pace-maker, I have been overtaken (for everything gets overtaken, one's co-runners and followers are so robust), that, in a word, I have arrived at the place where many people would, in the interests of their plans for the further development of musical history, be glad to see me—then I am obliged to mention one clear symptom of age which is present in my case: I can no longer hate as once I could; sometimes, and this is worse still, I can even understand without feeling contempt.

Schoenberg's foreword to the commemorative volume is dated 'Mödling, 20 August 1924'. Eight days later he married Gertrud Kolisch, the sister of his pupil and friend Rudolf Kolisch. The loving and devoted understanding this lady offered him was of fundamental importance in his subsequent development as a man and as an artist.

During this, Schoenberg's final stay in his native land of Austria, he composed three more works: the quintet Op. 26, for flute, oboe, clarinet, bassoon, and horn (the first performance of which has already been mentioned)—this was composed between April 1923 and August 1924; the Four Pieces for mixed choir, Op. 27 (September 1925 to end of the same year), and the Three Satires for Mixed Choir, Op. 28 (November 1925 to 31 December, 1925).

The wind quintet was the first long work Schoenberg composed entirely according to the twelve-tone method. The row e flat–g–a–b–c sharp–c–b flat–d–e–f sharp–a flat–f, together with certain subsidiary forms derived from it by a very simple process, is the sole basis for the thematic course of all four movements. The distinguishing feature of the basic set is that its second half, beginning on b flat, exactly follows the course of the first half (except for the very last tone), but a fifth higher. This means that the two halves are related in a way somewhat analogous to that of tonic and dominant in tonal music: and during the course of the work the two halves of the row are in fact often used in some such way, so that a type of entirely classical formal articulation becomes possible: the first movement (*Schwungvoll*) is a regular sonata movement, with an exposition, development, recapitulation and coda. Second comes a scherzo (*Anmutig und heiter, scherzando—* 'charming and gay, scherzando'), with two episodes, the second of which fulfils the function of the trio. The third movement (*etwas langsam, poco adagio*) is a ternary song form. The finale, a rondo, is perhaps a little harder to grasp, since on each of the rondo theme's three reappearances it is varied in a different way, besides which the episodelike sections are subjected to thematic work of a more intensive kind. The composer called this procedure, which in his later works became ever more highly developed and manifold, 'the principle of developing variation'.

Schoenberg dedicated the quintet to his grandson 'Bubi Arnold'. Berg made play with this dedication in his contribution to the U.E. *Yearbook* for 1926, '25 Years of New Music', when, in his 'committed reply to a non-committal questionnaire' (the questionnaire had solicited 'prospects for the next twenty-five years' in the development of music) he added the following words to a caricature of Beethoven's Ninth Symphony dating from 1847:

When the public produces and allows such things—and I strongly suspect that even nowadays they are still inclined to find this humorous attitude at least harmless, and to find my agitation on the subject a matter for bewilderment—when public opinion leaves behind such a record of itself, I flatly contest its fitness, and therefore its right, to judge the highest art, and to be the final arbiters in laying down such judgments. And once one has realised this, as I have, there is truly nothing for it but to flee from such contemporaries, into the remotest possible future. And then one sees the true point of a dedication with which Arnold Schoenberg sends into the world the work that takes his output into its second quarter-century. It is no mere act of grandfatherly affection, when he dedicates his wind quintet Op. 26 to an unsuspecting child; I believe he also means that this music, with which the unsuspecting child of our time is as much at a loss as is the 'Bubi Arnold' of today, may remain reserved for a time when the next generation but one, at least, will have matured; a time when what today seems merely like a prophecy will at last have turned into the incontrovertible truth.—What a 'prospect for the next 25 years'!

The four pieces for mixed choir, Op. 27, are the first practical application of the twelve-tone method to four-part vocal writing. This may also have been what prompted Schoenberg in the first three pieces (all sung unaccompanied) to use, with varying degrees of strictness, forms from the old polyphony (canon, etc.). In the first two pieces, whose words by Schoenberg himself, are printed on page 97 ('Unentrinnbar', and 'Du sollst nicht, du musst!'), the strictness of the canons matches the strictness of the philosophy of life expressed in the words. The theme of the third piece (*Mond und Menschen*, Moon and Men, Hans Bethge's translation of a poem by Chan Jo-su) gave rise to a copious use of mirror forms. The fourth piece (*Der Wunsch des Liebhabers*, The lover's wish) is also from Bethge's *Die chinesische Flöte*, the poet here being Hung So-fan, and makes a much simpler impression; even the basic set made it possible to produce reminiscences of tonal music; another contributory factor is the effect of the accompaniment (for mandoline, clarinet, violin, and cello), which makes frequent use of ostinato rhythms.

In a letter to Amadeo de Filippi (13 May 1941, *S.L.* 239) written in English a quarter of a century after the composition of the Three Satires, Schoenberg described how they originated: 'I wrote them when I was very much angered by attacks of some of my younger contemporaries at this time and I wanted to give them a warning that it is not good to attack me.' These 'younger contemporaries' were described in more detail in the foreword to the Satires, which contains passages such as this.

In the first place, I wanted to hit all those who seek their personal salvation along a middle way. For the middle way is the only one that does not lead to Rome. But it is used by those who nibble at dissonances—they want to count as modern, then—but are too cautious to draw the correct conclusions. . . . Next, the pseudotonalists, who think they may do anything they please, however much it shakes the foundations of tonality, so long as occasionally, at some fitting or ill-fitting moment, they offer a pinch of incense to tonality, in the form of a tonal triad. . . . Secondly, I am aiming at those who pretend they are trying to 'go back to . . .'. A person like that should not try to make people believe it is *he* who controls how far back he is soon going to find himself. . . . Since, moreover, we have already seen more than one 'Renaissance', proclaimed with a flourish of trumpets, quickly turn out to be based on a false pregnancy (unproclaimed), let me merely put on record that such people write, of their own free will, in the same needy way that is imposed on a poor conservatoire student. Thirdly: I have pleasure in also hitting the folk-lorists who—either because they have to (from an inability to summon up themes of their own), or even though they do not have to (since an existing musical culture and tradition could, if it came to it, stand even them)—apply to the naturally primitive ideas of folk music a technique suitable only to a complicated way of thinking. . . . Fourthly and finally, all the '. . . ists', in whom I can see only mannerists.

Schoenberg later resumed his polemic against the folklorists in his article 'Folkloristic symphonies', published in *Musical America* (February 1947). He ended the foreword to the Satires, with the following sentences, which read like a confession:

I cannot judge whether it is nice of me (it will surely be no nicer than everything else about me) to make fun of much that is well meant, in many ways talented, and in part worthy of respect, knowing as I do that it is certainly possible to make fun of everything. Much sadder things included. And much better fun! In any case, I am excused since, as ever, I have only done it as well as I can. May others find themselves able to laugh at it all more than I can, since I also know how to take it seriously! Perhaps I was trying to hint at that too!

The Three Satires are strict twelve-tone compositions. The texts are Schoenberg's own. The first two, *Am Schiedeweg* ('At the parting of the ways'—originally entitled 'Tonal or atonal?') and *Vielseitigkeit* ('Many-sidedness' or 'Versatility') are sung unaccompanied; in the third, *Der neue Klassizismus* (*Eine kleine Kantate*), an ensemble of viola, cello, and piano is closely interwoven into the contrapuntal texture. In all three pieces the old clefs are used; the second piece is also 'many-sided' in the literal sense, since if the two pages of music are turned through 180 degrees, the resulting musical text is identical with the original. As an appendix to the Satires, Schoenberg added three canons in C major, very complicated pieces with highly allusive texts. This was done in order to counter the frequently heard accusation that it was easier to produce contrapuntal subtleties in non-tonal music than in tonal, and to show 'that someone who wrote the present (twelve-tone) compositions does not absolutely have to have things made easy for him in that way, and that even with seven tones he can manage to produce a good deal that is, if not highly valued, at least counted difficult'. It should be noted that the third, six-part canon was dedicated ('with admiration') to George Bernard Shaw on his seventieth birthday.

During the latter half of 1924, an important turning-point in Schoenberg's life approached: on 27 June Busoni died. Since 1920 he had been in charge of a 'masterclass in musical composition', at the Berlin Academy of the Arts. At Franz Schreker's instigation, Leo Kestenberg, the musical counsellor to the Prussian Ministry of Science, Art, and Education, invited Schoenberg to move to Berlin and become Busoni's successor. The contracts are reprinted verbatim in Rufer's catalogue. Schoenberg's appointment aroused great astonishment in Vienna. There, in his native city, people suddenly realised how much and for how long they had been neglecting Schoenberg; now, his departure was strongly deplored, in public at least. Schoenberg found all the stir quite disagreeable, and when a journalist asked him to discuss the subject in an interview for a Viennese paper, he wrote to him, 26 September, 1925: 'My most pressing need is to depart from Vienna as unnoticed as I have always been while I was here. I desire no accusations, no attacks, no defence, no publicity, no triumph! only: *peace!*' (*S.L.* 86)

Because of an appendix operation in mid-November 1925, Schoenberg's departure for Berlin had to be delayed, and it was January 1926 before he took up his post in Berlin.

8 Berlin Variations with a Sombre Coda

Schoenberg's academic freedom in Berlin is illustrated by clauses 3 and 7 of his contract:

> 3. During the duration of the contract Mr Schoenberg undertakes to teach in Berlin for six months of each year. It is left to Mr Schoenberg to decide when he shall teach. The form taken by Mr Schoenberg's teaching is also left to him to decide. . . .
>
> 7. If because of concert- or lecture-tours outside Europe Mr Schoenberg shall be prevented from fulfilling his obligations within one contract year he will try to the best of his ability to make good the difference during the immediately ensuing academic year. . . .

During the whole of his stay in Berlin Schoenberg made ample use of the free time the contract gave him; but, on the other hand, as a member of the Academy's senate he also took a lively interest in all questions affecting its running, whether artistic or organisational, and he repeatedly put forward useful ideas. His master-class always assembled at his private residence, first in a pension on the Steinplatz, later at No. 17, Nussbaumallee, in the Charlottenburg district of Berlin, and finally at No. 3, Nürnberger Platz. Adolf Weiss, an American who was taught by Schoenberg both in Mödling and in Berlin, has described his teaching methods in an essay entitled 'The Lyceum of Schoenberg', published in the New York periodical *Modern Music*. One particularly original touch was that Schoenberg would first let his pupils discuss their compositions among themselves, before coming out with his own observations. Weiss also mentions that there were often violent arguments during such discussions, but that these greatly encouraged the remorseless honesty which Schoenberg himself practised, and which he absolutely demanded of his pupils. Recalling what Schoenberg had to say about orchestration—in which his overriding demand was for 'transparency'—Weiss particularly emphasises one maxim which Schoenberg often repeated: 'Rests always sound well!'

In his book on Schoenberg H. H. Stuckenschmidt, who was particularly close to Schoenberg as pupil and friend during these Berlin years, makes special mention of the following Berlin pupils, some of whom he had brought with him from Vienna: Winfried Zillig, Roberto Gerhard, Walter Goehr, Walter Gronostay, Peter Schacht, Adolph Weiss, Joseph Zmigrod (Allan Gray), Norbert von Hannenheim, Charilaos Perpessa, Erich Schmid, Nikos Skalkottas; and some who stayed only a short time, such as Marc Blitzstein, Henry Cowell, Rudolf Goehr, and —— Fried. There was also a Swiss pupil, Alfred Keller. Josef Rufer (b. 1893) had a special place within the Schoenberg circle; he had been a pupil since 1918, and, for 'technical' reasons, was also numbered among the pupils at the Berlin master-class, but in fact he was Schoenberg's assistant, his main function being to give elementary tuition to the majority of the composition pupils—Schoenberg did none of this during his Berlin years —and to familiarise them with Schoenberg's methods and academic views. Some of the most important contributions to our knowledge of Schoenberg's life and work have been made by Rufer: the manual *Composition with Twelve Tones*, the complete catalogue of Schoenberg's music, writings and paintings, and the supervision of the 'complete edition' currently in publication.

The first major work Schoenberg completed in Berlin was the Suite Op. 29, which he had already begun to write in Vienna during March 1925; he completed it on 1 May 1926, and dedicated it to his wife. The work is scored for seven instruments—E-flat clarinet (or flute), clarinet, bass clarinet (or bassoon), violin, viola, cello, and piano; its four movements—Overture, Dance-steps, Theme and Variations, Gigue—are based on forms found in the old suite. The theme of the third movement is a song, *Ännchen von Tharau*, by Heinrich Albert (1604–51), a tune that has become so popular as to be regarded as a folk-song. The work is composed according to the strict twelve-tone method, which, however, here achieved for the first time a complete freedom as far as moulding the course of the music is concerned. This is a special, and dialectical, step forward, as was pointed out by Theodor W. Adorno as early as May 1928, in a review of the work for the Berlin periodical *Die Musik*. As well as analysing its row-structure Adorno said this:

Constructive fantasy is still there; its freedom is unreduced, wide awake, and from the outset it illuminates the pre-existing forms and wants in the end to explode again whatever remnants of preordained existence wish to divert its path; it has to be autonomous, to be the sole arbiter of its own form. One must not imagine from this that Schoenberg has arbitrarily remembered a superseded style, and has proceeded to fill it in by means of twelve-tone technique. Rather, the objective power of Schoenberg's dialectic comes precisely from the fact that his *modus procedendi* in each work's predecessor makes that work's problems necessary, as if it were merely a matter of answering here the technical questions thrown up there—while the transition from question to answer already marks the transition to a new musical sphere. The motive power of this latest transformation is the question how to handle twelve-tone technique so that, with no diminution whatever in strictness, the course of the rows, and the rows themselves, are not perceptible, but disappear behind the resources of technique, thematic and compositional. The row is no longer to be thematic material, it constitutes simply the virtual thematicism, which is not manifest at all as such. As a result, a new loosening-up of the thematic characters is demanded, and this finds its close corollary in the work's looser forms. But at the same time, the strict logic of all the previous twelve-tone works continues to function. Twelve-tone technique has given up none of its strictness, it is merely that the possibilities of row division, combination and transposition have been so enriched that the full mobility of the earlier works has been recaptured.

The Suite was first performed in Paris on 15 December 1927, with Schoenberg conducting.

Schoenberg's next major piece of creative work after the completion of the Suite was literary—the drama *Der biblische Weg* (drafted mid-June 1926, first version completed 5 July: a second version dates from a year later). On 26 May 1933 he wrote about the work to the Jewish philosopher Jacob Klatzkin (*S.L.* 153):

The Biblical Way is a very up-to-date treatment (written in 1926–7) of the story of how the Jews became a people. Acquaintances of mine, who have thorough professional knowledge of this sort of thing, and to whom I showed it only recently, are enthusiastic, and agree with me that it would be a huge success in the theatre. Produced by someone such as Reinhardt, in London, it would probably have a very long run.[1] It is highly dramatic, stylistically the best thing I have written, and, although its profundities offer the superior kind plenty of food for thought, is vivid and theatrical enough to fascinate the simpler sort. You will forgive me for praising myself, but since it is now six years old, I am as objective about it as if it were not by me.

In 1967 an Italian translation of the drama was published in the Italian collected of Schoenberg texts (*Testi poetici e drammatici*, Feltrinelli). However, as from July 1927 onward Schoenberg showed it to some of his friends. A summary of its contents, and a farreaching, obviously authentic interpretation, form the central point of the essay contributed by Schoenberg's boyhood friend David Josef Bach to the 1934 commemorative volume. Bach referred to the two poems *Unentrinnbar* and *Du sollst nicht, du musst!* (cf pages 97, 153), which Schoenberg had set to music as Nos. 1 and 2 of the four pieces for mixed choir, Op. 27. Quoting the complete text of No. 2, Bach remarks,

This poem is a profession of faith. A confession that professes art and religion in one, since both spring from one root and culminate in one crown. . . . The play *The Biblical Way* provides access to the mysterious realm of this religion. The key this drama provides is only *one* key, and it by no means opens all the doors into the heavenly realm of union with the spirit.

Bach proceeds to link his summary of the plot directly to his interpretation of the drama:

The hero, or rather the main figure of this play in prose, is Max Aruns, a New Palestinian, who wants to found, in 'Ammon-Gäa', a new Palestine, a new kingdom, which will gradually attract to it all the Jews on earth, and will become God's kingdom. This is in the land of Ammon, in the midst of all the other African kingdoms. The goal is almost achieved, when Aruns comes to grief because of the imperfect nature of everything human. Not only through others' imperfections, but, as he realises, through his own imperfect nature, which

[1] Literally: 'Would probably spread through all the theatres'. L.B.

his death as a martyr redeems and lifts to the only level of perfection possible for humans. It is understandable that his monstrous plan aroused resistance from the non-Jewish world and, even more, among the Jews themselves; personal and general reasons play their part, material and ideological ones, inherited and acquired prejudices. And yet he is felled, not by the battle carried on with the material resources of power—for his death, too, is only a symbol—nor does he founder through treachery and intrigue, jealousy and revenge and all the other human passions and weaknesses, but through the fact that the weaknesses and sins of others can suck his blood. That is his ruin. He is betrayed by his own wife, but only because for a single moment he forgot the greatness of his task, and became entangled in things human, instead of following the bitter path of loneliness. Did he miss the true path? Did he in fact recognise it, but without the power to tread it? Or does he recognise it only in death, and follow it only through death? The true path is the *biblical* path. God has revealed it. Is one to take at its face value, and follow literally, the revelation found in the Bible, or is one to follow the spirit rather than the letter? *But is not the word the spirit itself, its condensation, solidification, the symbol of the idea?* So, for men, the true path is at the same time the wrong one, just as life intermingles with death. Destiny of man (and not only of the Jews): to spiritualise oneself, to bring about union in the spirit. This is, especially, the Jewish people's dream of God. 'We want to perfect ourselves in the spirit, to be allowed to dream our dream of God—like all the peoples of old, who have put matter behind them'—so says the new young leader Guido, after the death of the leader. The people is represented through Max Aruns. On him has fallen its destiny—to see the goal, to formulate it; to him has gone out the call to be a 'hero'.

Bach then extends the scope of his article to include the libretto of the opera *Moses and Aaron*, which Schoenberg had drafted in October 1928 (cf pages 177–9), and with profound perceptiveness relates the main figures of the two works:

First, one suddenly realises that in the single figure of Max Aruns there rage two personalities, Moses *and* Aaron, who are separated in the opera. Moses is the idea, Aaron is the word. To Moses has gone out the call which he can not deny—'for

Thou knowest the Truth!', as the Voice of the Lord replies to him. And later Moses himself says, 'Ineluctable law of thought forces to fulfilment!' That is taken from the field of religion and transferred to the field of art; the one pervades and illuminates the other. In religion, the law of thought is in an inconceivable God, an 'inexpressible idea with many meanings'. But as soon as it is expressed, it is falsified. Not only through the word of Aaron, whose fate is 'to say it worse than he understands it'; there is an Aaron of this kind within every man, even in Moses himself, just as 'Max Aruns' was nothing but the union of the two, made visible within one person. Because of this visible union he had to die.

Recent events in the Near East have made this drama, *The Biblical Way*, particularly relevant and topical. Its publication in the original German, and if possible also in English, seems of pressing urgency, as is its production on the stage.

In September 1927 Schoenberg spent some time in Vienna; on the 19th his Third String Quartet was given its first performance, by the Kolisch Quartet, in the second largest of the Konzerthaus's three halls. This work, commissioned by the American patroness of the arts, Mrs Elizabeth Sprague Coolidge, was composed, using the twelve-tone method, in February and March of the same year; it uses the method rather more freely than do its predecessors. For instance, in the first movement certain fragments of the basic set are repeated even before the whole row has been heard. It was this work which prompted Schoenberg once to warn Rudolf Kolisch that he attached little importance to strict analysis of his 12-tone works (27 July 1932; *S.L.* 143): 'I can't utter too many warnings against overrating these analyses, since after all they only lead to what I have always been dead against: seeing how it is *done*; whereas I have always helped people to see: what it *is*.'

About the turn of the year (1927–8) there was a series of important performances of his works abroad. On 30 November 1927 the *Gurrelieder* were given in Leningrad, conducted by Nicolai Malko, with members of the State Music Institute and the Leningrad Philharmonic Orchestra. The first

1 Edward Clark (cf note to page 62) was Schoenberg's only pre-1914 pupil from the English-speaking world. After the 1914–18 war (during which, as an Englishman in Germany, he was interned), he played an active role in British musical life, both as conductor and as a leading figure in the early days of the BBC's music output. In 1921 he conducted the first British performance of Schoenberg's 1st Chamber Symphony, Op. 9, with a distinguished ensemble including the young Leon Goossens and a cellist named 'G.B.' (later Sir John!) Barbirolli. Cf Asa Briggs (*The Golden Age of Wireless*, OUP, 1965), 'Edward Clark, who left the BBC in 1936, should have a key place in any history of twentieth-century British music. It was he who knew everything that was going on in the world of contemporary music —particularly in Europe—and everybody who was engaged in it. The BBC was involved from the 1920s onwards in the hazardous enterprise of introducing to the British listeners Schoenberg and Webern as well as Bartok and Stravinsky.' L.B.

Russian performance of this enormous work was such a success that it had to be repeated a few days later.

In December 1927 Schoenberg and his wife spent a few weeks in Paris. He had been invited by the Société Musicale Indépendante, and for them he conducted the Suite, Op. 29 (the work's first performance anywhere), *Pelléas and Mélisande*, the two Bach chorale preludes, and *Pierrot Lunaire* (twice), at two concerts in the Salle Pleyel, on 8 and 15 December. Marya Freund also sang four of the Op. 6 songs, and the Song of the Wood-Dove from the *Gurrelieder*. Schoenberg also lectured at the Sorbonne on the subject of 'Knowledge and Intuition'. After the concerts, which were greeted with storms of applause, but also with shrill whistles and shouts of protest, the Schoenbergs became so caught up in Parisian society that they had no chance of getting to know Paris, something they had been eager to do.

From Paris they went on to London, where the first performance of the *Gurrelieder* in English took place on 27 January 1928, with Schoenberg conducting. The promoters were the BBC, whose music department was headed by Edward Clark[1], a former pupil of Schoenberg (cf page 65). In a Viennese report of the performance it was said that:

The work had a success greater than that of any novelty in London during recent years. The Queen's Hall was full to overflowing, the leading personalities of the English musical world appeared, almost without exception, and at the end there broke out a sound of rejoicing rare indeed with the reserved English public. When almost an hour after the end of the concert Schoenberg left the building, an enthusiastic crowd of hundreds was awaiting him. This remarkable performance was simultaneously relayed by all the British radio stations.

On the return journey, there were concerts in Basle and Berne (during February), so that Schoenberg could look back with satisfaction on this tour abroad: 'Once again, after years of being ignored, a start at least.'

In March 1928 Schoenberg was back in Berlin. On the 24th, the Breslau City Opera gave the first performance in Germany of *Die glückliche Hand*. The conductor was Fritz Cortolezzi, the producer Herbert Graf, the stage sets were by Hans Wildermann. Schoenberg was very pleased with the performance.

The day before, Schoenberg's old friend Franz Schreker had celebrated his fiftieth birthday. There was a special edition of *Musikblätter des Anbruch* as a tribute to Schreker, and Schoenberg contributed the following sarcastic letter:

Dear Friend,

We both date from the good old days when unsympathetic people used to identify themselves by calling us 'newsounders'. How are we to adapt ourselves to a time when they now call us 'romantics'?

One thing we do know, however: they thought no better of us then, as 'newsounders', than of us as romantics; there were always people about who knew better than we did, even if they could do no better.

But where are they now, those who called us 'newsounders'? Who now calls them—anything?

Can we not be sure that those to whom we now, as romantics, have nothing left to say (what they could use they stole long ago)—that in another ten or twenty years they too will be where the opponents of our youth belonged from the outset?

Anyway: it seems we can wait; we can afford to.

Hear you[1] in twenty years!

Yours

1 March 1928   ARNOLD SCHOENBERG

[1] Idiomatic German does in fact use *Auf wiederhören* on the analogy of *Auf wiedersehen*; many a telephone conversation ends in that way. L.B.

Schoenberg spent the summer of 1928 on the French Riviera, at Roquebrune, Cap Martin. It was there that, in August, he completed the Orchestral Variations Op. 31, which he had begun in Berlin in the early spring of 1926. The final copy is dated 21 September.

Apart from its own artistic value, this work is specially important in Schoenberg's creative development because in it, for the first time since the Orchestral Songs, Op. 22 (1914–16), he used the resources of a large orchestra (a traditional symphony orchestra, with one or two additions). The intervening period having seen the full development of the twelve-tone method, in which doublings (hard to avoid when using a considerable body of instruments) are avoided on principle, it had become a great deal harder to write for a large orchestra. Discussing the Variations with Erwin Stein in 1928, Schoenberg emphasised that his way of scoring—a colouristic one—served principally to add expressive intensity, and to present the musical ideas more clearly. In his own words: 'It could be thought that, given my way of handling the orchestra, my works do not contain a single passage where there is a need to use five trombones, since there is no forte demanding their entry. And yet in many passages they are indispensable, in order to achieve complete clarity—a reason harder to recognise.' And in fact there are in the Variations several passages where four trombones and tuba are used in precisely the way Schoenberg describes here.

The contrast between the earliest twelve-tone compositions, for piano or chamber ensemble, and the Orchestral Variations is no mere external one determined simply by the increase in the number of instruments; the new method in turn exerted its own influence, and, once again, the entire layout of the work was affected.

This is already clear in the 'introduction' which precedes the twenty-four-bar variation theme; whereas in the earlier twelve-tone works the basic set was announced at the opening, and everything else developed from it, here it is only after a romantic opening (the work seems to 'dawn' on the listener) that the actual row is made to emerge, one tone at a time, from the general orchestral sound, and to fulfil two potentially useful functions: as a kind of 'expanded tonality', which determines the general sound character of the whole, and as carrier of the most important melodic motives, three of which are already present in the introduction, including the B–A–C–H motive (cf page 140), which acts as a secret motto dominating the Variations.

The variation theme (Molto moderato), consisting of all four forms of the row (basic set, retrograde inversion, retrograde, and inversion) is given out on the celli as a simple, strikingly rhythmicised melodic line, accompanied only by soft sustained chords from the rest of the orchestra. This is enough in itself to establish a strong contrast of sheer sound, both with the orchestrally luxurious introduction, and with the type of orchestration, rich in mixtures and subtle gradations, used throughout the actual variations. Formally speaking, the theme can be regarded as ternary song form (A–B–A), and this also determines the formal articulation in each of the nine variations, which are all either the same length exactly (24 bars), or of some length directly proportionate, such as 48 bars (Var. 4), or 24 plus 12 bars (Var. 6).

The nine variations vary the theme in two ways; variation of its own manifest musical form (fragmentation and re-rhythmicising of the melodic line, contrapuntal combination with countersubjects, new colouration using the sound palette of the symphony orchestra, and so on), and the interpolation of independent symphonic pieces whose musical character provides contrast or cumulative tension. There is then an extended finale (210 bars, as compared with the 252 covered by the variations), so that the whole makes up a large symphonic form whose unity derives from the basic set; the latter is the origin of all that happens in the work, but thanks to the changing character of the individual variations it appears in the greatest variety of musical guises.

Variation 1 (Moderato) feels like a prelude to an Adagio for wind and solo violin and cello (Var. 2); Var. 3 (Moderato) leads to the work's scherzo section, which consists of a variation (No. 4) in waltz tempo and a quick, stormy one in $\frac{3}{2}$ time (No. 5), dying away into an Andante (Var. 6) which, like Var. 2, uses wind and solo strings. Variation 7 is in the nature of a large-scale Adagio, and marks the work's expressive climax. The last two variations form a single unit; in quick tempo, they lead to the finale. This first sums up, as if reminiscing, many of the figures heard earlier, and eventually blows itself out in a lively presto where the variation theme is broken down into its motivic elements.

There is, however, something even more important to do than to demonstrate all the formal and compositional devices in the work; one must grasp its entirely new world of sound. In the Variations, Schoenberg kept the tightest possible rein on his truly demonic imagination, but, time after time, the elemental power of his original inspiration flashes forth from this brilliantly contrived work. What makes the Variations, Op. 31 a very important event in Schoenberg's entire output is this remarkable way it has of moving on two levels—the 'bistratification' of its sensory aspect.

The work's importance went quite unrecognised at its first performance (by the Berlin Philharmonic Orchestra under Furtwängler) on 2 December 1928. Part of the public demonstrated, hissing and whistling; Schoenberg regarded this as an 'oafish impertinence' against himself and the conductor. Six months passed, and then he wrote to Furtwängler (4 July 1929, *S.L.* 109): 'Frankly, I expected that you would repeat the piece at the next concert, showing the rabble that *you only do what you consider right*! . . . It is not my intention, in saying this, to try to make any conditions; for nothing is right in any such case but what one does of one's own free will.'

Schoenberg's next major work after the Variations took him into a new field (*S.L.* 107):

It is a cheerful to gay, even sometimes (I hope at least) comic opera: not grotesque, not offensive, not political, not religious. The music is as bad as mine always is; that is, appropriate to my intellectual and artistic condition. But it is also appropriate to the subject and therefore continually produces self-contained forms that are interrupted and linked by distinct (but naturally 'non-tonal') recitatives that do not set up to be melodic. There are several ensembles: duets and quartets.

This one-act opera, composed between 25 October 1928 and 1 January 1929, was given the title *Von heute auf morgen* ('From one day to the next'). The text was by Mrs Gertrud Schoenberg, whose authorship was concealed by the use of the pseudonym Max Blonda. In January 1930 I summarised the plot as follows for a Viennese daily paper:

1 Or 'The Man' (*Der Mann*)—cf *Die glückliche Hand*. L.B.

Five characters appear in the piece (which lasts some fifty minutes): The Husband[1] (baritone), the Wife and Her Friend (sopranos), the Singer (tenor), and the Child. The scene is laid in a modern bedroom. Husband and wife return home after an evening out, which they have apparently enjoyed; both are appropriately dressed. They talk about the evening's experiences. The husband has been greatly impressed by an old school-friend of his wife's, whom she had not seen for a long time, and who has been introduced to him during the evening. The wife talks about the famous tenor she has met at the party, who paid court to her so charmingly. The husband found him boring, 'with his endless trivial jokes'. A sharp exchange develops, in the course of which he admits that he is at that moment attracted less to his wife than to her friend. The wife makes things clear to him: 'I know this woman attracts only your curiosity; you hope for something fantastic, some miracle, behind the glittering mask. You are dazzled by every new thing that appears and acts fashionable. But once the novelty has worn off, you are left looking at a blank, disappointed. It's a bit late then to compare me with her!' He comes back strongly—'I'm not comparing. That would be ludicrous: she, a woman-of-the-world, and you, the model housewife.' The squabble develops further, and culminates in a canonic duet, both of them using identical words to complain of their dissatisfaction with their married life and declaring that from now on they will go their own way, extramaritally. Ignored by her husband, the wife now begins to 'transform' herself: having put on all the lights, she appears suddenly in an 'effect-ful negligé', and he is immediately fascinated. Playing the woman-of-the-world, she repels him, dances, forces him to drink champagne with her; he has to look after their child in the kitchen, all their noise having woken it. Suddenly the phone rings. It is the singer, calling from a bar and inviting the two of them to join him there. In a long flirtatious conversation the wife agrees, and changes into a long, elegant evening dress. The husband, jealous and deeply unhappy, refuses to go with her on this jaunt. By now the wife knows that her risky game has gone far enough; she makes her exit, reappearing in a simple working dress. The child, too, enters, and the three seat themselves cosily around the breakfast table. This idyll is interrupted by the appearance of the singer and the wife's friend, who have been vainly waiting in the bar. A long quartet develops, and finally the two 'seducers' take their leave, disappointed and poking fun at the married couple as 'faded theatrical figures'. The wife takes up this idea and remarks 'With them, the producer is fashion; but with us . . . love!' The husband: 'And, today, I don't even find them quite modern any more!' The wife: 'Well, that's bound to change from one day to the next!' The child: 'Mama, what are those—modern people?' And the curtain falls.

When the opera was about to go into production for its first performance, Schoenberg wrote a long letter to Wilhelm Steinberg, who was conducting the work, and gave in great

detail his views about casting and rehearsals (4 October 1929).
In the final sentence he went on to give his overall view of
the work:

The tone of the whole should really be very *light* throughout.
But it will be permissible, necessary even, for people to feel,
or sense, that one or two things are hidden behind the simplicity
of these goings-on; that the aim is to show, using everyday
figures and goings-on, how, far beyond the bounds of this simple
marital incident, the merely modern, the fashionable, lives
only 'from one day to the next', from insecure hand to greedy
mouth—in marriage, but at least equally in art, in politics, and
in people's views about life.

The first performance was on 1 February 1930, at Frankfurt-on-Main. It had a mixed reception from the public and
the press. Schoenberg had obviously overestimated listeners'
receptivity to his 'gay' music. Work and performance alike
were very perceptively assessed on 4 February by the Viennese critic Max Graf, writing in *Der Tag*:

The music of Schoenberg's new opera is entirely dominated
by his new twelve-tone style. The vocal parts, too, take part in
the motivic work. The result is a closely woven fabric of vocal
and orchestral parts, consisting of melodic figures that are now
energetically sweeping, now tersely rhythmic, but in either
case utterly characteristic of Schoenberg; a fabric completely
free in its rhythm, which changes from bar to bar. From time
to time ensembles are interpolated, and these show a strict
constructive form: man and wife squabble in a canon by
inversion; the final quartet for husband, wife, lady-friend and
singer is an ingenious double canon. But all these constructive
forms are not intellectual, abstract, but alive, a special mani-
festation of Schoenberg's ever-active fantasy, which in this
new work displays the greatest freshness and a marvellous
clarity of disposition. The music of the opera is full of rhythmic
energy, full of life, with no recourse to anything familiar; it has
grown on its own ground. Only in a few passages does the
complete orchestra make itself heard. Mostly it is broken down
into groups of solo instruments, a chamber orchestra in which
all the parts are essential, with no dressing-up, each instrument
an individuality. All the new, self-made artistic resources are

used by Schoenberg, with a certainty and superiority that are imposing. Everything in this opera is done with skill, the kind of skill possessed only by a great mind that can do as it likes. No trace of the clever, superficial handicraft that so often passes for art. A new type of fantasy has created a new style, a new expression, a new music. The difficulties of performing such a work, which has hurried far ahead along music's path, 'from today to tomorrow',[1] are inconceivable. In performing it, the Frankfurt Opera celebrated its historic day, and all the difficulties were brilliantly overcome. Schoenberg's marital comedy was sung with a naturalness which seemed to give the lie to any suggestion that Schoenberg melodies are tongue-twisters, and played as naturally as if it were by Ludwig Fulda.[2] Else Gentner-Fischer as the wife, Benno Ziegler as the husband, Anton M. Topitz as the Wagner-tenor, and Elisabeth Friedrich as the friend were equally excellent, a finely balanced ensemble. The Opera's young director, Wilhelm Steinberg, of whom Schoenberg has said that he (Steinberg) knows the score better than he (Schoenberg) does himself, conducted the orchestra with astonishing certainty and freedom. My son Herbert Graf, as the Frankfurt Opera's senior producer, looked after the production; the sins of the father are evidently inheritable, since it was the father of Schoenberg's producer who years ago became the first critic to speak up loudly on the composer's behalf, when his first string quartet was performed in Vienna. Who could have imagined, when the readers of a weekend[3] supplement were exhorted to take note of the name Schoenberg, the development that has led Schoenberg to his latest opera!

1 The literal translation of the opera's title.
L.B.

2 A successful contemporary writer of light comedies.
L.B.

3 Literally, 'Monday', that being the day when such supplements appeared in Vienna.
L.B.

The opera was performed only a few times in Frankfurt. On 27 February 1930 it was heard once more, conducted by the composer, over the Berlin Radio. Then the tragic course of world events caused it to disappear for more than twenty years. On 20 December 1952 Hermann Scherchen brought it to life again at the Teatro San Carlo in Naples, where it formed part of a double bill with *Salome*. I was the producer, and Teo Otto designed the sets. The public were part amused, part repelled. There were, however, no demonstrations, and the scheduled number of performances for the season could be given. Since then only a few opera houses have tried the work out.

On 26 April 1929, in Vienna, there was a performance that afforded Schoenberg great pleasure: *Pierrot Lunaire* was given by highly talented students from the Vienna Conservatoire, under their Rector, the composer Franz Schmidt (cf page 79). It was one of the best performances of the work I have ever heard, and had powerful repercussions among Vienna's younger musicians.

At almost the same time, Schoenberg's works also formed the central point of a concert promoted by final-year students of the Berlin conservatoire; the composer and his interpreters received a tumultuous ovation.

A year later, early in June 1930, *Erwartung* and *Die glückliche Hand* were at last performed in Berlin, indeed at the principal opera house, that on the Platz der Republik. The conductors were Zemlinsky and Otto Klemperer, the designers Teo Otto and Oskar Schlemmer. The producer in both works was A. M. Rabenalt, but Schoenberg himself provided important ideas about production in a long letter to the Intendant (14 April 1930). The programme book reprinted an article by Schoenberg which had appeared shortly before, in the monthly *Der Querschnitt* (Cross-Section). It was entitled 'My Public'. Schoenberg began by telling of his early experiences with the public, and the resistance he had always encountered from the so-called 'experts'. He went on:

I take it to have been the expert judges, not the art-lovers, who received my *Pierrot Lunaire* with such hostility when I performed it in Italy. I was indeed honoured that Puccini, not an expert judge but a practical expert, made a six-hour journey, despite his illness, to hear my work, and afterwards said some very friendly things to me. That was good, strange though my music may have remained to him. But on the other hand it was characteristic that the loudest disturber of the concert was identified as the director of a conservatoire. He it was, too, who proved unable, at the end, to bridle his truly Mediterranean temperament—who could not refrain from exclaiming 'If there had been just one single honest triad in the whole piece!' Obviously his teaching activities gave him too little opportunity to hear such honest triads, and he had come hoping to find them in my *Pierrot*. Am I to blame for his disappointment?

I have to conclude that the Italian public may not have known what to make of my music. But the image of a concert where there was hissing—in twenty-five years I have seen it so often that I may be believed—was always as follows: in the front third of the hall, roughly, there was little applause and little hissing; most people sat unconcerned, many stood looking round in amazement or amusement toward the parts of the hall further back, where things were livelier. There the applauders were in the majority—there were fewer unconcerned, and a few hissers. But the most noise, both applause and hisses, always came from the standing space at the back and from the galleries. It was there that the people instructed or influenced by the expert judges went into battle against those who were impressed.

. . . That was how I saw the public, and in no other way, except when, as today with my older works, they applauded. But besides a number of very pleasant letters I receive now and then, I also know the public from another side. Perhaps I may end by relating a few pleasing little experiences. When just drafted to a reserve company during the war, I, the conscript, who had had many a bad time, once found myself treated with striking mildness by a newly arrived sergeant. When he addressed me after we had drilled, I hoped I was going to be praised for my progress in all things military. There followed a blow to my soldierly keenness; surprisingly the tribute was to my music. The sergeant, a tailor's assistant in civil life, had recognised me, knew my career, many of my works, and so gave me still more pleasure than by praising my drill (even though I was not a little proud of that!) There were two other such meetings in Vienna: once when I had missed a train and had to spend the night in a hotel, and again when a taxi was taking me to a hotel, I was recognised, the first time by the *night porter*, the other by the *taxi-driver*, from the name on the label of my luggage. Both assured me enthusiastically that they had heard the *Gurrelieder*. Another time, in a hotel in Amsterdam, a *hired man* addressed me and said he was a longstanding admirer of my art; he had sung in the choir in the *Gurrelieder* when I conducted the work in Leipzig. But the prettiest story last: a short while back, again in a hotel, the *lift-man* asked me whether it was I who had written *Pierrot Lunaire*. For he had heard it before the war (about 1912), at the first performance, and still had the sound of it in his ears, particularly of one piece where red jewels were mentioned (*Rote fürstliche Rubine*). And he had heard at the time that musicians had no idea what to make of the piece—the sort of thing that was quite easy to understand nowadays!

It strikes me that I need not alter what I believe about the semi-ignorant, the expert judges: I may continue to think they lack all power of intuition.

But whether I am really so unacceptable to the public as the expert judges always assert, and whether it is really so scared of my music—that often seems to me highly doubtful.

Other compositions Schoenberg completed between 1929 and 1931 were: the two piano pieces Op. 33a and b (between the end of 1928 and October 1931)—two short pieces (40 and 68 bars) written strictly according to the twelve-tone method, and the last he wrote for piano solo; the 'Accompanying Music for a Film Scene', for small orchestra, Op. 34 (October 1929–February 1930)—this has three 'phases': 'Danger threatens', 'Panic', 'Catastrophe', and the piece achieves a powerful expressiveness and an extraordinary range of colour, using the resources of twelve-tone technique; the Six Pieces for male-voice choir, Op. 35 (April 1929–March 1930), of which the first five are written according to the twelve-tone method, while the sixth is entirely tonal, ending with a d-minor triad. The text of all the pieces is Schoenberg's own, and their titles are: *Hemmung* (Inhibition), *Das Gesetz* (The Law), *Ausdrucksweise* ('Manner of speaking', or 'Mode of expression'), *Glück* (Fortune, Luck, or Happiness), *Landsknechte* (Troopers), and *Verbundenheit* (Obligation); as always with Schoenberg, their content is akin to a personal confession. In the sixtieth-birthday volume, Schoenberg's pupil Josef Polnauer made a thorough analysis of *Verbundenheit*, and it was precisely when he came to point out its tonal relationships that some highly ingenious musical symbolism came to light; Polnauer ended his perceptive analysis by pointing out something very remarkable and significant:

However, the first three bars of the main part (first bass) stand out strikingly in manner from the remainder of the piece. They seem like nothing so much as the beginning of a cantus firmus, and an old, quite specific cantus firmus! Are these not the opening notes of 'L' Homme armé'?—of the melody which was handed down by the old Netherlanders and their successors, handed down from generation to generation, as a 'master-greeting'; as a slogan of *spiritual alliance and obligation;*[1] a recurring 'tribute to art', in terms of especially pious, meaningful work?

Apart from composing these pieces, Schoenberg was also intensely occupied from 1930 onward with his opera *Moses and Aaron*, which will later be discussed at length (cf pages 177-83).

Among Schoenberg's literary productions from this period one should mention, above all, his contribution to the tribute to his old friend Adolf Loos, published in Vienna for the latter's sixtieth birthday (10 December 1930). Schoenberg paid homage, formulated very tersely but in an absolutely convincing way, to the three-dimensional view that lay behind Loos' work as an architect, and he ended with an energetic attack on the 'experts':

It is certainly bold of a layman to make such assertions, which he can, after all, support only by saying 'I have the impression . . .' And yet I dare do so: because what is new in Loos manifests itself as the new aspect of a loftier view of things—and the performance of a genius can have no nobler origin: the natural disposition of a genius. And here there are no accredited experts who could refute me.

In the early spring of 1931, the Berlin Radio adopted an idea of Schoenberg's, and broadcast a series of Portraits of Musicians, in each of which an important musician had a discussion with a critic who held opposing views, and a neutral observer. The first portrait was devoted to Schoenberg, whose opponent was Heinrich Strobel, with Eberhard Preussner as the neutral observer. Strobel began the discussion by admitting that the sound of Schoenberg's later works was something to which he could attach no meaning, since he found it impossible to make out any logical cohesion without looking at the score. He gained clear impressions only from the early works, but in these he saw 'only the last exaggeration of romantic subjectivism', so that he could not regard them as 'new'. Schoenberg replied that he had absolutely no

1 '*Verbundenheit* in Schoenberg's text for Op. 35 No. 6 means primarily 'obligation'. Polnauer here also makes play with one of the word's other meanings.
L.B.

reason to be ashamed of carrying on the great German musical tradition; that he would not think of repudiating his early works, but rather saw in them the foundations of his artistic and moral existence. He regarded his double counterpoint, freedom of phrase lengths and absence of primitive sequences—all of which were constantly latent in his earliest works—as an extension of his predecessors' way of composing.

From the very outset he had rejected subjectivism, since the psychological background of a work is a purely private matter, and has nothing to do with the work of composition. He was obliged, on the contrary, to lay claim to logic in his work, but only the logic of 'strictest observance'—not the sort of generally practised 'logic' conveyed by the colloquial use of the word. In defending his twelve-tone method Schoenberg quoted examples from earlier times, and pointed out that even Goethe, in arguing with Zelter, had opposed the exclusive dominance of diatonicism; he also mentioned the church modes and certain folk-songs which likewise are based on non-diatonic scales. The twelve-tone method, he said, was particularly important because it forced the composer, before deciding on a basic set, to try and envisage the probable course of his entire work, modifying its themes and its row structure in an appropriate way. To show the usefulness of the twelve-tone method, he quoted, as a practical experience, the fact that singers, once they had grasped the basic set, could easily deliver all the melodic figures that occur in the piece. Schoenberg ended his reply by reminding historians that their glosses on history should not be extended to cover the epoch that lay closest to them, and recalled the amusing fact that in their own times, even the works of Mendelssohn and Schumann had been regarded in Vienna as 'intellectual North German music'. A comprehensive understanding of his work could, he said, be hoped for only from an idealistic younger generation of the future, who would be tempted by its mysteries and so would come under its spell.

Shortly before this, in a draft of an article dated 24 February 1931 and entitled 'National Music', he had considered at some length the close links between his work and the great German musical tradition, links which he emphasised at the beginning of the broadcast discussion. The first reference to this document was in a lecture by Josef Rufer, at a public session of the West Berlin Academy of the Arts, in 1957. An expanded version of it is included on pages 138 and 139 of Rufer's catalogue. Probably these notes—or at least the final section, which follows here—were connected with the article, intended for a French periodical, on 'My models' (cf Rufer's catalogue). Here is the final section of Schoenberg's draft, 'National Music':

My teachers were primarily Bach and Mozart, and secondarily Beethoven, Brahms, and Wagner.

From Bach I learned
1. To think contrapuntally, i.e. the art of inventing musical figures that can be used to accompany themselves.
2. The art of producing everything from one thing, and of relating figures by transformation.
3. Disregard for the 'strong' beat of the bar.

From Mozart
1. Inequality of phrase lengths.
2. Coordination of heterogeneous characters to form a thematic unity.
3. Deviation from even-number construction in the theme and its component parts.
4. The art of forming subsidiary ideas.
5. The art of introduction and transition.

From Beethoven
1. The art of developing themes and movements.
2. The art of variation and of varying.
3. The multifariousness of the ways in which long movements can be built.
4. The art of being shamelessly long, or heartlessly brief, as the situation demands.
5. Rhythmically: the displacement of figures onto other beats of the bar.

From Wagner
1. The way it is possible to manipulate themes for expressive purposes, and the art of formulating them in the way that will serve this end.
2. Relatedness of tones and chords.
3. The possibility of regarding themes and motives as if they were complex ornaments, so that they can be used against harmonies, in a dissonant way.

From Brahms

1. Much of what I had unconsciously absorbed from Mozart, particularly odd barring, and extension and abbreviation of phrases.
2. Plasticity in moulding figures; not to be mean, not to stint myself when clarity demands more space; to carry every figure through to the end.
3. Systematic notation.
4. Economy and yet richness.

I also learned much from Schubert and from Mahler, Strauss and Reger too. I shut myself off from no one, and so I could say of myself: 'My originality comes from this: that I immediately imitated everything I saw was good. Even when I had not first seen it in someone else's work.' And I may say: often enough I saw it first in myself. For if I saw something I did not leave it at that; I acquired it, in order to possess it; I worked on it and extended it, and it led me to something new.

I am convinced that eventually people will recognise how intimately this 'something new' is linked to the loftiest models that have been granted us. I venture to credit myself with having written truly new music, which, being based on tradition, is destined to become tradition.

From 1930 onward it became apparent that Schoenberg's poor physical condition could no longer cope with the rigours of the Berlin winter. He made ample use of the free time his contract allowed him, and for the most part confined his periods of teaching in Berlin to the spring and autumn months. After brief periods spent recovering in Baden-Baden, Lugano and Territet (on Lake Geneva), he stayed, for preference, in Barcelona, where he was looked after by his pupil Roberto Gerhard and Gerhard's Austrian wife. The orchestra there, of which Casals was the founder and permanent conductor, gave him great pleasure; he conducted it successfully in a concert of his own works, and also managed to secure an invitation to Webern to appear as guest conductor.

In Barcelona he also had ample opportunity to play tennis, a sport he much enjoyed and which he also played as much as possible in Berlin. When he had to give up the game, in 1942, he made the regretful note, 'I feel that even now I should not have given it up. I ascribe the improvement in my asthmatic condition to the need to breathe very deeply when running after a ball or returning it strongly.'

He stayed in Barcelona from October 1931 to May 1932. A happy event coloured the final stages of this long stay; on 7 May 1932 his daughter Nuria was born—the first child of his second marriage.

Not until June did he begin teaching again, at his flat in Berlin (No. 3, Nürnberger Platz).

In his book, *Arnold Schoenberg*, H. H. Stuckenschmidt has written evocatively about the atmosphere of this flat:

This apartment, in a central quarter of the new West Berlin, was Schoenberg's last permanent residence in Europe, and it completely corresponded to the taste of its owner. His desk had been designed by Schoenberg himself, and he also himself made a small stepladder, worked in a spiral around a vertical axis. Among the furnishings of the music room were a piano and a harmonium, also a guitar and a mandoline, instruments which were frequently used for trying out sound effects. One large room was almost exclusively furnished with a ping-pong table; here Schoenberg played table tennis with his wife and friends—a game in which he excelled. He demonstrated a lively interest in new inventions, new materials and similar matters. For his dining table he preferred chromium to silver because of its characteristic colour.

Chess too was often played in Schoenberg's home. But it was typical of him that he found the conventional game with its sixty-four squares and thirty-two pieces insufficient. He invented an enlarged game which he called 'Hundred-chess' with ten times ten squares. To the usual chessmen he added a bishop[1] and an admiral; the number of pawns was increased to ten.

[1] The piece known in English as a Bishop is called a Runner (*Läufer*) in German. L.B.

Schoenberg's major creative work during 1930–32 was the composition of the opera *Moses and Aaron*. He drafted the text of the work, which was originally conceived as a three-part oratorio, between 3 and 16 October 1928; he later rewrote it a number of times. The first musical sketches are dated 'Berlin, 7 May 1930. Schoenberg began work at the score on 17 July in Lugano, having made a note the previous day: 'Row drafted'. At the end of Act 2 there is a note 'Barcelona, 10 March 1932'; only a few bars of Act 3 were

Schoenberg's entry in his score of Moses *and* Aaron
on completion of Act II.

sketched. Rufer has provided exact chronological details of the numerous interruptions, varying in length, to which Schoenberg's work on *Moses and Aaron* was subjected. Schoenberg himself provided a very informative report about his way of working, in a letter from Territet to Berg, who had informed Schoenberg of the completion of Act 1 of his own opera *Lulu*. Here is part of Schoenberg's letter (8 August 1931, *S.L.* 128):

So you have one act of an opera finished too, have you? So have I. Almost 1000 bars it runs to. But I've already got 250 of the second act too. . . . Oddly enough I'm working in just the same way: the libretto being definitely finished only during the composing, some of it even afterwards. This proves an extremely good method. Of course—and I dare say you have done the same—this is possible only if one starts with a very exact notion of the whole thing, and what takes some doing is not only keeping this vision vivid all the time but intensifying it, enriching it, enlarging it, in the working out of details! . . . I want to try very hard to get the opera finished before going back to Berlin. It isn't going as fast as I hoped at the beginning when I reckoned with a *daily* average of twenty bars. . . . Main reason: the libretto and the choruses. . . . Then I'm slowed up still more by writing out a complete score from the start, which of course takes a lot of time. But still, the advantage is that I'll have finished the whole job when I've composed the last note. There's only one thing I'm afraid of: that by then I'll have forgotten everything I've written. For even now I can scarcely recognise the parts of it I composed last year. And if it weren't for a kind of unconscious memory that always automatically brings me back to the right track of ideas, both musically and with the words, I wouldn't know how the whole thing should come to hang together organically at all. . . .'

In a letter (15 March 1933; *S.L.* 151) to the Viennese poet Walter Eidlitz, who had sent him his play about Moses, *Der Berg in der Wüste* ('The mountain in the desert', 1923), Schoenberg spoke of the vision that had guided him when he conceived his text: 'The elements in this tremendous subject that I myself have placed in the foreground are: the idea of the inconceivable God, of the Chosen People, and of the leader of the people.'

The authentic source of the story treated in Schoenberg's text is to be found in Exodus 2, 3, and 32; however, Schoenberg interpreted and developed the story in an entirely personal way. The first act has four scenes, leading from the calling of Moses to the decision by the people of Israel to go forth out of Egypt. From the Burning Bush, God speaks to Moses (who shrinks back before the boldness of his task), telling him that Aaron will go with him as a doughty helper. In the dialogue between the two brothers, their contrasted spiritual personalities emerge clearly, and the contrast is of decisive importance for the entire drama: Moses, the thinker, the inarticulate mystic, close to God, whose truly 'illuminated' faith grasps the essence of the invisible God in all His profundity; Aaron, the eloquent man of the real world, who is able to perceive God's existence and make it perceptible to others only through signs and wonders. And indeed the Israelites, who at first reject any idea of being directed by an invisible God, are persuaded to revolt and depart toward the Promised Land only thanks to three miracles performed by Aaron: he changes Moses' staff into a snake, strikes his hand with leprosy and then cures it, and finally turns water into blood. At the opening of Act 2, the people and their spiritual representatives, the seventeen Elders, are waiting impatiently for Moses, who has not yet returned from the Mount of Revelation; there follows the bloodthirsty 'orgy of drunkenness and dancing' before the Golden Calf which Aaron has created in order to appease the people; the anger of Moses, who destroys the idol; and finally the great confrontation of Moses and Aaron, in which Moses shatters the tables of the law entrusted to him on the mountain. Led by a column of smoke, the people side with Aaron and set off toward the Promised Land. Moses sinks to the ground in despair:

> So I am defeated!
> So it was all madness, all that I have thought,
> and it can and may not be said!
> O word, thou word, which I lack!

The third act, which Schoenberg never set to music, consists of a single scene, in which Moses pronounces judgment on Aaron. The latter's guilt lies in the fact that by the force of his words and miracles he has alienated the people—and himself—from the true Divine Idea, their role as the people chosen to serve that Divine Idea in freedom. However, Moses sets Aaron free, but once the latter is freed of his shackles, he collapses and dies. The poem ends with the powerfully prophetic words addressed by Moses to the people of Israel:

> Always, when you mingle among the peoples
> and use your gifts, which you are chosen to possess
> in order to fight for the Divine Idea,
> and you use your gifts for false and petty ends,
> competing with foreign peoples, to share in their low
>   pleasures,
> when you leave the desirelessness of the desert
> and your gifts have led you to the topmost heights,
> you will always be cast down again from your misguided
>   success,
> back into the desert. . . .
>
> But in the desert you are invincible
> and will attain the goal:
> united with God.

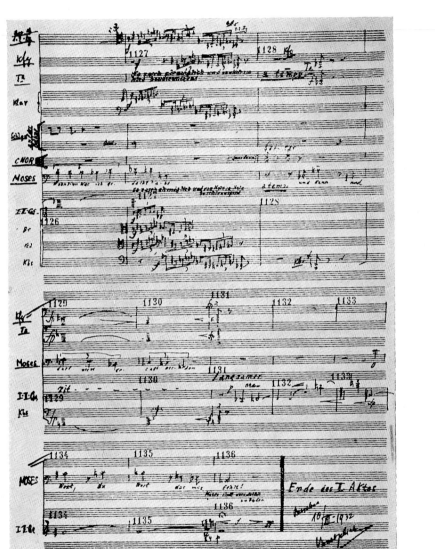

The final page of the score of
Moses and Aaron

Schoenberg during a rehearsal,
with Rudolf Kolisch and
members of the Kolisch
Quartet

These final words of the poem apply even to later developments in the history of the Jewish people; Schoenberg sensed these and wished his opera to make them comprehensible as a musical prophecy.

In finding music to convey this message, Schoenberg called on all the experience and achievements of a long life of sacrifice—on everything he had laboured for during a career as man and artist, whose outward course had been dramatic, while its inner aim had been the highest spiritual unity. The work's structural unity is ensured by a twelve-tone row (a–b flat–e–d–e flat–d flat–g–f–f sharp–g sharp–b–c); every one of the opera's 2000-and-more bars can be related to this row. However, within this strictly organised system, the wealth of sounds and forms is unprecedented; at the beginning the strangely 'glassy' vocal colour of the opening scene before the Burning Bush (Moses, six solo singing voices and six speaking voices), and the sharp differentiation between the voices of Moses ('speaking voice', as in *Pierrot Lunaire*), and Aaron (highly expressive tenor cantilenas); later, the marvellous polyphony of the people's choruses, the whispering voices of the crowd waiting for Moses' return, the ecstatic cries of those who sacrifice themselves to the Golden Calf, the bold depiction of Aaron's miracles, and the rhythms of the dance orgy, which in their apparent primitivity seem a suitable re-creation of the 'primal biblical landscape'. The foundations of the whole work are thematicism—its transformations use every subtlety of the art of variation, and it achieves extreme flexibility of musical gesture—and an instrumental colour sense whose wealth of nuance is inexhaustible. Karl H. Wörner's book *Schönberg's Moses and Aaron* (London, Faber, 1963) contains detailed formal and thematic analyses of the work's most important points, as well as an English translation of the entire text.

Even these few hints should be enough to give an idea of the musical and scenic problems the work presents in production. Schoenberg was well aware of these problems, as is shown by the seven closely written pages of performing indications excerpted in Rufer's catalogue; they end with the important exhortation, 'Characterisation must never be achieved at the expense of good tone production!'

Since in later years a number of Schoenberg's instrumental works have been arbitrarily made into ballets, his remarks to Webern about the Dance round the Golden Calf are specially important (12 September 1931, *S.L.* 129):

It was a very great deal of work getting the scene 'Dance round the Golden Calf' worked out properly. I wanted to leave as little as possible to those new despots of the theatrical art, the producers, and even to envisage the choreography as far as I'm able to. For all this sort of thing is in a very bad way nowadays, and the highhandedness of these mere minions, and their total lack of conscience, is exceeded only by their barbarity and feebleness. But now I've solved the problems of the greater part of it and hope to have it all finished soon. You know I'm not at all keen on the dance. In general its expressiveness is on a level no higher than that of the crudest programme music; and the petrified mechanical quality of its 'beauty' is something I can't stand. Anyway, so far I've succeeded in thinking out movements such as at least enter into a different territory of expression from the caperings of common-or-garden ballet. Let's hope I shall be able to see it through. . . .

Remarkably enough, a concert performance of the 'Dance round the Golden Calf' was to be the first occasion on which any of the opera was heard in public. Hermann Scherchen conducted it in Darmstadt, on 2 July 1951, at the Summer School For New Music. The telegram telling of the piece's great success, and saying that it had immediately had to be played again, during the same concert, was one of the last things to give Schoenberg pleasure shortly before he died.

Shortly before that, a performance had been planned at the Florence 'Maggio Musicale', but this never took place. All the same, the eventual first performance of the whole work owed a lot to Scherchen. When at the end of 1952 the North German Radio, Hamburg, began to make plans, and received a microfilm of the music from Mrs Schoenberg, Scherchen received one of the two enlarged copies; from this, a short score only, he produced a conductor's score, altruistically and purely out of his love for Schoenberg's works. He had already printed the score of the Dance round the Golden Calf in 1951, at his own expense. The second copy went to

Winfried Zillig, who used it to make the vocal score required for rehearsal purposes. At the end of 1953 rehearsals could begin, involving some twenty solo singers, the choirs of the Hamburg and Cologne Radios, the choir of the Hamburg state conservatoire of music, and the joint symphony orchestra of the North-West German Radio, augmented to some 160 members. Since Scherchen was on tour abroad, the principal conductor of the Hamburg Radio, Hans Schmidt-Isserstedt, was entrusted with the task of conducting the performance; Zillig made himself available as assistant. After months of preparatory work, Schmidt-Isserstedt was taken ill only a few days before the concert. Hans Rosbaud took over, and conducted the performance in the Hamburg Musikhalle, on 12 March 1954; thanks to his long-standing familiarity with Schoenberg's whole output, and his (in the best sense) virtuoso conducting technique, the work was a complete success. It was an historic event in the history of music!

Hans Rosbaud was also responsible for the work's first stage production, which took place in the Zürich City Theatre on 6 June 1957, as part of the I.S.C.M. Festival. The producer was Karl Heinz Krahl, the theatre's director at that time; the sets were by Paul Haferung. The rehearsals stretched over the entire season and involved about 350 choral rehearsals and fifty orchestral rehearsals. This prompted Rosbaud to recall a conversation with Schoenberg in 1931 about the likely difficulties of staging the opera; finally the composer confessed: 'Since I can't reckon on a performance of the work for a few decades, I didn't feel obliged to avoid difficulties in the choral and orchestral parts!'

Despite an excellent musical performance, the work had a very mixed reception at this Zürich première; a few shrill whistles mingled with respectful applause from the majority of the public, but even well-disposed observers found the effect not wholly satisfying, because of considerable deficiencies in the production. At later productions (Berlin, conducted by Hermann Scherchen, produced by Gustav Rudolf Sellner, sets by Raffaelli; London, conducted by Georg Solti, produced by Peter Hall, sets by John Bury), one's intuition that *Moses and Aaron* is one of the most important operas of our time turned into complete certainty.

Early in 1954, before the Hamburg performance, Winfried Zillig published an essay 'Arnold Schoenberg, seeker after God' (in the *Frankfurter Hefte*), recalling the lines from Rilke's *Book of Hours* (*Stundenbuch*, Book 2, No. 16), which Schoenberg had set at the end of 1914 as the first of his Op. 22 songs:

Alle welche dich suchen,
  versuchen dich.
Und die, so dich finden,
  binden dich
an Bild und Gebärde.
  Ich aber will dich begreifen

All who attempt to find you,
  tempt you,
And those who find you,
  bind you
To image and gesture.
  I, though, want to be knowing
  [you in the way Earth knows][1]

Zillig said of the third, uncomposed act of *Moses and Aaron*:

Perhaps it was humility that forbade him to complete this work. Perhaps, in his search, he sensed the temptation to bind to image and gesture whatever he had found. For one thing we do know of him, with absolute certainty: he 'wanted to be knowing' . . . And this desire 'to be knowing' found the most gripping possible expression in the first two acts of the opera.

After completing the second act of *Moses and Aaron* Schoenberg spent one more year in Europe, a year filled mostly with literary work rather than composition, in addition, of course, to his teaching. Like everyone else, he was well aware of the increasingly grim, threatening turn events were taking in Germany, though he naturally had no more idea than most people of what was to burst upon the country within a few months. On 27 July 1932 he wrote to his son-in-law Rudolf Kolisch (*S.L.* 143): 'The elections are over and done with, anyway; I'm curious to see what's going to come of it all. I simply can't imagine.'

Early in 1933 Schoenberg completed his arrangement of a work by the Viennese composer Georg Matthias Monn (1717–50); as early as 1912 he had come to know the works of Monn, and of his brother Johann Christoph Monn (1726–82) (cf page 85). The concerto, dedicated to Casals, was published in New York in 1936, under the title 'Concerto for violoncello after the concerto for clavicembalo composed in 1746 by Georg Matthias Monn (1717–50)'. Schoenberg described his 'free adaptation' in a letter to Casals (20 February 1933, *S.L.* 150):

I think it has turned out a very brilliant piece. Anyway I went to *very* special trouble with the *sound* of it and am very pleased with the result. In certain respects the piece is less soloistic than a concerto of Monn's would be; for very often the cello's function is rather like a chamber-music soloist's, whose brilliant playing produces very beautiful and interesting sound. For the rest, I was mainly intent on removing the defects of the Handelian style (prevailing in the original work). Just as Mozart did with Handel's *Messiah*, I have got rid of whole handfuls of sequences (rosalias, *Schusterflecke*), replacing them with real *substance*. Then I also did my best to deal with the other main defect of Handelian style, which is that the theme is always best when it first appears and grows steadily more insignificant and trivial in the course of the piece. I think I've succeeded in making the whole thing approximate, say, to Haydn's style. In harmony I have sometimes gone a little (and sometimes rather more) beyond the limits of that style. But nowhere does it go much further than Brahms, anyway there are no dissonances other than those understood by the older theory of harmony; and: it is nowhere atonal.

Schoenberg originally intended to conduct the first performance of the concerto in London in 1934, with Casals. But this plan never matured, and the first performance did not take place till 7 December 1935, in London, the soloist being Emanuel Feuermann.

The last composition Schoenberg completed in Berlin (in January and February) was a set of three songs for low voice and piano, to texts by Jakob Haringer (born in Dresden in 1883, died in Zürich in 1948); *Sommermüd, Tot*, and *Mädchenlied* (Summer Weariness; Dead; Song of a Girl). These remained unknown until 1952, when an American publisher printed them as Schoenberg's Op. 48. This high opus number is explained by the fact that in the troubled times after his emigration Schoenberg forgot about this work, and only remembered it much later. Although they are twelve-tone compositions these last songs of Schoenberg's often recall the vocal music of his earlier days, and with their tender, expressive melodic lines and their absolutely transparent accompaniment they are numbered among his most attractive works. They deserve special attention from singers.

On 12 February 1933 Schoenberg delivered a radio lecture to open the Frankfurt-on-Main 'Brahms Year'; this he later considerably revised, publishing it under the title 'Brahms the Progressive' in his book *Style and Idea*. It is one of his most important and original works of musical theory.

From Frankfurt Schoenberg went on to Vienna, where on 15 February he addressed the *Kulturbund* on the subject of 'New and outmoded music, or Style and Idea'—a lecture also included in *Style and Idea*. The May number of the Viennese musical periodical *23*, which had appeared under my editorship since 1932, contained a report of the lecture by Rudolf Ploderer, which made use, as far as possible, of Schoenberg's own words. It ran:

The shape of the lecture was clearly determined by the double contrasts expressed in its title—on the one hand, new and outmoded music, on the other style and ideas. The music acknowledged as new, permanently new, is music which expresses an idea. Music that does not fulfil this requirement is outmoded even as it comes into the world, and has no claim to respect. Pseudohistorians, who confuse symptoms with causes, have come up with the idea of 'new music', one that has ominous overtones. They overlook the fact that, in the course of time, any way of writing deadens the senses, a fact enough in itself to lead to phenomena such as the wavelike alternation of homophonic and contrapuntal periods. Alongside this one finds the inner compulsion of creative wealth, the compulsion to accommodate the maximum of content in the minimum of space. The conquest of an ever-expanding realm of sound is the field within which music has developed. The outmoded is whatever no longer fits the conditions of life as it is lived. We rightly find pathos, long hair and candles no longer suited to the style of our time. But there is no form of life which could make romantic music, in the broadest sense, superfluous. People have tried to write 'music for use'—but, for lack of use, it has necessarily become 'ideal' again. Style is the sum of the qualities possessed by the producer and the thing produced. Style without subject-matter is nothing, therefore style can be established in advance. All artistic creation is spiritual vision, and therefore the formation of ideas, and Schoenberg confesses that he has always conceived his compositions in terms of ideas. He is not one of the masters who has fallen straight from heaven—straight onto his head. The idea can wait—it is timeless.[1] New Music is a new musical idea in a new dress. Eternal, never-ageing art will therefore always be able to rest in itself: 'L'art pour l'art!'.

After the lecture there was a convivial gathering at the Hotel Meissl and Schadn, on the Neuer Markt. Schoenberg was in the best of moods, and none of his Viennese friends and pupils can have had any idea that this was the last time they would see him in this life.

As a farewell to his Austrian homeland, he gave an interview, which was reprinted in the Viennese weekly *Radiowelt*; the subject was 'Modern music on the radio', and it is reprinted as an appendix to this book (pp. 243-4).

On 1 March 1933, shortly after his return to Berlin, Schoenberg took part at a meeting of the Academy's Senate, in which the composer Max von Schillings (1868–1933), then president of the Academy, made known the government's wish that the Jewish influence in the Academy should be eliminated. Schoenberg's immediate reaction was to say that he never stayed where he was not wanted, and he walked out of the meeting.

In a letter to the Academy on 20 March Schoenberg drew the appropriate conclusions from this incident:

Pride, and awareness of what I have achieved, would long ago have prompted me to withdraw of my own accord. For when I accepted the Academy's flattering proposals, I did so because I was flattered in my ambitions as a teacher, and was reminded of my duty—to propagate what I know; and because I knew what I can do for my pupils.—But I have done that, and more; anyone who has been my pupil has been made to sense the seriousness and morality of a view of art which will do him credit in all the circumstances of life, if he can maintain it!

Pointing out that his move to Berlin had meant the sacrifice of a 'very respectable private position' in Vienna, he demanded

[1] An instance of Schoenberg's 'delight in paradoxes'. In everyday German, if a person or thing 'hat Zeit', it 'has time', i.e. it can wait. But in this case the idea 'has *no* time' is outside time, timeless, so it can wait. L.B.

his salary until 30 September 1935, as stipulated by his contract, as well as compensation for the expense of moving back to Vienna. He added:

One who, like myself, stands in an unassailable position in matters political and moral, and who, by losing his field of activity, has been most deeply injured in his artistic and manly honour, should not, on top of all that, have his economic position endangered—indeed, threatened with disaster.

Despite the conditions laid down in his contract of 28 August 1925 Schoenberg's salary was paid him only until the end of October 1933. On 17 May of that year he left Berlin, going initially to Paris.

9 Initial Experiences as an Exile

The first thing Schoenberg did in Paris was try very hard to put his economic affairs on a firmer footing. In a letter (27 May 1933) to Roberto Gerhard in Barcelona, he reported that he was negotiating with Casals and a concert promoter about guest appearances to conduct in Spain, and that he was looking for a publisher for the Cello concerto after Monn, for *Moses and Aaron*, and his play *Der biblische Weg*. None of these efforts proved fruitful. His return to the Jewish religion —having had a Catholic upbringing, he had become a Protestant at the age of eighteen—which took place as quietly as possible on 24 July, in Paris, led to further plans. In Alban Berg's papers I found a copy of a fragmentary letter from Schoenberg to Webern, dated 4 August 1933; in this letter, Schoenberg wrote at length about his plans:

You are right when you say it is hard to remain inactive at a time like this. You and I are somewhat differently placed, though, when it comes to the question of activity. For fourteen years I have been prepared for what has now happened. During this long time I have been able to prepare myself for it thoroughly, and have finally cut myself off for good—even though with difficulty, and a good deal of vacillation—from all that tied me to the Occident. I have long since been resolved to be a Jew, and you will also have sometimes heard me talk about a play (*The Biblical Way*); I could not say more about it at that time, but in it I have shown the ways in which a national Zionism can become active. And now, as from a week ago, I have also returned officially to the Jewish religious community; indeed, we do not differ in the matter of religion (my *Moses and Aaron* will show this), though we do when it comes to my views on the need for the church to adapt itself to the demands of the modern way of life. It is my intention to take an active part in endeavours of this kind. I regard that as more important than my art, and am determined—if I am suited to such activities—to do nothing in future but work for the Jewish national cause. I have begun already, and almost everyone I have approached in Paris has agreed with my idea. My immediate plan is for a long tour of America, which could perhaps turn into a world tour, to persuade people to help the Jews in Germany. I have been promised powerful support. Things are going forward somewhat slowly. For things are as they seem always to have been with me: someone who has been impressed by

what I have said, and has believed me, is rarely able to pass on
his impression to a third party, so prompting him to believe;
for what I have said seems to depend not only on my actual
words, but on the way I say them—something very hard to
reproduce; so the third party remains sceptical until he has me
in his ears at first hand. I shall, then, have to speak at large
gatherings (loud-speakers) and over the radio. That is why I
do not yet know how much time I shall be able to spend working here, nor whether I shall be able to complete *Moses and
Aaron*, or to revise my drama *The Biblical Way*. At the moment
I am trying to complete the String Quartet Concerto after
Handel, for the Kolisch Quartet, since there is some chance that
I may find an English publisher for it (at a low fee, but I am
glad all the same, since I must at all costs find some money),
and it is, moreover, to have its first performance in London in
November. Incidentally, I am to go to Prague for the Zionist
Congress, about August the 20th; perhaps I shall go via Vienna.
To be honest—glad though I should be to see you all, and my
children and grandchildren, I do not greatly look forward to it...

Schoenberg would have looked forward even less to the
journey—which in fact he never made—had he seen the
report in Vienna's *Acht-Uhr-Blatt* on 31 July 1933, about his
return to Judaism. It ran:

We think religion is not a private matter. *Paris Soir* says that
in the last few days the composer Arnold Schoenberg and his
wife have returned to the Jewish faith, as a way of protesting
about the persecution of the Jews in Germany. This shows the
true face of these liberal Jews' religious depths and metaphysical roots. For them, faith is a tool like any other, a means to
an end. No more than that. What Mr Free-thinker Schoenberg
has done looks brave (though one should not overlook the fact
that his step can also be taken as a 'retreat forwards'). In reality
it is a manœuvre. The sum total of all his past views meant so
little to him that he could throw them out double-quick, and
by the same token his new faith will mean no more to him than
a cloak thrown about his shoulders, to be blown away again
by the next shift in the wind of opinion. These liberal gentlemen
are always carrying on like that; you can tell them by the fact
that they never stay in one place for long. Once upon a time,
when the world was still rational and 'bourgeois', this was
tolerated or overlooked or not even noticed; nowadays, when the

world is being reborn out of a spirit of firm affirmation, the spirit of truth to one's own nature, each tactical attitude unmasks a mimicry that has played itself out. Indeed, if Arnold Schoenberg had quietly and reflectively returned, in a spirit of confession, to the synagogue, we should have felt respect for him, for then the events in Germany would merely have been what prompted his return; but as it is, religion has once again been debased, and made to serve political ends.

As a comic postscript to this paper's pathetic exclamations, it should be said that Schoenberg's return to the Jewish faith had indeed taken place as quietly as possible, with only four people present: Schoenberg and his wife, the Rabbi, and a certain Dr Marianoff, whom Schoenberg later suspected of having identified himself with 'tout Paris'.

The Schoenbergs spent August and September of 1933 at Arcachon, a spa in the Gironde, not far from Bordeaux. It was there that, on 16 August, he completed his 'free transcription', for string quartet and orchestra, of Handel's Concerto grosso Op. 6 No. 7, which he had begun in May, shortly before leaving Berlin. The first performance was in Prague on 26 September 1934, by the Kolisch Quartet and the Prague Radio Orchestra, conducted by Karel B. Jirak. Schoenberg made no progress with his other plans for Arcachon—the completion of *Moses and Aaron* and the revision of *The Biblical Way*. Negotiations about a teaching position in the U.S.A. caused him to return to Paris at the end of September.

It was from there that he wrote to his cousin Hans Nachod that his publicity campaign among world Jewry would be carried out from America, and that he intended to found a United Jewish Party, also to run a newspaper in furtherance of his aims. However, he wished to keep his other plans secret from everyone. At the beginning of October, his engagement at the Malkin Conservatoire in Boston and New York was finally agreed. On 25 October he left France, arriving in New York on 31 October.

The details of Schoenberg's first 'American year' are covered by his own report dating from November 1934, a strongly stylised document covering three closely-typed foolscap pages, which he sent to some of his friends and to those who had been associated with the commemorative volume on his sixtieth birthday (cf pp. 194–5)—the report was sent as an addendum to his official letter of thanks (cf pp. 195–6). This marked a return to an earlier habit of his: in order not to repeat himself in a large number of letters, he would send his friends duplicated 'journals' with an account of his life and work. Having been one of those involved with the sixtieth-birthday tribute, I too had the honour of receiving this first report from America. Much of it is confidential, but excerpts will be given here.

Not long after his arrival in New York, an official reception was given for him:

The League of Composers arranged a concert (only chamber music, though), and a very big reception—2000 people were said to be there; I had to shake hands with certainly 500 of them, and the Committee of Honour was said to include everyone in New York interested (in any way) in art. Soon after, there was another reception, also a very noisy affair, but I can not recall who gave it.

Schoenberg was very disappointed in the Malkin Conservatoire when he discovered that it was only a small teaching institution, unable to raise even its own student orchestra, and that he had to teach in both Boston and New York, which meant many very tiring journeys. There were, moreover, only a few pupils—twelve to fourteen in the two cities—and most of these were beginners, since his enrolment on the staff had been announced too late, and the fees demanded were too high, bearing in mind the conditions at that time. On the other hand, he said:

The actual teaching I enjoyed. Even the more mature pupils had covered the ground work very inadequately, but all the same I had two really talented ones and a few with some talent. Apart from this, so much new material had been accumulating in me during the previous months that I was able to tell my pupils really a great deal that was quite unknown to them, and surprised them very much.

On 12 and 13 January 1934 Schoenberg was to have conducted two concerts by the Boston Symphony Orchestra, including his *Pelléas and Mélisande*. But immediately after the final rehearsal he was suddenly taken ill, and had to withdraw; he did not manage to give the concert until 16 March. Of his illness and its consequences he said:

At half past two on the afternoon of Friday, 12 January, I had an attack of coughing in the lift of our house; I tore something, and this gave me such violent pains in the back and chest that I could not move, even though I was bandaged. I had already been ill since the early days of December (as soon as the bad weather set in), but was able to keep going, more or less, and carry out my duties to some extent, thanks to medicaments which obviously did me harm. The climate there is very bad, you see, and was particularly so that winter. Within twelve or twenty four hours the temperature will go down by 60 or more degrees Fahrenheit, i.e. 34 Centigrade. In March this sort of sudden change of temperature started again, and I had a horrible attack of asthma, made worse on this occasion by irritation of the heart. . . . I then had to take great care of myself in April, May, and June, but during the summer, spent in Chautauqua, I recovered very quickly, though not enough to be able to risk another winter anywhere near New York.

Schoenberg's contract with the Malkin Conservatoire expired in May 1934. He declined all further offers of posts in the eastern states because of his state of health, and later, on 3 October 1934, when he was already in Hollywood, he refused an invitation from the Juilliard School of Music, America's largest and most respected musical academy.

10 'And, for all that, I Pray'

On Schoenberg's sixtieth birthday—13 September 1934—
he was in the midst of preparations to move to the west coast,
having become convinced that there he would find a climate
better suited to his state of health. His 'report' says the following about the birthday itself: 'I was able to enjoy it all
extraordinarily, and was fully content, even though we
passed the day without any kind of ceremony and with not
a single guest. The first to greet me were Trude and Nuria,
then came the many telegrams, the letters, and the fabulous
Festschrift; this all gave me far more pleasure than the public
could ever provide.'

The 'Festschrift' (Universal Edition's 'commemorative
volume', already mentioned several times) contained various
contributions by Schoenberg himself—his poem *Verbundenheit* (cf pp. 172–3), a fragment from his 1912 memorial
tribute to Mahler, and facsimiles of the opening of his very
first song, composed in 1893, also of a page from the score of
Moses and Aaron. The contributors covered a wide range;
naturally, all Schoenberg's oldest friends and pupils were
represented—Berg with an acrostic on the letters of 'GLAUBE,
HOFFNUNG UND LIEBE' (Faith, Hope, and Charity); Webern
with a brief introduction to some of Schoenberg's aphorisms;
Zemlinsky with the reminiscences of Schoenberg's youth
already quoted on pp. 4–10; David Josef Bach (cf pp. 3–4),
Oskar Adler (cf pp. 250–2), Egon Wellesz, Eduard Steuermann, Heinrich Jalowetz, and Paul Stefan. More recent
pupils who contributed were Erwin Stein, Paul Amadeus
Pisk, Olga Novakovic (cf page 195), and Josef Polnauer (cf
pp. 172–3), while the younger generation were also represented by three of Berg's pupils—Theodor Wiesengrund-
Adorno, Hans Erich Apostel, and myself. Alma Maria
Mahler recalled the time a quarter of a century earlier when
she first heard of Schoenberg from her teacher Zemlinsky;
her husband, the writer Franz Werfel, also added a tribute,
as did the Viennese poetess Hildegard Jone. There were
brief tributes from Darius Milhaud and Willem Mengelberg,
and an article in which Alois Haba related Schoenberg's
achievements to the exploration of new musical material by
himself and other Czech composers. A Polish composer,
Josef Koffler, wrote of three decisive 'encounters' with

Schoenberg (whom he had never met)—the first consisting of his discovery of the *Harmonielehre*, which had had a profound effect on his life. A twenty-year-old metal-worker, Karl Schulhofer (a pupil of Pisk's), also wrote in comparable terms about the *Harmonielehre*. The longest single contribution was from the distinguished author Hermann Broch—a highly technical article on 'Irrational cognition in music'. The other two contributors were Erhard Buschbeck (a producer at the Vienna Burgtheater), with a Rilkesque poem entitled *Musik*, and, posthumously, Rudolf Ploderer (cf page 39). The prevailing mood of the Vienna Schoenberg circle at that time is very beautifully reflected in the contribution by a distinguished pianist, Olga Novakovic:

As we celebrate the sixtieth birthday of Arnold Schoenberg, who lives far away from us, distance (temporal and spatial) suddenly means nothing; he is among us, and we are around him. We are caught up, not in recollection, but in the *presence* of his active power. To have been Schoenberg's pupil means to *be* Schoenberg's pupil; it means—despite the wandering and error which, having no fears as to the outcome, he so loved in us—that we have had etched into us the criterion that tells the genuine from the false, and makes the truth one's goal, in art and in life. Art and life? In him, we could hardly tell them apart. In his vicinity, art and life were interwoven, and became *one*. Little everyday things took on symbolic value, became a metaphor for lofty things. But lofty things, whose living source he pointed out to us, drew near. Honoured master, when once you were unwilling to leave for the summer, because of your pupils, you said, 'As one gets older, one doesn't always need to go to the mountains. A scrap of meadow seen in passing conjures up a vision of the whole landscape.' Just such a scrap of meadow is ours—since you are not here—in our communal celebration of your birthday, which we are spending with gratitude, joy, and hope, our eyes turned to past, present and future alike.

In Schoenbert's official letter of thanks (*S.L.* 163) to those who had sent him greetings he said:

On my fiftieth birthday many people felt an urge or necessity to make a declaration of sympathy with me, and even of adherence to me; on my sixtieth many felt they were now free of this wearisome compulsion, while others, under the compulsion of Nordic ideology, attained the same freedom, even though against their will; on my seventieth—that is as far as I presume to envisage the future—the circle of those who do not regret my first birthday will perhaps be still smaller; but it is to be hoped that those who address me then will be only such as do it of their own free will, and of those only such as recognise some achievement in the few little things I have jotted down.

I have for a long time known that I cannot live to see widespread understanding of my works, and my far-famed resoluteness is a matter of dire necessity arising from the wish to see it for all that. I have set my goal far enough ahead to be sure that the reluctant and even the resistant will some day have to arrive there. For, after all, parallels—as mathematics assure us—do meet at such points, if one only has the patience to wait long enough.

It is perhaps expected that now that I am in a new world I should feel its amenities to be ample compensation for the loss I have sustained and which I had foreseen for more than a decade. Indeed, I parted from the old world not without feeling the wrench in my very bones, for I was not prepared for the fact that it would render me not only homeless but speechless, languageless, so that to all but my old friends I could now say it only in English: supposing they wished to hear it at all. On the other hand, here one does live like a fighting cock.[1] For here I am universally esteemed as one of the most important composers: alongside Stravinsky, Tansman, Sessions, Sibelius, Gershwin, Copland, etc., . . . etc., . . . etc., . . . And so I can safely count on my seventieth birthday turning out just as I have prophesied.

I am nevertheless set on living to see it. For if, besides my domestic happiness, there then really remain these friends who give me so much joy and each single one of whom makes me proud of the force, courage, intelligence, originality, and knowledge with which he can express his reasons for saluting me: then I can congratulate myself on the occasion even now.

The fact that I can be proud of having such friends determines the measure of my gratitude. But how deeply from the heart it comes is something I could really express only in music.

His 'report' describes his first home in California (5680, Canyon Cove, Hollywood):

1 'live like a fighting cock': the corresponding German phrase is 'live like the Lord God in France', and Schoenberg continues: 'where He would have even more difficulty in getting a labour-permit than here' (footnote by translators of the *Selected Letters*).

We have a very charming little house, not too large, furnished, with many amenities customary here but hardly known at all in Europe. Once we can have our furniture—it is still in Paris, because the German government has so far refused to pay the balance of my salary for 22 months—we shall probably rent an unfurnished house. This will be still cheaper, and we shall also look for one rather more into the hills, where there is still less damp and more sun. . . . Los Angeles (Hollywood is a sort of Floridsdorf or Mödling[1] of Los Angeles, only with the difference that here they produce those splendid films, whose highly unusual plots and wonderful sound give me so much pleasure, as you know) is a completely blank page, so far as my music is concerned.

Schoenberg goes on to complain bitterly about the way his music was ignored by American conductors—native and immigrant—naming as the one exception Frederick Stock (1872–1942) of Chicago; at other points the report also contains further sharp attacks on particular conductors.

The first work Schoenberg composed in America was a Suite for String Orchestra, which he completed on 26 December 1934. This work, with its five movements—Overture, Adagio, Minuet, Gavotte, and Gigue—was the first since the F-sharp-minor Second String Quartet, completed in 1908, in which he used a key-signature: the Suite is in G major. Schoenberg foresaw that this 'relapse' into tonality would cause his whole output to be misunderstood, and he drafted a foreword to the Suite, omitted when the work was published (New York, 1935), but printed by Rufer in the catalogue. Slightly abridged, it runs:

I was prompted to write this piece when Professor Martin Bernstein, of New York University, provided me with some gratifying impressions and perspectives in the matter of American high-school orchestras—what they aim at, what they manage to do, and how successful they are. I became convinced that the encouragement of such aims is a matter of interest to every composer, particularly to every modern composer, and quite particularly to myself. Here it is that the basis for a new artistic climate—spiritual and intellectual[2]— can be created; here, that a younger generation can be given

[1] Floridsdorf is an industrial suburb of Vienna, immediately north of the Danube, where Schoenberg spent much of his youth; Mödling is a suburb to the south, where he later lived. L.B.

[2] Schoenberg's word is *Geistigkeit*; as often in his writings, both possible meanings of *geistig*—spiritual and intellectual—are probably implied. L.B.

the chance of getting to understand the new fields of expression and the resources fit to serve them. So my task was set. I had to do as follows: within a harmonic idiom conducive to modern feelings—and without, for the moment, putting students in jeopardy through the 'poison of atonality'—I had here to prepare them for the modern technique of playing: fingerings, bowings, phrasing, intonation, dynamics, rhythm—all of that was to be demanded, without insuperable difficulties, being offered. But hints of modern intonation, composition technique, counterpoint and phrase structure were also needed, if the student is gradually to acquire a sense that melody, to count as such, need not mean the kind of primitive symmetry, lack of variation and lack of development such as are the delight of the mediocre in every land and among all peoples; rather that here, too, there already exist higher forms, belonging not merely technically but *spiritually and intellectually* in a higher artistic category. . . . Here, the genuine and true teachers, prophets, and propagators of a culture—that is to say, genuine and real leaders—must be given the opportunity, which they surely desire, of bringing their pupils up to have the deepest respect for artistic capacity,[1] and of making certain things clear to them: that the maintenance of a culture depends on growth—because, like all that lives, it can live only so long as it is still growing. But as soon as it stops developing it dies, withers. So that the only reason why anything technical or spiritual can, artistically speaking, be worthy of conservation is that it forms a first stage in a new step forward, in new life; and that it is worth conserving only then, and *only for that reason*. Perhaps, after all the above, it is superfluous to mention that this piece does not signify *any repudiation* of what I have created up to now.

1 *Vermögen*, which here also implies 'things already achieved' (*ein Vermögen* = a fortune).
L.B.

It was by no means superfluous! Time and again, this suite and other late tonal works have been taken by uncomprehending or hostile people as arguments for the idea that Schoenberg had seen the senselessness of his 'atonal' and twelve-tone compositions, and had returned, repentant, to tonality. To refute this assertion one need only quote the closing words of Schoenberg's essay 'On revient toujours' (1949), included in *Style and Idea*:

But a longing to return to the older style was always vigorous in me: and from time to time I had to yield to that urge.

This is how and why I sometimes write tonal music. To me stylistic differences of this nature are not of special importance. I do not know which of my compositions are better: I like them all, because I liked them when I wrote them.

We know of various more or less amusing experiences during Schoenberg's early American years in Hollywood, from two sources; Walter H. Rubsamen's article 'Schoenberg in America' (*Musical Quarterly*, October 1951), and Hans W. Heinsheimer's book *Menagerie in F sharp* (1947). Rubsamen relates:

On the occasion of his election to the American Society of Composers, Authors and Publishers (ASCAP), he was invited to a dinner given by the Los Angeles Section of the Society, and found himself sitting between two Tin Pan Alley song writers recently transferred to the film capital. During dinner Schoenberg's conversation with his neighbours was rather limited, but after he had been formally introduced to the entire membership, one of the song-writers turned to him and said confidentially: 'You know, Arnold, I don't understand your stuff, but you must be O.K., or you wouldn't be here.' Schoenberg loved to tell this story, for he remained constantly amazed at the easy familiarity of the Broadway–Hollywood confraternity, and was sufficiently aware of his own importance in the field of serious music to be ironically amused at the manner of his admission to the sacrosanct company of the commercially successful. As it turned out, the royalties from ASCAP, subsequently increased in most generous fashion, were a boon to the composer during the last years of his life.

Why did he not dip into the pot of gold and compose film scores? . . . Schoenberg came close to writing music for a Hollywood film only once, when the M.G.M. producer Irving Thalberg sought to engage him as composer for *The Good Earth*, the screen version of Pearl S. Buck's novel about China. Having heard *Verklärte Nacht* on records and having been told that the *Encyclopaedia Britannica* contained an article about Schoenberg, Thalberg was so impressed that he sent a representative to inquire whether the composer would be interested in writing such a score. According to Oscar Levant's account of the incident (confirmed by Mrs Schoenberg), the composer seemed indifferent to the proposal, whereupon Thalberg's emissary warmed up to his subject in most persuasive fashion. Describing the climactic scene, he said, 'Think of it! A terrific storm is going on; the wheat field is swaying in the wind, and suddenly the earth begins to tremble. In the midst of the earthquake, Oo-Lan gives birth to a baby! What an opportunity for music!' Schoenberg paused for a moment, then said mildly, 'With so much going on, why do you need music?'

However, he was persuaded to pay a visit, accompanied by his wife, to Thalberg at the latter's office. Heinsheimer takes up the story:

After he and his wife arrived at M.G.M. there was some confusion because Thalberg kept Schoenberg waiting for twenty minutes, but it shows the awe-inspiring grandeur of Hollywood, and of M.G.M. in particular, that Schoenberg, who had *never* waited for anybody in all his sixty-one years, *threatened to leave but actually did not*. However, these twenty minutes might have played an essential part in setting the stage for the following historical scene.

Finally the great Thalberg arrived and apologised to the great Schoenberg. Then he asked him what his terms would be for writing music to *The Good Earth*.

'My terms are very simple,' said Schoenberg. 'I want fifty thousand dollars and an absolute guarantee that not a single note of my score will be altered.'

Here endeth the story and any relationship between Arnold Schoenberg and the moving-picture industry.

The fifty-thousand-dollar fee is not the point of the tale. Thalberg probably raised an eyebrow, but only one, and this one only slightly. Money is no consideration if anybody really wants anything in Hollywood. But that a greenhorn (and Schoenberg, with his sixty-one years and all the professional trimmings, was just that as soon as he crossed the heavily guarded border into Culver City) wanted to go home, write a score, and then have it put in a picture, this really rocked Hollywood to its very foundations.

In the summer of 1935 Schoenberg obtained a post as Professor of Composition at the University of Southern California. He was very disappointed by the small size of his classes, most of whose members were amateur music-lovers and not professional musicians. But, as ever, he adapted his teaching so that it exactly suited his listeners, speaking above all of 'understanding' music, and trying above all to develop in his listeners 'a sound capacity to distinguish between value and non-value' in musical works (*S.L.* 168). The American composer Oscar Levant (b. 1906) took private lessons from him about then, and in his book of chatty reminiscences, *A Smattering of Ignorance* (New York, 1940), he tells how, during Schoenberg's early days in Hollywood, countless film composers, allured by his great reputation as a composer and music teacher, came to him, hoping to learn, within the space of a few weeks, a handful of useful technical tricks; they were sorely disappointed when he insisted on teaching them harmony, counterpoint and chorale harmonisation. There was an amusing incident with a young man who had been commissioned to compose film music for an aeroplane scene, and wanted Schoenberg to give him advice on how to do it. Schoenberg thought for a moment, then said 'Airplane music?—Just like music for big bees, only louder!' Ever afterwards, he used to call the background music typical of films 'big-bee music'.

In the autumn of 1936 Schoenberg was able to improve his position a good deal; he was appointed as Professor of Music at the much larger and more famous University of California in Los Angeles (U.C.L.A.), where he taught until 1944. Although U.C.L.A.'s upper age limit for its teachers was sixty-five, an exception was made in Schoenberg's case, and he was allowed to remain until seventy. Rubsamen tells us about his teaching at the University:

During the years at U.C.L.A. (until his retirement in 1944, when he was named Professor Emeritus), Schoenberg taught a variety of lecture classes and seminars, ranging all the way from elementary counterpoint to graduate classes in composition and advanced theory. Popular with the students, even though his German accent in the early years made the lectures a bit difficult to understand, he taught entirely without notes, pacing up and down nervously with his hands clasped behind his back. The smaller classes and seminars gave ample opportunity for an interchange of ideas, but in lecture classes the students participated only by turning in written assignments. Schoenberg's models were Bach, Beethoven, Mozart, Haydn, Schubert, Schumann, and Brahms; rarely did he refer to other composers. In all the basic classes he taught students to use traditional, tonal means—only advanced composers in graduate seminars were allowed to write atonally, and then only if they so desired. From 1936 until his death the composer had a series of three hard-working assistants—which meant disciple, amanuensis, and general factotum: at first it was Gerald Strang who fulfilled these duties; then, from 1939 until 1946, Leonard Stein, and finally, during the last years of the composer's life, Richard Hoffmann.

Because many of his students were taking music only as a second study—a fact which would perhaps have prompted many another leading composer to refuse to teach these 'laymen'—Schoenberg made a very remarkable and successful experiment; he taught even the laymen composition—not in order to make them into composers, but because he thought this was the way to build up their sense of form and their understanding of logical musical development. One sees how important he found this idea from the fact that he wrote a short textbook on the subject (*Models for Beginners in Composition*) as well as an essay 'Eartraining through composing', which later appeared in *Style and Idea*.

In 1936, so as to be near the university, Schoenberg moved with his family to a pleasant house of their own, at 116, Rockingham Avenue, in the Brentwood Park district; there he taught his private pupils, and also held courses after his retirement. The family led a busy social life; local residents and many artists exiled from Europe all went to make up the circle.

About this time, Schoenberg formed a cordial friendship with one young composer in particular: George Gershwin (1898–1937). Rubsamen relates:

Schoenberg's friendship with Gershwin until the latter's untimely death in July 1937 was one of opposites, yet each composer had the greatest respect for the other's abilities and talents. Schoenberg esteemed Gershwin as one who naturally expressed the feelings of the masses in music, while the younger man studied the elder's works and listened avidly to whatever Schoenberg recordings he could obtain. They often met socially, Schoenberg's passion for tennis contributing indirectly to the friendship, for once a week he and a party of friends went to play on the private court at the Gershwin house. Oscar Levant tells amusing stories about these tennis sessions, which Schoenberg never missed, even on the day in 1936[1] when his son Ronald was born. Incidentally, Ronald is an anagram of Arnold, which gives a hint of Schoenberg's superstitious nature. His last child, Lawrence Adam, born in 1941, was to have been called Roland, but Mrs William Dieterle, wife of the film director, persuaded the Schoenbergs against it for astrological reasons, whereupon the boy was given two names including all of the letters in Arnold except 'o'. Of the composer's three hobbies—tennis, ping-pong, and bookbinding— the first afforded him the keenest pleasure. I remember often playing with him, Weiss, Stein, and others, for he preferred doubles, so that he would not have to run around as much (he was in his mid-sixties at the time). Towards the end of his tennis-playing activities, we learned to hit the ball directly at or close to him, so that he could participate fully. If aware of this little trick, he gave no sign.

There are two lasting memorials to the Schoenberg-Gershwin friendship: the extraordinarily speaking likeness of Schoenberg painted by Gershwin not long before his death, and the essay Schoenberg wrote for the symposium on Gershwin edited by Merle Armitage and published in 1938. Schoenberg also paid the following radio tribute to Gershwin:

George Gershwin was one of this rare kind of musicians to whom music is not a matter of more or less ability.

Music to him was the air he breathed, the food which nourished him, the drink that refreshed him. Music was what made him feel, and music was the feeling he expressed.

Directness of this kind is given only to great men, and there is no doubt that he was a great composer. What he achieved was not only to the benefit of a national American music but also a contribution to the music of the whole world.

The first two works Schoenberg completed in California— at times working on both at once—were the Concerto for Violin and Orchestra, Op. 36, begun in the summer of 1934 and completed on 23 September of that year, and the Fourth String Quartet, composed between 27 April and 26 July 1936. The violin concerto was dedicated to Webern, and first performed at a concert by the Philadelphia Orchestra on

[1] In fact 26 November 1937. W.R.

6 December 1940 (with a second performance on the 7th): the soloist was Louis Krasner, and the conductor Stokowski. The Fourth String Quartet, like the Third, was commissioned by Mrs Elizabeth Sprague Coolidge, and dedicated to the Kolisch Quartet, who gave the first performance in Los Angeles on 9 January 1937.

The Concerto for Violin and Orchestra has three movements—Poco allegro, Andante grazioso–Adagio, Allegro alla Marcia. So far as its solo part is concerned, it must be the most technically difficult in the entire repertoire so far. Schoenberg, who was particularly fond of this work, once said of it that the soloist really needed a left hand with six fingers; he held, however, that these immense technical difficulties, which are never there merely for the sake of showy virtuosity, were likely to raise the general level of the performer's technique, and also to lead him toward an understanding of the work's musical structure. Except that a few short motives are occasionally repeated, the Concerto is written strictly according to the twelve-tone method; at the very beginning, the basic set (a–b flat–e flat–b–e–f sharp–c–c sharp–g–a flat–d–f) is divided between phrases for the soloist and orchestral interpolations; soon, however, the solo violin takes it up and elaborates on it in a forthright manner, using the basic set and its inversion. The orchestra, using treble wind, four horns and tuba, timpani, percussion and strings, plus xylophone and glockenspiel, offers a highly colourful complement to the absolute thematic dominance of the solo part.

After the Amsterdam String Quartet had performed the Fourth String Quartet in Zürich on 6 November 1949, Willi Schuh discussed the work in the *Neue Zürcher Zeitung*, making an important point about its position within Schönberg's total output:

In an article of this length, it would be as pointless to try even to hint at the richness of its musical content as to examine the details of its structure, and of the problems that arise in connection with its twelve-tone technique (which is used with sovereign mastery). Let us be content to say that this large-scale work in four movements—as ever, the string quartet forms a climax, a summing-up, especially for a Viennese

master—is a work which speaks equally strongly for Schoenberg as a 'traditionalist' and as a pioneer in new realms. The
middle movements are perhaps the most accessible at a first
hearing; the 'comodo' scherzo, developing from hints of a
most tender minuet or Ländler, and the largo movement, which
begins with a very striking unison recitative, and which is
laid out with splendid musical imagination—this movement,
moreover, follows the example of the severely contoured
opening movement in announcing the basic set as a theme (the
row is: d–c sharp–a–b flat–f–e flat–e–c–a flat–g–f sharp–b).
The 'dynamic' expressiveness this quartet wrings from con-
structivism seems clearly related to that of the First D minor
Quartet, Op. 7, from 1905. For example, in the first movement
the traditional layout of first subject, transitional ideas, second
subject, etc. is strictly adhered to. And throughout almost the
entire work the music has a memorability, a striking quality,
such as one would not have expected in view of its enormous
density and wealth of relationships; the reasons for this are
the very clear distinction between main and subsidiary parts;
the pregnant rhythms both of the themes themselves and of
their accompanying ideas; and the energetically accentuated
articulation both of the ideas in each section and of the formal
complexes as a whole. This Fourth Quartet can be reckoned
Schoenberg's most important statement in the field of chamber
music.

Between 1 August and 8 September 1938, Schoenberg
composed a work closely linked to the Jewish liturgy, but
subtly using all the skill he had developed over his entire
career: *Kol Nidre*, for speaker, mixed chorus and orchestra,
Op. 39. It was first performed, with Schoenberg conducting,
on 4 October 1939, in Los Angeles.

The work was written at the suggestion of a Los Angeles
Rabbi, Jakob Sonderling. The passionate devotion with which
Schoenberg addressed himself to his great task is shown not
only by the extraordinary expressive power of his music,
but also by his intense efforts to clarify the problems presented by the text, and to ensure that the original liturgical
melody remained unaltered. He wrote at length about his
labours (22 November 1941: *S.L.* 187) to the composer Paul
Dessau, who at that time lived in New York. The sarcastic
remark quoted at the end of the following excerpt from

Schoenberg's letter refers above all to Max Bruch's composition of 1881, 'Kol Nidrei—Adagio for cello and orchestra or harp, after Hebrew melodies, Op. 47'—a work which was once very popular.

The difficulty of using the traditional melody has two causes:
1. There actually isn't such a melody, only a number of flourishes resembling each other to a certain degree, yet without being identical and also without always appearing in the same order.
2. This melody is monodic, that is, is not based on harmony in our sense, and perhaps not even on polyphony.
I chose the phrases that a number of versions had in common and put them into a reasonable order. One of my main tasks was vitriolising out the cello-sentimentality of the Bruchs, etc. and giving this DECREE the dignity of a law, of an 'edict'. I believe I succeeded in doing so.

The Hebrew words Kol Nidre mean 'all vows'. They are the first words of an old liturgical text sung in the synagogue on the Day of Atonement, Yom Kippur; basically, the text was meant to declare invalid all vows made contrary to the Mosaic faith, and to receive repentent sinners back into the Jewish religious community. While this text was often taken to refer to any kind of sinful vows and oaths, Schoenberg emphasised in his version, which deviates somewhat from the traditional one, that it is a question only of those sinful vows that run counter to the Jewish belief in God. Acting on a suggestion from Rabbi Sonderling, Schoenberg prefaced the liturgical text with a story, told by a speaker, referring to a legend in the Cabbala, according to which God, having created light, crushed it to atoms; these are spread throughout the world, and can be perceived only by the faithful, including repentant sinners. The text of the piece is in English, but the original Hebrew is retained for the invocations of Divine and earthly authority.

The musical form follows that of the text, in being divided into two parts; after an orchestral prelude that rises from the depths of darkness, the Rabbi delivers his powerful and sharply accented proclamation, in which there are extraordinary pictorial effects (still within the bounds of strict thematic development) at the point where the text refers to the light's being 'crushed to atoms'. The *Kol Nidre* itself is treated as a strikingly rhythmic dialogue between the Rabbi and the choir. The latter reinforces the speaker's most important remarks by repeating them in a way that is thematically the same, but differently scored. The work, organised entirely around the tonal centre G, dies away with the quiet call 'We repent': it is one of the most impressive things Schoenberg ever wrote.

Schoenberg completed his Second Chamber Symphony a year later than *Kol Nidre* (on 12 October 1939), but, perhaps to indicate that its conception dated from earlier, he gave it an earlier opus-number—Op. 38. He had begun to compose the work in August 1906, immediately after completing the First Chamber Symphony, Op. 9. So thirty-three years had elapsed (though he had also worked on the piece in 1911 and 1916) when Schoenberg resumed work on it at the suggestion of the conductor Fritz Stiedry; at that time, all but a few bars of the first movement and a third of the second movement were already composed. He wrote to Stiedry:

For a month I have been working on the Second Chamber Symphony. I spend most of the time trying to find out 'What was the author getting at here? Indeed, my style has greatly deepened meanwhile, and I find it hard to reconcile what I then rightly wrote, trusting my sense of form and not thinking too much, with my current extensive demands in respect of 'visible' logic. Today that is one of the major difficulties, for it also affects the material.

Schoenberg wanted also to compose a third movement (Adagio) as a kind of 'epilogue', and at the end of January 1940 he sketched approximately eighty bars of this; but he abandoned the attempt, realising that the musical and 'psychic' problems had been exhaustively presented in the first two movements. The work, in E flat minor and G major, belongs entirely to the sphere of 1906 onward, so far as its thematic aspect is concerned. Schoenberg's empathy with this far-distant sphere is truly astonishing. The forces used (strings, double wind without trombones) are greater than those in the First Chamber Symphony, and in many passages the sound is correspondingly more opulent. The first performance of the work was on 15 December 1940, at a New York concert of the New Friends of Music, conducted by Stiedry.

Schoenberg may well have been prompted to resume work on the Second Chamber Symphony when in 1935 he arranged the First one for symphony orchestra, giving the work's structure many new touches by the addition of subsidiary and accompanying parts. This version was published by Schirmer, New York, as Op. 9b.

Schoenberg again turned to an earlier world when in the summer of 1937 he orchestrated Brahms' G-minor Piano Quartet, Op. 26; the arrangement contains no element of recomposition. In an English letter written during March 1939 (*S.L.* 181. Eng.) to the music critic Alfred V. Frankenstein he discussed his arrangement, which was first performed on 7 May 1938, in Los Angeles, conducted by Klemperer:

My reasons:
1. I like this piece.
2. It is seldom played.
3. It is always very badly played, because the better the pianist, the louder he plays and you hear nothing from the strings. I wanted once to hear everything, and this I achieved.

My intentions:
1. To remain strictly in the style of Brahms and not to go farther than he himself would have gone if he had lived today.
2. To watch carefully all these laws which Brahms obeyed and not to violate any of those which are only known to musicians educated in his environment.

How I did it:
I am for almost fifty years very thoroughly acquainted with Brahms' style and his principles. I have analysed many of his works for myself and with my pupils. I have played as violist and cellist this work and many others numerous times: I therefore knew how it should sound. I had only to transpose this sound to the orchestra, and this is in fact what I did.

Shortly after Klemperer had conducted the first performance of the orchestration of Brahms' Quartet, Schoenberg himself conducted the work—which he used jokingly to refer to as 'Brahms' Fifth'—in San Diego, California. In the autumn of

1937 he took part in a music festival held in his honour at Denver, Colorado; the Kolisch Quartet gave two concerts including all his published string quartets, and at a third concert works by his pupils—Berg, Webern, Gerald Strang and Oscar Levant—were performed. At the end of 1939 he delivered two lectures to the annual congress of the Society of American Music Teachers. On 11 April 1941, at a simple ceremony in Los Angeles City Hall, Schoenberg and his wife acquired American citizenship—an additionally important event for him because he was now able to intervene even more authoritatively on behalf of refugees from the Third Reich. Already—particularly after the Austrian Anschluss—he had been very active obtaining affidavits and jobs for those who had been persecuted. He gave compelling artistic expression to his hatred of dictatorship in the *Ode to Napoleon Buonaparte*, composed early in 1942 (cf pp. 211–13).

Because of war conditions, there were no official celebrations on Schoenberg's seventieth birthday (13 September 1944); he had to content himself with private messages of congratulation, and he expressed his thanks on 3 October in the following duplicated letter:

Dear Friends,

    For more than a week I tried composing a letter of thanks to those who congratulated me on the occasion of my seventieth birthday. Still I did not succeed: it is terribly difficult to produce something if one is conceited enough to believe that everybody expects something extraordinary at an occasion like this.

But in fact the contrary might be true: at this age, if one is still capable of giving once in a while a sign of life, everybody might consider this already as a satisfactory accomplishment. I acknowledged this when my piano concerto was premièred and to my great astonishment so many were astonished that I still have something to tell. Or perhaps, that I do not yet stop telling it—or that I still am not wise enough to suppress it—or to learn finally to be silent at all?

> Many recommend: 'Many happy returns!'
> Thank you, but will this help?
> Will I really become wiser this way?
> I cannot promise, but let us hope.

Having turned seventy, Schoenberg had to retire from his teaching post at U.C.L.A. Since he had only been a member of the University for eight years, he received a very small pension—38 dollars a month!—quite insufficient to provide for himself and his family. Nor was his income from performances of his works and private teaching adequate to cope with his difficulties. Although his state of health was anything but satisfactory, he even considered emigrating to New Zealand, as is shown by a letter written on 17 October 1944 to an uncle of his wife who lived there (*S.L.* 194). In January 1945 he applied unsuccessfully for a grant from the Guggenheim Foundation, in order to be able to complete the musical works, and works of musical theory, which he had begun. In fact he had to sell some of his manuscripts to the Library of Congress in Washington to help himself out of his difficulties.

In all this outward distress, he was sustained by the thought of the spiritual mission he had to fulfil. He wrote (8 December 1944, *S.L.* 196, Eng.) to the American composer Roger Sessions: 'I want my message to be understood and accepted.'

The works Schoenberg composed between 1941 and 1943 carry an important part of this message, and in them he broke much new ground.

Between August and October 1941 he composed his first work for organ solo: *Variations on a Recitative*, Op. 40. The work was commissioned by a New York publisher who was bringing out a series of contemporary organ works. It is based on the key of D minor, and a characteristic feature is its bold, strongly modulating harmony. The recitative theme, introduced in the bass, contains all twelve tones of the chromatic scale; it consists of thirty six tones in all, grouped in three- and six-note motives. The theme is followed by ten variations of widely varying character, followed by a virtuoso cadenza and an ingenious closing section that uses a version of the theme together with its inversion. Since Schoenberg was, as ever, concerned above all with clarity of part-writing, he expressed much dissatisfaction with the complicated registration employed by the work's first performer and subsequently included in the printed edition; aiming at colour effects he had not envisaged, it was the work of Carl Weinrich, organist of New York's Princeton University Church, who gave the work its first performance there early in 1944. Schoenberg later wrote a long letter to a Berlin musicologist, at whose instigation the work was to be performed in the church of St Paul, Berlin-Zehlendorf, in May 1949; the letter (reprinted complete in Rufer's catalogue) expresses at some length his views about composing for the organ, views formed decades earlier. He said, among other things: 'I regard the organ as, above all, a keyboard instrument, and I write for the hands to suit what they can do on a keyboard. I am little interested in the organ's colours; for me, colours of any kind are there only to make the idea clear—the motivic and thematic idea, and perhaps its expressiveness and character.' In keeping with his views about the 'linear nature' of organ composition, he developed the idea of having the 'giant instrument' played by several performers at several different consoles, so as to obtain expressiveness of a genuinely dynamic rather than merely colouristic kind.

About a fortnight before he began working on the organ variations, Schoenberg drafted the beginning of a strictly twelve-tone organ 'sonata' (the only time the title 'sonata' appears in his works), but after composing fifty bars he abandoned the work in favour of the variations. Glenn E. Watkins, who has made an exact analysis of the opening of the sonata (in the New York periodical *Perspectives*, 1965), points out interesting connections between this work and the Piano Concerto, Op. 42, composed a year later.

Byron is said to have written the *Ode to Napoleon Buonaparte* within the space of a few hours (it has sixteen nine-line stanzas!), when in 1814 he heard of Napoleon's abdication at Fontainebleau. In it he expressed all his contempt for his former hero, who had now come to so shameful an end. When, shortly after, his publisher asked him, in order to circumvent a certain tax regulation about printed matter, to make the poem somewhat longer, he added another three stanzas setting up George Washington, true founder of the U.S.A., as a figure of light contrasting with the sombre figure of the ruthless dictator. Schoenberg first came (in 1941) to know a German translation of the original version, and saw in

Napoleon a symbol for Hitler; he immediately sketched out the work. According to Mrs Gertrud Schoenberg, he was deeply moved while setting to music the final three stanzas which he found soon afterwards. In this additional section Washington, the ideal counterpart to Napoleon, proved the occasion for some sharp musical contrasts. The following passage (stanza 2, preceded by the final two lines of stanza 1) particularly struck Schoenberg as a prophetic anticipation of Hitler's miserable end:

> Since he, miscalled the Morning Star,
> Nor man nor fiend hath fallen so far.
>
> Ill-minded man, why scourge thy kind
>   Who bow'd so low the knee?
> By gazing on thyself grown blind,
>   Thou taught'st the rest to see.
> With might unquestion'd—power to save—
> Thine only gift hath been the grave
>   To those that worshipped thee;
> Nor till thy fall could mortals guess
> Ambition's less than littleness!

Schoenberg set the original English text, which was to be delivered by a reciter; he envisaged a 'very musical singer'. The ensemble consists of string quartet and piano. The work's first performance was in an orchestral version, on 23 November 1944 (New York Philharmonic Symphony Orchestra, with Mack Harrell as speaker and Eduard Steuermann as pianist, conducted by Arthur Rodzinski), and for the occasion Schoenberg added a double-bass part reinforcing the bass line. But, as he explicitly emphasised, he preferred the work to be performed with one instrument to a part.

The whole work is composed with the aid of the twelve-tone method, but the basic set (e–f–d flat–c–g sharp–a–b–b flat–d–e flat–g–f sharp) permits frequent tonal references, and even a weighty ending on a chord of E-flat major, possibly an allusion to Beethoven's *Eroica* Symphony, a work which is in that key and which was originally meant as a tribute to Napoleon. In overall form, the work has the effect

Schoenberg
with his family
in Los Angeles

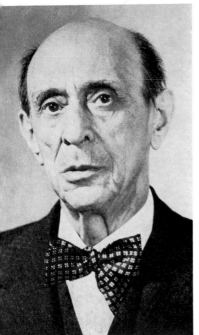

One of the last
photographs
taken of the
composer

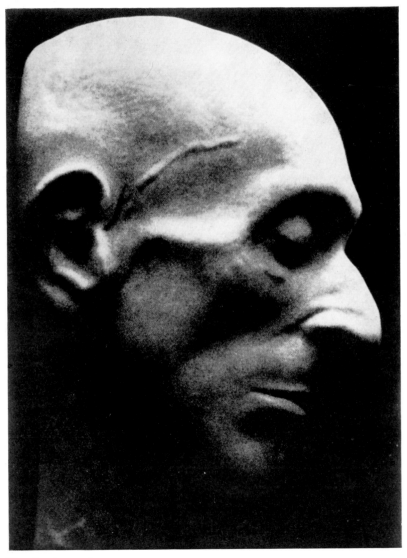

The death-mask,
made by Anna
Mahler on
14 July 1951

of a large-scale symphonic movement; the instrumental ensemble serves not only to highlight the strikingly accented vocal part, but also leads a richly varied life of its own, in long preludes, interludes, and postludes.

The Piano Concerto, Op. 42, composed between July and December 1942, may be regarded as one of the outstanding proofs that strict twelve-tone technique is reconcilable with well-nigh 'romantic' expressiveness—the only condition, naturally, being that the creative gifts involved must, like Schoenberg's, combine supreme artistic skill with the imagination of a genius. The work plays without a break, but falls clearly into four movements, and its abrupt changes of mood can well be summed up by the brief notes jotted down by Schoenberg for his pupil Oscar Levant, who was originally to have given the first performance. For the first part (Andante) Schoenberg wrote 'Life was so easy'; for the second (Molto allegro), 'But suddenly (*sic*) hatred broke out'; for the third (Adagio), 'a serious situation was created', and for the fourth (Rondo giocoso), 'but life goes on'.

The first performance was on 6 February 1944, at the N.B.C. studios in New York, with the N.B.C. Symphony Orchestra conducted by Stokowski; the soloist was Eduard Steuermann.

Schoenberg's next work, in its original version, also occupies a special position in his output. In October 1944 he wrote to the conductor Fritz Reiner (*S.L.* 195):

This is not one of my main works, as everybody can see, because it is not a composition with twelve tones. It is one of those compositions which one writes in order to enjoy one's own virtuosity and, on the other hand, to give a certain group of music lovers—here it is the bands—something better to play. I can assure you—and I think I can prove it—technically this is a masterwork. And I believe it is also original, and I know it is also inspired. Not only can I not write ten measures without inspiration, but I wrote this with really great pleasure.

The work, composed in the summer of 1943, has the title Theme and Variations for wind band, Op. 43a; Schoenberg composed it at the suggestion of his friend Carl Engel, President of the music publishers Schirmer Inc., New York;

his primary aim was a 'pedagogic' one—to offer amateur wind bands something of a genuine and artistic nature, instead of the dubious arrangements they mostly had to play. The work is in G minor, with a theme, seven variations and a finale, and demands a forty-three-piece band, plus percussion and double-bass. In moulding its themes Schoenberg laid special stress on immediate comprehensibility. Much of it is very difficult to play; the part-writing is extremely rich and varied, and transparent.

Schoenberg made a version of the work for symphony orchestra (Op. 43b) simultaneously with the original version; this symphonic version follows exactly the same course, thematically speaking; to compare the two versions' refinements both of composition-technique and of colour is an extraordinarily instructive and delightful experience. The first performance of Op. 43b was given on 20 October, 1944, by the Boston Symphony Orchestra under Koussevitsky.

At the beginning of 1945 Schoenberg appeared twice in San Francisco as guest conductor. On the first occasion he conducted *Transfigured Night* at the Ballet Theater—the work had been made into a ballet entitled *Pillar of Fire*, with choreography by Anthony Tudor, and had had many very successful performances. This success was a good thing, not only economically, but because it helped Schoenberg to attain a certain popularity, apparent from the frantic applause that greeted his appearance on the rostrum. There was again enthusiastic approval shortly after, when he conducted the San Francisco Symphony Orchestra in *Pelléas and Mélisande* and the Five Orchestral Pieces, Op. 16. These successes, and similar ones with works from his 'romantic' period, prompted him, in 1949, to remark ironically, 'This raises the hope that at my next anniversary, in let us say fifty or seventy-five years, I might be celebrated by performances of works of my last period' (letter in English to James Fassett, quoted by Rubsamen).

In the summer of 1945 Nathaniel Shilkret, the conductor of the popular radio concerts in Los Angeles, invited Schoenberg to compose the prelude for a work in many movements, to be entitled *Genesis*, which was to contain passages from the

Book of Genesis set for chorus and orchestra. Since Stravinsky, Castelnuovo-Tedesco, Milhaud, Ernst Toch, Alexandre Tansman, and Shilkret himself had already been commissioned to compose the parts that had a textual basis, Schoenberg used the choir to sing wordless vocalises in his Prelude, which dealt with the creation of the world out of chaos. He said the extraordinarily complicated structure of the work, which took him seven days to compose (he completed it on 30 September 1945), was meant to give an idea of the 'technical' difficulties at the creation of the world. The Prelude, Op. 44, was first performed on 18 November 1945, in Los Angeles, conducted by Werner Janssen.

Willi Schlamm, a German political writer who had emigrated to America, invited Schoenberg to collaborate with him on a New York periodical, *New Magazine*; Schoenberg not only replied (26 June 1945, *S.L.* 203, Eng.) with several proposals for articles, but added the following statement of principle about his attitude to political parties:

I believe in the right of the smallest minority.

Because democracy often acts in a manner resembling dangerously something like a 'dictatorship of the (very often extremely small) majority', it is impossible, in spite of the freedom of the press, to publish ideas which do not fit into the frame of one of the greater parties; ideas whose truth might manifest itself only in five, ten, thirty, hundred years; perhaps only at a time, when, to their author, they have become already obsolete!

In the same letter, Schoenberg made some very critical remarks about musicologists who 'do not much more but explore in a sterile manner the musical past'. In his view, musicologists' main task was to develop the theory of musical composition, which not only assists research into the language of music, but also—and this struck Schoenberg as the most important point—furthers understanding of how musical forms are organised.

In fact Schoenberg's teaching ever since the beginning of the century had been a practical example of such 'ideal' musicology. We can see this at its clearest in two textbooks on which he lavished much time and care during his final years. He only completed one of them, *Structural Functions of Harmony*, in 1946; his textbook on counterpoint was to have been a long work in three sections, but only the first part was left in a form which could be made fit for publication—this task was carried out by Leonard Stein, Schoenberg's last assistant but one, who had already helped a good deal with *Structural Functions of Harmony*. Both works were published posthumously—*Structural Functions of Harmony* in 1954, and *Preliminary Exercises in Counterpoint* in 1963.

Structural Functions is a most important extension of the principles developed in the *Treatise on Harmony* of 1911 and 1921. The thread running through the entire book is the principle of monotonality, that is, the principle that all the musical events in a piece must be derivable from a single realm of tonality. To provide a foundation for this principle Schoenberg introduced the idea of 'regions'—an extension of the idea of 'degrees' which had played a leading role in his *Harmony Treatise* and also in earlier works of musical theory. Six regions have to be taken into account: three (tonic, dominant and subdominant) have a major character, and three (doric, mediant minor and subdominant minor) have minor character. This produces noteworthy further developments of the harmonic formations earlier produced on the individual degrees of the scale. In the main part of the book, the usual schematic tables of chord progressions are replaced by examples (most of them fairly long) from specific musical works (J. S. Bach to Schoenberg's own early music). This is where Schoenberg's genius for 'illumination from within' is overpoweringly evident; in each of almost a hundred examples, he demonstrates compositional traits that are new and essential to the overall form; these have to do either with surprising harmonic relationships, or with bold extensions of tonality. Finally (in analogy to 'Models for Beginners', but in a much more comprehensive way) Schoenberg demonstrates how the harmonic progressions shown have been used for various creative purposes (symphonic introductions, transitions, and what he called 'elaborations', free rhapsodic formations, recitative-accompaniments, strophic variations in songs, etc.). The accompanying text is kept to a minimum almost throughout, and the musical text, together with the indications of degrees and regions, is left to speak eloquently for itself. In the brief closing chapter 'Apollonian evaluation of a Dionysian epoch', there is a further rapid survey—this time purely in words, without musical examples—of the whole development of harmony as experienced by Schoenberg and his 'master pupils'. There is a discussion of the idea of beauty, which takes up again a theme critically examined almost forty years earlier, in the *Harmony Treatise*. Here Schoenberg says:

Beauty, an undefined concept, is quite useless as a basis for aesthetic discrimination, and so is sentiment. Such a *Gefühl-saesthetik* (aesthetic of sentiment) would lead us back to the inadequacy of an obsolete aesthetic which compared sounds to the movement of the stars, and deduced virtues and vices from tone combinations.

And the exposition of the *Structural Functions of Harmony* ends with the prophecy of a future 'harmonic lore'[1] of twelve-tone music:

Is then a composer with twelve tones at a greater disadvantage than his predecessors because the evaluation of the chords which he produces has not yet been carried out. . . ? One day there will be a theory which abstracts rules from these compositions. Certainly, the structural evaluation of these sounds will again be based upon their functional potentialities. But it is improbable that the quality of sharpness or mildness of the dissonances—which, in fact, is nothing more than a gradation according to lesser or greater beauty—is the appropriate foundation for a theory which explores, explains and teaches. . . . Theory must never precede creation: 'And the Lord saw that all was well done.'

In discussing *Preliminary Exercises in Counterpoint* we must be content to say that in its 200 and more pages the five traditional species of simple polyphonic writing are very thoroughly treated, in two, three and four parts, each musical example and each remark providing evidence of Schoenberg's genius for teaching, and of his method, which was aimed, above all, at enabling the pupil to make an independent critical judgment of his own attempts. The two draft fore-words (neither, unfortunately, was completed) are of great general interest. In the first, written in 1936, Schoenberg discusses the relationship between counterpoint—for which he rules out the possibility of any 'eternal law'—and harmony and the art of variation; to him, 'part-writing' is only a 'craftsman's' tool for realising artistic aims—one of many compositional procedures, all of which are constantly develop-ing further. The second foreword contains a sharp attack on methods of instruction in counterpoint setting up Palestrina's style as the ideal of perfection which the pupil must try with all his energy to attain; it ends with the words:

It may not be wholly wrong to assert that, once a pupil has known even once the satisfaction that can be released in him by perfection, he will never forget it. But, on the one hand, why should the pupil try to produce imperfect imitations of a style when an author's works can make him know the radiance of perfection better than he ever could in his own stumbling efforts? And, on the other: music reached its peak of perfection in Bach! Neither Beethoven nor Haydn, nor even Mozart, who came nearest to it, ever achieved such perfection. But, it seems, this perfection does not produce a style that a pupil can imitate. This perfection lies in the idea, the basic conception, not in the working-out. The latter is merely the natural sequel to the profundity of the idea, which is the kind of thing that can be neither imitated nor taught.

Early in 1946 Schoenberg gave a number of lectures at the University of Chicago (these were included in *Style and Idea*), and he gave a further demonstration of his 'passion for teach-ing' in a long letter (*S.L.* 202, Eng.), to the University's Chancellor, in which he made detailed proposals for the foundation of a music department. But in the summer his many activities were rudely interrupted by a catastrophic event, of which he gave an account in a report about his physi-cal troubles, begun in August 1950:

Now I must describe the extraordinary event which I call my 'fatality'. On August 2 (1946), our house-doctor tried a new medicament for my asthma: benzedrine. An hour or two later, during the midday meal, I suddenly felt sleepy and went to bed, something very unusual for me. At about ten o'clock in the evening I woke up, jumped out of bed and ran to a chair which I have been using during asthmatic attacks. I began to feel fierce pains throughout my body, particularly in the chest and around the heart. After trying for half an hour to find a doctor, a friend sent Dr Lloyd-Jones, our present house-doctor, who then saved my life. He gave me an injection of Dilaudid, to reduce the pains. This immediately helped; but ten minutes later I lost consciousness, and my heart-beat and pulse stopped. In other words, I was practically dead. I have never found out how long it lasted. All I was told was that Dr Jones made an injection directly into my heart. It was three weeks before I recovered. I had about 160 penicillin injections; my heart and lungs were examined, X-rays taken, and there were sometimes three or four doctors there at once, discussing my case . . .

Only a few weeks later Schoenberg too 'discussed' his case, in his own way: between 20 August and 23 September 1946, he composed the String Trio, Op. 45, which had been commissioned by Harvard University; the work reflected his illness and recovery. Rubsamen related certain details to do with its form, as narrated by Schoenberg himself:

So literal is the description that it even includes reminiscences of the hypodermic needle—this the composer told Weiss. . . . The string trio is a twelve-tone composition. Schoenberg manipulates short fragments of the basic row to produce the themes of this extremely complex work, which is divided into three parts connected by episodes, the last part being a condensed repetition of the previous sections. Passages full of turmoil alternate with those of repose, reflecting both his suffering during the illness and the subsequent surcease from pain. All the technical devices in the repertory of the virtuoso violinist are called for, yet these are used so fragmentarily that the display element is entirely lacking.

For almost a year Schoenberg composed nothing more. In May 1947 he received a signal token of esteem when the National Institute of Arts and Letters, New York, awarded him a grant of a thousand dollars, with a covering letter couched in terms of the deepest respect. Schoenberg recorded a speech of thanks in English, and the record was sent to the

Institute on 22 May 1947. Here is the text of the speech
(*S.L.* 214):

Mr President, ladies and gentlemen,

I am proud about the formulation under which this award
has been given to me. That all have I endeavoured to accomplish during this fifty years is now evaluated as an achievement,
seems in some respects to be an overestimation.

At least not before could I sum up—that is: while it still
looked like a pell-mell of incoherent details—at least then did
I fail to understand it as a direction leading towards an accomplishment. Personally I had the feeling as if I had fallen into an
ocean of boiling water, and not knowing how to swim or to get
out in another manner, I tried with my legs and arms as best
I could.

I did not know what saved me; why I was not drowned or
cooked alive. . . .

I have perhaps only one merit: I never gave up.

But how could I give up in the middle of an ocean?

Whether my wriggling was very economical or entirely
senseless, whether it helped me to survive or counteracted it—
there was nobody to help me, nor were there many who would
not have liked to see me succumb.

I do not contend it was envy—of what was there to be envious?

I doubt also that it was absence of goodwill—or worse—
presence of ill-wishing.

It might have been the desire to get rid of this nightmare, of
this unharmonious torture, of these unintelligible ideas, of this
methodical madness—and I must admit: these were not bad
men who felt this way—though, of course I never understood
what I had done to them to make them as malicious, as furious,
as cursing, as aggressive;—I am still certain that I had never
taken away from them something they owned; I never inter-
fered with their prerogatives; I never did trespass on their
property; I even did not know where it was located, which were
the boundaries of their lots, and who had given them the title
to these possessions.

Maybe I did not care enough about such problems; maybe I
myself failed to understand their viewpoints, was not consider-
ate enough, was rough when I should have been soft, was
impatient when they were worried by time-pressure, was ridi-
culing them when indulgence was advisable, laughed when they
were distressed . . .

I see only that I was always in the red—

But I have one excuse: I had fallen into an ocean, into an ocean of overheated water, and it burned not only my skin, it burned also internally.

And I could not swim.

At least I could not swim with the tide. All I could do was swim against the tide—whether it saved me or not!

I see that I was always in the red. And when you call this an achievement, so—forgive me—I do not understand of what it might consist.

That I never gave up?

I could not—I would have liked to.

I am proud to receive this award under the assumption that I have achieved something.

Please do not call it false modesty if I say:

Maybe something has been achieved but it was not I who deserves the credit for that.

The credit must be given to my opponents.

They were the ones who really helped me.

Thank you.

The abrupt, often incomplete sentences used by Schoenberg to express his gratitude give an idea of the deep inner excitement filling him at the time. This was caused not only by the aftereffects of the severe physical crisis he had just been through, but also by the shattering effect of the news about Nazi atrocities, many details of which were only then beginning to become known. His mind constantly turned, above all, to the victims of anti-semitic persecution—including many of his friends and relations—and he wanted to leave a musical memorial to them.

These were the inner reasons that prompted him, between 11 and 23 August 1947, to compose his Op. 46, *A Survivor from Warsaw*, for speaker, male voice choir and orchestra. The outward occasion was a commission from the Koussevitzky Music Foundation of Boston, and this was also the reason why the work was dedicated 'to the memory of Natalie Koussevitzky'. The steady deterioration of Schoenberg's eyesight meant that he could only write the work down in short score, on music paper with specially wide staves. From this short score, the French conductor René Leibowitz, who was on a visit to Los Angeles at the time, prepared the full score. Leibowitz, who has been of great service in making

Schoenberg's music better known and understood, also conducted the first European performance of *A Survivor from Warsaw*, in Paris. (The first performance had taken place in Albuquerque, New Mexico, conducted by Kurt Frederick.) In a German newspaper (15 November 1949) Leibowitz wrote about the work and the deep impression it made on the performers at the Paris première:

After I had conducted the first European performance of *A Survivor from Warsaw*, in a radio concert, one of the audience came up to me and said, 'Whole volumes, long essays, many articles have been written about this problem, but in eight minutes Schoenberg has said far more than anyone has been able to do before.'

I believe that is really so; Schoenberg's work most acutely comprehends and reflects the particular tragedy that is its subject—and, in a general sense, the tragedy of our time. It is a work that achieves the highest synthesis of extra-musical and purely musical elements, a work which makes our present-day fate clear to the listener by musical means, on the other hand rising to an extraordinary artistic level precisely through its treatment of this fate.

It is not easy to describe the work so that people have an idea of it. But one thing is certain: it would be wrong to say that Schoenberg's starting point in *A Survivor* was 'purely human' or 'purely musical'; both sources contributed simultaneously to his inspiration. The work's composition was prompted by the story of a *real* survivor from the Warsaw Ghetto; a few years later, he came to Schoenberg and told him the following story:

I cannot remember everything, I must have been unconscious most of the time; I remember only the grandiose moment when they all started to sing the old prayer.

The day began as usual. Reveille when it still was dark —we were assembled and brutally treated. People got killed.

The sergeant shouted that the dead should be counted, so that he knew how many he had to deliver to the gas-chamber. The counting started slowly, irregularly. Then it began again: one, two, three, faster and faster, so that it sounded like a stampede of wild horses, and—all of a sudden —they began singing the Shema Yisroel.

Schoenberg used the story verbatim.[1] It is told by a speaker, in a typical Schoenberg 'speech-song'. The orchestra is heard

1 The story is in fact considerably condensed here.
L.B.

first; a few short, very terse motives suggest the military background. The tragic element is there at once: in the economy of texture, in the remorselessness of the composition itself. And it remains so when the orchestra accompanies the speaker; but it would be wrong to regard this as merely programmatic, 'descriptive' music; the musical construction is absolutely autonomous. Here twelve-tone technique is used strictly, handled in a radical way, and it leads to quite new principles of variation which, for lack of a better word, I would be inclined to call 'a-thematic'. At the moment when the counting begins, a mighty build-up also begins, a crescendo from pianissimo to treble forte, together with a big accelerando. Then, suddenly, the prayer is heard: unison men's voices, doubled by a trombone—a strict cantus firmus, surrounded by rich polyphony in the orchestra. The coda is very short, and the whole breaks off in a powerful orchestral tutti. . . . One is left bewildered, having heard so much in such a short time.

It was the extraordinary newness of the work that so gripped my audience. Many of them came to me with tears in their eyes, others were so shocked that they could not even speak, and only talked to me about their impressions much later. But not only the audience were impressed in this way; from the first rehearsal onward, the entire orchestra and chorus were so moved that there was none of the usual resistance one tends to meet in rehearsing a new work of such difficulty. Rehearsals proceeded in the greatest calm, and with a seriousness I have but rarely met.

Schoenberg and his family spent the summer of 1948 at Santa Barbara, where despite his precarious state of health he held classes in musical analysis and composition at the recently founded Music Academy of the West; he also gave a public lecture. About this time he also arranged three German folk-songs for four-part unaccompanied choir, and these were published the following year as Op. 49, Nos. 1-3. The basis for these songs was the first three of four German folk-songs, from the fifteenth and sixteenth centuries, arranged by Schoenberg in 1928–9 for voice and piano at the request of the German state commission that was bringing out a book of folk-songs for young people; the book appeared in 1930, and included Schoenberg's arrangements. Naturally, both versions were completely tonal; in the original version, the old church modes, in which the melodies were written, are duly observed.

In March 1949 he composed a one-movement piece, the Fantasy for Violin with piano accompaniment, Op. 47, which was to prove his last instrumental work. It makes great technical demands and it is also remarkable because of the way it was composed. Schoenberg first wrote it down as a violin solo, and the piano accompaniment was only added once the violin line was definitely settled. The demands this way of writing made on Schoenberg's mastery of composition can be imagined, since the Fantasy adheres strictly to the twelve-tone method. The work's basic set (b flat–a–c sharp–b–f–g–e–c–g sharp–d sharp–f sharp–d) is also remarkable: if one inverts it, beginning a fifth lower, the second six tones are exactly those of the first half of the basic set, though in a different order; naturally, the same applies to the other half of the row (cf page 234). Schoenberg dedicated the work to the memory of his friend Adolf Koldofsky, who had given the first performance (accompanied by Leonard Stein) on 13 September 1949—Schoenberg's seventy-fifth birthday—in Los Angeles.

In Los Angeles Schoenberg was on friendly terms with Thomas Mann, who had settled in California in 1941. Their friendship came to an abrupt end late in 1948. The cause was Mann's novel *Doctor Faustus*—'the life of the German composer Adrian Leverkühn, as narrated by a friend'—published in 1947. The conflict became public when on 1 January 1949, the *Saturday Review of Literature* published an open letter from Schoenberg to Mann, together with the latter's reply. Schoenberg's letter began:

In his novel *Doctor Faustus* Thomas Mann has taken advantage of my literary property. He has produced a fictitious composer as the hero of his book; and in order to lend him qualities a hero needs to arouse people's interest, he made him the creator of what one erroneously calls my 'system of twelve tones', which I call 'method of composing with twelve tones'.

Mann sent me a German copy of the book with a handwritten dedication, 'To A. Schoenberg, dem Eigentlichen'. As one need not tell me that I am an 'Eigentlicher', a real one, it was clear that he wanted to tell me that his Leverkühn is an impersonation of myself. . . . Much pressure by Mrs Mahler-Werfel had still to be exerted to make Mann promise that every forthcoming copy of *Doctor Faustus* will carry a note giving me credit for the twelve-notes composition. I was satisfied by this promise, because I wanted to be noble to a man who was awarded the Nobel Prize. But Mr Mann was not so generous as I, who had given him good chance to free himself from the ugly aspect of a pirate. He gave an explanation: a few lines which he hid at the end of the book on a place on a page where no one ever would see it. Besides, he added a new crime to his first in the attempt to belittle me: he calls me '*a* (a!) *contemporary* composer and theoretician'. Of course, in two or three decades, one will know which of the two was the other's contemporary.

The explanation appended by Mann to his novel ran:

It does not seem supererogatory to inform the reader that the form of composition delineated in Chapter xxii, known as the 12-tone or row system, is in truth the intellectual property of a contemporary composer and theorist, Arnold Schoenberg. I have transferred this technique, in a certain ideational context, to the fictitious figure of a musician, the tragic hero of my novel. In fact the passages of this book which deal with musical theory are indebted in numerous details to Schoenberg's *Harmonielehre*.[1]

In *The Genesis of a Novel*,[2] his account of his life while writing *Doctor Faustus*, Mann refers to this explanation as follows:

From now on the book, at Schoenberg's request, is to carry a postscript spelling out the intellectual property rights for the uninformed. This is being done a bit against my own convictions—not so much because such an explanation knocks a small breach into the rounded, integral world of my novel, as because, within the sphere of the book, within this world of a pact with the devil and of black magic, the idea of the twelve-tone technique assumes a colouration and a character which it does not possess in its own right and which—is this not so?—in a sense make it really my property, or, rather, the property of the book. Schoenberg's idea and my *ad hoc* version of it differ so widely that, aside from the stylistic fault, it would have

[1] From the English edition, trans. H. T. Lowe Porter, Secker & Warburg, 1949.

[2] Trans. Richard and Clara Winston. New York, Knopf; London, Secker & Warburg, 1961

seemed almost insulting, to my mind, to have mentioned his name in the text.

Mann's reply in the *Saturday Review* ended as follows:

Instead of accepting my book with a satisfied smile as a piece of contemporary literature that testifies to his tremendous influence upon the musical culture of the era, Schoenberg regards it as an act of rape and insult. It is a sad spectacle to see a man of great worth, whose all-too-understandable hyper-sensitivity grows out of a life suspended between glorification and neglect, almost wilfully yield to delusions of persecution and of being robbed, and involve himself in rancorous bickering. It is my sincere hope and wish that he may rise above bitterness and suspicion and that he may find peace in that assurance of his greatness and glory!

Peace was eventually restored between Mann and Schoenberg, as is shown by the letter sent by Mann to H. H. Stuckenschmidt on 19 October 1951, and published by the latter as a preface to the second edition of his book on Schoenberg. The relevant sentences in the letter are:

The opportunity of another personal meeting with Schoenberg, who had been ailing for some time, did not arise after all. Suffice it to say that I was absolutely determined not to increase his hostility, but to allow it to remain one-sided and never to say a bad word about him, and that this determination finally won the day. That I was so determined was sufficiently clear from my reply to his letter to the *Saturday Review of Literature*, and I reinforced my decision in a personal letter[1] which I sent him, when somewhat later he published a very strange attack on me in an English periodical[2]—an article which the editors of the publication called a 'character document'. It did in fact document his character—as did all his pronouncements, which of course one cannot but reverence. To my letter he replied that I had made reconciliation, and that we should bury the hatchet. Yet he did not wish to perform this act in public, since those who had supported him in the 'Faustus' affair might be disappointed. Some special occasion, perhaps an eigthtieth birthday, might arise, where the peace treaty could be made public.

Alas, he did not live to see this.

1 The letter ended: 'However determined you are to be my enemy, you will not succeed in making me into yours.' Schoenberg's reply (S.L. 249) was completed on 9 January 1950. W.R.

2 *Music Survey*, Autumn 1949.

Schoenberg had not appeared in public since his severe illness in August 1946. Early in 1949 he felt better for a time, and even thought about a trip to Europe; his heart was set on celebrating his 75th birthday with his old friends. His doctors raised no medical objections to the trip; but he himself was obliged to write on 8 May 1949 (*S.L.* 238) to Josef Rufer:

Subjectively things are at such a pass that I really cannot. I dare say what I am suffering from is something of no interest to a doctor because it can't either be operated on or alleviated by taking medicine. But for me it is really awful. I suffer from asthma, I suffer from giddiness, and I also have stomach troubles; cramps of all sorts, and pretty violent ones at that. . . . I don't think I can risk the journey . . . and am very sad that I can't come over.

He was, however, able to attend the special concert given by the Los Angeles Chamber Orchestra, conducted by Harold Byrns, and during the interval he received from the Austrian Consul-General for the Western States a memorial album symbolising honorary citizenship of the City of Vienna. According to Rubsamen, in his brief speech of thanks he referred ironically to the fact that this same Vienna had so eagerly embraced the Nazis in 1938, and had waited a very long time to recognise the greatness of one of its sons.

There was, however, no trace of such irony in the letter of thanks he sent on 5 October (*S.L.* 247) to the Mayor of Vienna:

It was with pride and joy that I received the news that I had been given the freedom of the city of Vienna. This is a new, or rather, a renewed, bond, bringing me closer again to the place, its natural scenery and its essential character, where that music was created which I have always so much loved and which it was always my greatest ambition to continue according to the measure of my talents.

Perhaps I may cherish the hope that this honour bestowed on me by the Burgomaster and the Senate of the City of Vienna is due to recognition of that profound desire and of the intensity with which I have striven—however little it may amount to— always to give of my best.

And so I should gladly live to have the opportunity of exercising the right of free entry into the city where I spent so many years. Then I shall not fail to call on you, Herr Bürgermeister, in order personally to express my thanks for this enhancement of my birthday celebrations.

There were two publications to celebrate the birthday. One was a special Schoenberg number of the monthly magazine *Stimmen* published in Berlin by H. H. Stuckenschmidt and Josef Rufer, which gave pride of place to two important autobiographical fragments by Schoenberg himself: *Rückblick* (see page 1) and *On revient toujours* (see page 198). It also contained analytical studies by Rufer, Stuckenschmidt and Peter Gradenwitz, an essay 'Schoenberg in the U.S.A.' by Roger Sessions, personal recollections by the singer Margot Hinnenberg-Lefevre (Mrs Stuckenschmidt), Winfried Zillig and Fritz Stiedry, and tributes from Luigi Dallapiccola, Boris Blacher, Paul Dessau, Werner Egk, Wolfgang Fortner and Karl Amadeus Hartmann. The other commemorative volume was a special issue of the Australian musical periodical *Canon*, which contained a 'twelve-tone' poem by Rudolf Kolisch and contributions from Dika Newlin, René Leibowitz, Paul Amadeus Pisk, Otto Klemperer and Eduard Steuermann.

Schoenberg expressed his thanks in a handwritten letter (*S.L.* 261), facsimiles of which were sent to all those who had taken part in the tributes. It ran as follows:

To gain recognition only after one's death . . . !

In these last few days I have met with much personal recognition, which has given me great pleasure because it testifies to the respect in which I am held by my friends and other well-disposed people.

On the other hand, however, I have for many years been resigned to the fact that I cannot count on living to see full and sympathetic understanding of my work, that is, of what I have to say in music. I do indeed know that more than a few of my friends have come to feel at home with my mode of expression and are familiar with my ideas. It is likely then to be such as they who will fulfil what I prophesied in an aphorism exactly thirty-seven years ago: 'The second half of this century will spoil by overestimation whatever the first half's underestimation left unspoilt.'

I am somewhat embarrassed by all these hymns of praise. But I nevertheless also see something encouraging in them. For: Is it so much to be taken for granted if in the face of the whole world's resistance a man does not give up, but continues to write down what he produces?

I do not know what the great have thought about this. Mozart and Schubert were young enough not to have to come to close terms with this problem. But Beethoven, when Grillparzer called the Ninth a jumble, or Wagner, when the Bayreuth scheme seemed about to fail, or Mahler, when everyone found him trivial—how could they go on writing?

I know only one answer: they had things to say that had to be said. Once, in the army, I was asked if I was really the composer Arnold Schoenberg. 'Somebody had to be,' I said, 'and nobody else wanted to, so I took it on, myself.'

Perhaps I too had to say things—unpopular things, it seems —that had to be said.

And now I ask you all, all of you who have given me real joy with your congratulations and tokens of esteem, to accept this as an attempt to express my gratitude.

My heartfelt thanks!

After these birthday celebrations Schoenberg was rarely seen outside his own home; he sensed a marked decline in his physical powers. Almost the only occasions that could make him venture into the world had to do with his son Ronald's tennis; he followed his progress in the sport with passionate interest.

Rubsamen tells of a remark very characteristic of Schoenberg's attitude to emigration:

In his Sunday column of 14 May 1950 Albert Goldberg of the *Los Angeles Times* published a note from Schoenberg that throws light on an interesting and controversial subject, the influence of America upon emigré composers. An unnamed musician who had lived in the United States for a decade had emphatically expressed the belief to Goldberg that the work of most refugee composers had changed since they had lost contact with their native countries; that most of their music written in America did not equal what had been composed previously; and that he personally 'felt a little below his proper level' in the United States. The critic thereupon wrote to several prominent emigré composers living in Southern

California, inquiring whether they felt the same way, and asking them to state frankly whether separation from the homeland had affected the quality and character of their work. Schoenberg replied that his own moves to France, Spain, and America had had no effect whatsoever upon his music. In his own inimitable English: 'If immigration has changed me—I am not aware of it. Maybe I would have written more when remaining in Europe, but I think: nothing comes out, what was not in. And two times two equals four in every climate.'

A few months later, on 2 August 1950 Schoenberg made the last entry in the book which had become the record of his state of health:

I seldom have severe attacks, but my shortness of breath is more or less chronic. I only feel free of it for four or five hours a day, and almost every night I wake up short of breath. I then cough, often for three or four hours, and only when I am sufficiently exhausted can I get to sleep again—only to go through it all again the next night. For some months now I have not dared to sleep in my bed but in a chair. I have had various courses of treatment. I have been treated for diabetes, pneumonia, kidneys, hernia, and dropsy. I suffer from exhaustion and dizziness, and my eyes, which used to be extraordinarily good, make it hard for me to read.

The last compositions Schoenberg completed were in April 1949, *Dreimal tausend Jahre* ('Thrice a thousand years'), for unaccompanied four-part choir, Op. 50a, to a text by Dagobert D. Runes, and at the beginning of July 1950, Psalm 130, *De profundis*, for unaccompanied six-part choir, Op. 50b. Both are twelve-tone compositions. Op. 50a first appeared in the periodical *Prisma* (Stockholm, 1949), and had its first performance in Fylkingen (Sweden) by a chamber choir conducted by Eric Ericson. Op. 50b was composed at the suggestion of Chemjo Vinaver, the editor of an *Anthology of Jewish Music*, who sent the composer the original Hebrew text, and English translation of it, and a number of Chassidic songs. Schoenberg, however, retained only certain rhythmic details of the liturgical melodies, and set the Hebrew text to music as his own inspiration dictated, giving the vocal parts alternatively pure singing parts and speech-song. The first performance was on 29 January 1954, in Cologne, by the choir of the West German Radio conducted by Bernhard Zimmermann. Schoenberg dedicated the work to the State of Israel.

During 1950 and 1951, in Los Angeles, Schoenberg also came into contact with leading figures from the Israeli world of musical education. In the spring of 1951 he was elected Honorary President of the Israel Academy of Music in Jerusalem. In the letter (26 April 1951, *S.L.* 257) in which he thanked the Academy's director for his appointment, he recalled that for more than fourteen years it had been his 'dearest wish to see the establishment of a separate, independent State of Israel. And indeed more than that : to become a citizen of that State and to reside there.' In this letter Schoenberg also expressed the hope that he could be of use to the Academy with further explanations and advice—the relevant passage is also very important as his final confession on questions of musical teaching in the widest sense:

I have no words to express how much I should like to make my contribution by taking charge personally, and by teaching at this Academy. I have always had a passion for teaching. I have always felt the urge to discover what can most help beginners and how they can be made thoroughly acquainted with the technical, intellectual, and ethical demands of our art; how to teach them that there is a morality of art, and why one must never cease to foster it and always combat to the utmost any attempt to violate it.

I am unfortunately compelled to resign these hopes. But it seems to me that the half-century by which my experience exceeds that of many of my colleagues entitles me to explain what I would have endeavoured to make of this Academy if I had the good fortune and still had the strength to tackle it today. . . .

I would have tried to make this Academy one of worldwide significance, so that it would be of a fit kind to serve as a counterblast to this world that is in so many respects giving itself up to amoral, success-ridden materialism: to a materialism in the face of which all the ethical preconditions of our art are steadily disappearing. A universal model must not send forth anyone who is only semiqualified. It must not produce any instrumentalists whose greatest skill is merely skill, merely the ability to adapt itself completely to the general craving for entertainment.

Those who issue from such an institution must be truly priests of art, approaching art in the same spirit of consecration as the priest approaching God's altar. For just as God chose Israel to be the people whose task it is to maintain the pure, true, Mosaic, monotheism despite all persecution, so too it is the task of Israeli musicians to set the world an example of the old kind that can make our souls function again as they must if mankind is to evolve any higher.

On 23 April 1951 (*S.L.* 256) Schoenberg wrote to London to his boyhood friend Oskar Adler, about a collection, 'Psalms, Prayers, and other Conversations with and about God', on which he was working, and added, 'So far there are twelve of them—but I have material for fifty or more: our contemporaries' religious problems'.

Schoenberg completed the texts of only fifteen of the Psalms; he wrote a mere five lines of a sixteenth one—on 3 July 1951. In 1956 Schott's published the entire material for the collection—texts, sketches, and facsimile and printed scores of the first psalm, edited by Rudolf Kolisch, so the scope of the project can easily be seen.

Schoenberg himself called the work *Modern Psalms*. He originally gave his first psalm the number 151, which shows that he wanted his work to continue the series of 150 psalms contained in the Bible, but in a modern context. The dates of origination show that the sixteen texts fall into two groups: the first ten were written between 29 September 1950 and 9 February 1951, the remaining six between 28 March and 3 July 1951. Composition of the first psalm was begun on 2 October 1950.

This psalm acts rather as a portal admitting one to the entire collection, and it lays the greatest stress on the idea underlying Schoenberg's entire religion—prayer as the essential means of union with God. The text runs as follows:

O Thou my God, all peoples praise Thee and assure Thee of Thy loftiness.
But even if I do, or not, what can it signify to Thee? Who am I, to believe that my prayer is necessary?

When I say 'God', I know that I mean by this the Sole, All-powerful, Omniscient and Unimaginable One, of whom I neither can nor may make unto myself an image. On whom I neither may nor can make the least claim, who will fulfil my most fervent prayer or not notice it.
And, for all that, I pray, as everything that lives prays; for all that, I beg for grace and wonders; fulfilments.
For all that, I pray, since I would not be deprived of the felicitous sense of unity, of union with Thee.
O Thou my God, Thy grace has left us prayer as a means of contact, a blessed means of contact with Thee, as a bliss which gives us more than would all fulfilment.

The Italian composer and writer Roman Vlad has pointed out (*Melos*, September 1957) the deep spiritual connection between this psalm and the final words of the third act of *Moses and Aaron* (which Schoenberg never set to music): 'United with God'. But the connection goes further, also taking in Gabriel's final speech from part 2 of *Jacob's Ladder* (which Schoenberg also never set). There, taking up a reference to a quotation from Balzac's *Séraphita*, Gabriel says, 'Whoever prays has become one with God. His desires alone still separate him from his task. But the union need not cease; it is not interrupted by guilt'.

It is possible to give a brief account of the themes touched on in the other nine psalms of Group I, since Schoenberg mostly emphasises them in the opening lines. No. 2 is a meditation on the role of prayer in the machine age; No. 3 is a prayer asking God for justice, for Man may be tempted to think, 'Why should *I* be just, when nothing but injustice happens to me?' No. 4 contrasts the acts of good men, who act without prospect of any reward, and the dealings of the bad, who are richly rewarded by the Devil; No. 5 is a defence of the Jews, the 'Chosen People' already stricken with so many sorrows, against the accusation of arrogance. No. 6 is an attack on the philistinism of scientific atheists who show contempt for miracles because they 'reveal what is unprovable'; No. 7 rejects the assertion that God no longer performs miracles, and offers a new definition of the term 'miracle'. No. 8 glorifies God's ten Commandments; No. 9, the longest piece in the collection, treats the tragedy inherent in the fact

1 The technical
details of the row are
as follows.

1. The only
intervals it
contains are
semitones, whole
tones, and major
and minor thirds.
2. The intervals of
its second half
(consequent)
make this the
retrograde of its
first half (ante-
cedent).
3. In the Violin
Fantasy Schoen-
berg had already
used a row whose
antecedent, trans-
posed down a
fifth and inverted
provided the
tones of the
consequent (cf
page 224), but
this 'miracle set'
offers even
greater possibili-
ties, since there
are *three*
different inver-
sions of the
antecedent which
provide the tones
of the conse-
quent: those by
transposition
down a minor
third and a
major seventh,
as well as by a
major fifth.
Moreover, the row
ends a tone lower than
it began, so, in view of

cont. on next page

that Jesus has never been adequately treated in the Jewish
version of history (for Schoenberg, Jesus was 'undoubtedly
the purest, most innocent, most selfless, most idealistic being
who ever walked this earth; His will, His entire thought and
aims were directed toward men's salvation, in that he leads
them to the true belief in the Sole, Eternal, All-powerful
One'). No. 10 treats of love between the sexes.

Schoenberg did not number the Psalms in the second group;
they are listed here in the order in which they were written.
1. The Chosen People are comforted in sorrow and persecution by the Lord's promise that 'His seed shall be numberless
as the sand on the sea-shore'. 2. This psalm (completed after
Nos. 3-5) is headed 'Why for Children?', and praises childlike
faith as a 'fragmentary sense of Eternity and Infinity', a
consciousness most adults are deprived of. 3. A discussion
of the evil that has come upon men because of their excessive
lust. The psalm ends with a touch of scepticism uncharac-
teristic of Schoenberg: 'But perhaps atomic fission was given
to us, to exterminate us and our evil'. 4. Prayer as an expression of humility, i.e. 'subordination to the Omniscience of
the Almighty'. 5. A discussion of the guilt that comes of
love's excesses, and the nature of a religious way of life that
could succeed in reforming humanity. 6. The few extant lines
of this final sketch are: 'The prohibition of in-breeding, incest,
is based on the fact that it destroys the race. National in-
breeding, national incest, is just as dangerous to the race as
that of the family and the tribe.'

Rudolf Kolisch's edition of the first Psalm, which Schoenberg began to compose on 2 October 1950, provides us with
facsimiles not only of the short score, covering fifteen pages,
but also of the fourteen sketches that have been preserved,
and of the scheme for the rows. The basic set (e–d sharp–c–a
flat–c flat–g: f–a–f sharp–b flat–c sharp–d) is an unusual
one; Schoenberg had chanced upon it some time earlier, and
the Rufer catalogue reprints his comments on this 'miracle
set'. Its effect, in his own words is to 'offer a greater variety
than double counterpoint of all sorts. Of course you have to
invent your theme as ordinarily, but you have more possibilities of producing strongly related configurations which in
sound are essentially different'.[1]

The tempo-marking for the piece is Adagio; only a small orchestra is used (double wind, with one trombone; strings, percussion), a speaker (speech-song), and four-part mixed choir. The texture is extraordinarily transparent; Schoenberg's last musical entry is at bar 86; here only the soprano part is noted down, to the words 'Und trotzdem bete ich'—'And, for all that, I pray'.

Throughout his life Schoenberg looked on 13 as a fateful number. In his later years he showed a steadily increasing aversion to it. On Friday, 13 July 1951, at 11.45 p.m., he died. Apart from a nurse, only Mrs Schoenberg was present, and it was to her that he spoke his last word: 'Harmony.'

2 above, when it is transposed down a whole tone the antecedent becomes *identical in pitch* with the consequent of the original set—a literal retrograde. And so on for all further transpositions down a tone. In fact the row is used only at the five pitches mentioned (original pitch and the four transpositions), so that only two six-note groups occur in its whole course. Hence the 'strongly related configurations' to which Schoenberg referred.
L.B.

Appendix 1 / Self-analysis

Early in 1931 the German psychologist Julius Bahle sent the following letter to a number of composers in Germany and other countries:

Following my recent study *Zur Psychologie des musikalischen Gestaltens* (On the psychology of the musical formative process, Leipzig 1930) I now intend to carry out a further piece of research devoted principally to song composition, this being probably the field in which the musical-artistic creative process is easiest to investigate. In connection with this I shall also treat the problem of the text, one which is so important to composers. This can only be done in a methodically irreproachable way if I can interest a large number of recognised contemporary artists in this problem and its great cultural-historical importance, and persuade them to co-operate in its solution. For this reason I take the liberty of asking you for your most valued co-operation. I realise how great a favour you would be doing me, the more so since I am asking a creative artist to expend his valuable time in this research. But I hope that your co-operation will to some extent provide its own compensation, since a detailed description of your creative process helps your contemporaries and successors to understand your art.

In order to acquire as faithful an insight as possible into the entire course of musical production and its various phases, it would be necessary for composers to provide an exact self-analysis of their creative process, like André Gide's report on his literary creative work in the *Diary of the Coiners*.

These considerations of scientific method make a simple questionnaire inadequate. I would therefore ask you to set to music, at a suitable time, one at least of the enclosed eight short poems, and to report at length on how this composition came about—the purpose being to avoid the major defects of statements about artistic creation which are often speculative and theoretical and couched in very general terms, and to let the actual psychological processes involved come more to the fore. The immediate description of a concrete case also makes self-observation a good deal easier, and offers the maximum assurance that the psychological facts of the case will be pinned down in an irreproachable and exact way. Moreover, such an investigation provides highly interesting comparative material about composers' individual creative procedures when dealing with identical subject-matter. Although I had in mind settings of the poems as a 'Lied' in the strict sense, choral settings need not be ruled out on principle.

236

Should you, however, find none of the texts selected suitable, then I would ask you, when setting a text of your own choice, to observe yourself in the way indicated. Should your time be currently taken up with work on some large-scale project, then an analogous report about the latter would also be of the greatest value.

I take the liberty of enclosing a list of guide-lines for self-observation, worked out according to scientific principles. . . .

Bahle's eight short poems covered a wide range of subjects and moods: they were a nature poem, a work song, a lullaby, a travel song, a prayer, an amusing anecdote, a social-revolutionary poem, and a metaphysical poem. Of the thirty-two composers who answered Bahle's enquiry briefly or at length, twenty-seven sent in compositions, eighteen of which were settings of the poems provided by Bahle. He published a thorough analysis of the material provided by his 'long-distance' experiment in his book, *Der musikalische Schaffens-prozess. Psychologie der schöpferischen Erlebnis- und Antriebs-formen* (The musical creative process. Psychology of experience and stimulus among the creative, Leipzig 1936, revised edition Constance 1947). In the foreword to the second edition he also told of the violent attacks made on him in the Third Reich because of his researches. After publishing these results of his researches, Bahle produced another important work, *Eingebung und Tat im musikalischen Schaffen. Ein Beitrag zur Psychologie der Entwicklungs- und Schaffens-gesetze schöpferischer Menschen* (Talent and deed in musical creation. A contribution to the psychology of the laws governing development and creation among creative people, Leipzig 1939).

From the outset Schoenberg was very interested in Bahle's researches. Being overburdened with other work, he could not bring himself to compose a short song as requested, with a report on the creative process; but he answered at length the seven questions put by Bahle in his 'guidelines', also an eighth question. Only a few sentences from his reply were included in Bahle's book (pages 76, 206, and 207). However, Dr Bahle very kindly placed the whole of Schoenberg's reply at my disposal, and allowed me to reprint it. I must thank him very much for making possible the first publication of this important text, which is here translated complete, together with Dr Bahle's questions.

1. BAHLE. What was the nature of your psychic processes as you read through the poems, and what prompted you to choose or reject the various poems?

SCHOENBERG. Inward stirrings: certainly corresponding to the content of the poem. In choosing: inspiration, a state of feverish excitement; preceding the real conception of ideas. In rejecting: indifference, or contradiction, criticism, often also the feeling, 'I cannot express that'.

2. BAHLE. What are the most important phases in the composition of a song?—please list as precisely as possible the order in which they occur, the point in time at which each one occurs, and the conditions governing their occurrence.

SCHOENBERG. Stage I: Unnameable sense of a sounding and moving space, of a form with characteristic relationships; of moving masses whose shape is unnameable and not amenable to comparison.

Stage II, which since my earliest youth I have called' translating the poem into "everyday music" '. Perhaps this has always been a musical 'through-fantasising' along emotional lines, one in which (particularly during my youth) the real, personally coloured invention of figures had not yet begun.

Stage III: Here, frequently, a large or small number of themes soon also appear, often proving unusable. The real themes, however, often appear only during a second working run (if one may so name it); in this, the sense of inspiration should indeed be no less marked, but as a whole the process is governed by a greater degree of consciousness.

Stage IV: This is the point at which I begin a more detailed working-out (often with a sense that it is still too soon), either by means of short sketches with varying degrees of finality and unequal value; often, though, I in fact write the piece straight down, sometimes with some difficulty, but mostly very fast; and certainly guided by the initial conception.

Stage V: With longer works, I often come to a halt once or twice in the middle. This is sometimes because I have 'got on to the wrong track', but often it may perhaps be slight fatigue, since I seldom need to alter anything when I resume work four or five days later.

3. BAHLE. In what way and to what degree is your musical creation dependent on the literary source?

(a) How far is the composition the expression of the moods

and emotional or value experiences released (directly or indirectly) by the poem?

(*b*) How far is the composition the representation of the poem's ideational content, of any objective happenings, fantasy ideas, or anything similar?

(*c*) In giving form to the piece, were the poem's features—rhythmic, acoustical, and those of speech melody—used, and if so to what extent?

SCHOENBERG. Once one has reached the stage of real composition, which is already a technical matter, one has overcome any dependence on the subject-matter, its content, artistic value, etc. Details can momentarily create difficulties, but these will no longer be basic ones. For all of that has already been settled at the time of conception—at that time, I have the feeling that my music is 'the music *for this* text.' That answers part (*a*) of the question, without my needing to consider the matter in any greater detail. I arrive at the appropriate musical expressive resources by intuition; in any case, *without outward intention.* Naturally, it may often happen that some particular pointing of the text, underlining, emphasis, and so on, comes from the technical field, but (I can assure you) this hardly ever happens in a dry, technical way, for even technical things must *occur* to one (*einem einfallen*)![1]

Einfall = inspiration. L.B.

(*b*) What has been said above has probably answered this question. I can offer the following explanation of my sense of 'the music *for this* text': ideas, moods, emotions in the poem are, like figures in music, nothing but the expression of some basic fact concealed behind the whole, and this could equally be represented in a different material: in words, rhymes, sounds, but also in colours, forms, and marble.

(*c*) At conception, all the poem's perceptible characteristics certainly found a reflection. So far as I know, I do not consciously consider the rhythmic and acoustical factors. However, in my case the element of speech melody has the greatest influence on the shape and line of my vocal parts, though at the moment I could not say much of a theoretical nature about this. Here I do not need consciously to do much extra. Perhaps, as a disciple of Wagner, I was trained along these lines; but perhaps a feeling for a singing voice is a natural talent.

4. BAHLE. In what way and to what extent is the poem merely an occasion, excuse, stimulus, for and to production from purely musical points of view, and what would the latter be?

SCHOENBERG. In my earlier days (since, for a long time now,

I have only very exceptionally set anyone else's texts) I always used to look for a particular poem, and often, certainly, its content (mood and emotions) had to match preconceived ideas of my own. All the same, I often ended up by choosing something quite different, perhaps because it matched a musical idea that was in my mind; a theme, waiting for someone to help it into the world. For I know over and over again that I was after texts for music I wanted to write. This was in fact how I came to write my own texts; texts for imaginary music. I must confess at this point that the intellectual working-out of a poetic plan then often led, despite my good intentions and every precaution, to formulations which would have deterred me from setting them had they been written by anyone else; quite especial efforts and concentration are then required to overcome such difficulties, and often I begin by losing heart. So, in such passages, I myself run counter to my own wish that guided me in formulating my poems—for these are always supposed (and I am getting steadily more successful at it) to be 'texts for music that is in my mind'. To sum up: the words are often an occasion, an excuse, a stimulus. What really draws me to them is my musical need. I must add one thing only, *à propos* 'stimulus': certain texts are in fact often very well suited, if I may put it in this way, 'to send the music on its adventures'. For the special quality of a material subject certainly also lends its impress to some special quality of the musical figures; I am often very vividly aware of this, and here I believe that this particular type of musical idea was to be invented by following the path along which the poem's special quality guided the imagination.

5. BAHLE. Before you composed the song, was any compositional material already present, which had not yet been used in a work, and can you say how this originated and what its relationship to the text is?

SCHOENBERG. Hardly. I can remember only one single instance when for a new work I took over a theme invented in some other context. Principally because musically speaking I was very fond of it, and it had a related mood.

6. BAHLE. Is your composition ruled by any aesthetic norms, guidelines or principles, and of what kind are they?

SCHOENBERG. No. Aesthetic questions are unknown to me. But, as regards so-called composition with twelve tones, this is a method more of a craftsmanly nature, which exerts no decisive influence on either the work's structure or its character. The question is simply, 'how the material is treated'—in the sense of a particular way in which one exploits its conditions so as to give it form. But most important as such.

7. BAHLE. As your setting came into being, what was the influence, the role, of compositional material

(*a*) from the past (which older composers?)

(*b*) of the present (which contemporary composers or schools?)

(*c*) from your own earlier works?

SCHOENBERG. The compositional material existing outside myself is certainly influential in various ways, even if unconsciously. Often, certainly, one even sets oneself formal assignments like those set themselves by our creative predecessors. Sometimes, too, it happens consciously; who would not like, just once, to achieve a structure whose postulates were as richly artistic as those of everything by Bach; who would not like, sometimes, to match Beethoven's spirit, fire and dynamism, or to be as graceful, nimble and clear as Mozart? And certainly one will venture into a field of expression where one has already tried one's hand: one hopes to put things more successfully.

8. BAHLE. What were the psychological motives or principles behind your stylistic changes?

SCHOENBERG. The psychological motives behind my stylistic *development* (I have to put the question thus, instead of saying 'stylistic changes')? What I know in the matter is as follows: I was driven onward by the need for *brevity, precision, definition,*[1] *and clarity*. I had the sense that I was now saying it *better*, more *clearly*, more *unambiguously*, more *personally*.

[1] *Schärfe* (lit. 'sharpness'), which also means 'severity'. L.B.

The transition from composition which still emphasised key (while always containing many dissonances) to one where there is no longer any key, any tonic, any consonances, happened gradually, in accordance not with any wish or will, but with a *vision*, an *inspiration*; it happened perhaps instinctively.

Considerations such as enhanced performance, reminiscences, inhibitions, satiety, revulsion, and so on, never entered my mind. On the contrary: I always *greatly* regretted that I suddenly found myself debarred from continuing in the style, for instance, of my Chamber Symphony, since it struck me that there were still immeasurable and unexploited possibilities here. I thus had, unfortunately, to abandon works I had almost completed; for instance I have tried in vain, time after time, to complete a second Chamber Symphony, which is very nearly ready. I still hope to do so.

Has the psychological basis of my creation altered? Not at

241

all, I believe. For reasons unknown, I sometimes had to work very hard at something, but mostly it was very easy. At times, when working on something extraordinarily difficult, I had a sense of merely transcribing what already existed; at others, I could not put my finger on the reason why—without being any the worse for it—something (the end of *Die glückliche Hand*, for instance) was causing so much trouble and making such slow progress.

Appendix 2 / Modern Music on the Radio

An Interview.[1]
First, an excerpt from the editorial introduction:

Arnold Schoenberg recently visited Vienna to give a lecture. We took the opportunity of getting him to state his attitude to the radio, from the special point of view of the art he has inaugurated, and asked him a series of questions, which this artist answered in the sharply pointed way characteristic of him. What makes Schoenberg's replies so noteworthy is that here we have the words of a man who has always followed his own path with iron consistency, who has never compromised for opportunist reasons, and who is in the habit of calling a spade a spade.

Question 1.
Is modern music suited to the radio, and how might the one perhaps be adapted to the other?
Answer.
This touches on questions of musical technique, radio technique, and taste. I would ask of the radio that it reproduce everything as it actually sounds. But this particularly affects the highest and lowest registers. Unfortunately, with most transmitters one hears only the upper parts (I call this sort of sound 'a lady sawn in half'), and only a few stations, for example those in Britain and Italy, satisfy me in this respect. Modern music is for the most part 'thinly scored'. That should really make it very suitable for broadcasting—more so than, say, music from the eighties and nineties of the last century. So it is hardly for modern music to adapt itself, particularly since it has another virtue that suits broadcasting conditions—it is mostly quite short.

Question 2.
How could one educate the public for modern music?
Answer.
It will be no more possible now than it ever was to educate the whole of the public for modern, or, to put it better, serious art-music. Rightly or wrongly, it is not everyone's business to concern himself with difficult and profound things, just as these things are not thought of with everyone in mind. But the part of the public that is to be won over could and should be won over as soon as possible. The way to do this: many,

1 From *Radiowelt*, an 'illustrated weekly for all: official organ of the Association of Austrian Radio-Amateur clubs, and of the Association of experimental transmitters. 10th year, Vol. 15, Saturday 8 April 1933, Vienna.'

frequently repeated performances, as well prepared as possible. I have long been pleading that an hour should be given over to modern music, at a time when its opponents will not greatly begrudge it; for example, an hour late at night, once or twice a week, perhaps after eleven. That could be handed over to modern music with no envious reactions.

Question 3.

The running of concerts and music in general, and the way in which radio music is run?

Answer.

I find it fitting to remind the radio of an obligation: a moral obligation to which it pays too little regard. Since there is so much music—good or bad—to be heard on the radio, the public is not forced to rely solely on going to concerts. This has certainly played no small part in causing concerts to be so badly attended. The radio should make the most extensive amends to artistic life for this harm done; the harm is not merely material, but in the highest degree artistic! What amazes me about the radio's activities is that it makes so little use of its chance to arrange quite short performances, perhaps of a single work. In concert life one has to travel a long way to the concert hall, and one will not do so for a single piece. But this difficulty disappears in the case of the radio!

Question 4.

What are your views on the aptness of electrical instruments?

Answer.

No doubt at all: this aptness is something which must in principle be regarded as important. But—it has to be said—for the moment their efficiency is still very problematic. The reason for this is not the incapacity of inventors, but the misguided spirit of industry, which does not allow inventions to mature until they are perfect from the artistic point of view, but provides inventors with money only for very dubious purposes: what they are to produce is not an instrument serving art, but something which can be mass-produced and thrown cheaply onto the market, and which can be brought out at least once a year in a new fashionable version that makes the earlier ones valueless, until the whole world loses interest. That is a sad and hope-destroying phenomenon.

Appendix 3 / 'Supposing Times were Normal'

The preface drafted by Schoenberg in 1936 for my early monograph on Berg consisted of two sections. The second, discussing Berg as pupil, has appeared in my later biography of Berg. Here is the first part of the preface which Schoenberg never completed because of other pressing work. In any case, his highly characteristic remarks are important, and generally applicable not merely to Berg's own life but to the whole period during which they were written.

Supposing times were normal—normal as they were before 1914—then the music of our time would be in a different situation. A free younger generation, coming freely to their own decisions, and choosing their own path, would stand enthusiastically behind it; like every previous generation, they would do their duty—that of placing the new, as yet unacknowledged treasures of art in their rightful place alongside all that has already come to be acknowledged.

Before 1914, the young were brought up to do that; 'bred' or not, they proved equal to every challenge, and they had to face challenges enough. And they were highly esteemed for it. And rightly: they had proved that when the mind and character are given an intellectual education in culture and art, one is very well fitted to be a war-hero.

If only, nowadays, it were just the same old situation: that mankind wants new slogans to keep it happy, no more than that, nothing else but that. However, slogans have come to be acted on; whereas no-one used to imagine any consequences, nowadays the consequences will be unimaginable.

Presentday youth, too, believes in a mission: that of fighting for some kind of change in the structure of the state, a change that has long been on the way. Nobody who has observed the bewildering fluctuations from one extreme to the other during the last few decades can deny that such a faith is justified. It announces unmistakably that society is caught up [*two words illegible*] for an improved system of equipoise.

But these ideas and aims, and the stimulus to work toward them, do not stem from this younger generation; they have been taken over from the intellectual province of the men who were about forty in 1914.

Here too, remarkably, this same intellectual upbringing

nowadays written off as 'decadent' (a fashionable slogan already obsolete twenty-five years ago) has proved no obstacle to an unexpected change in the spiritual climate.

Intellectuality, worship of the spirit, idealism, materialism, realism and romanticism have neither harmed nor helped, neither furthered nor hindered.

It is difficult, then, to acquire such a modicum of spiritual culture; it is, however, infinitely easier to shake it off again—so that, at most, the illusion of it remains.

Here we are speaking not only of art and morals but also of politics; justification enough for a few somewhat light-headed remarks about convictions, and attitudes of mind resulting from them. No one would willingly be convicted of having no attitude, and by now few people dare even to have incorrect ones. Attitudes of mind are therefore replaceable, and need not be based on conviction. It would be better still if convictions could also be handed in and exchanged for others. But one can not, factually speaking, exchange 'twice two $= 4$' for '$= 5$' —only linguistically, but the latter loophole is pitilessly exploited. To change conviction is, after all, wrong only linguistically; politically, it can look extremely upright. One slaps a coat of political distemper on a conviction one has worn for years (but which has now proved unusable), and on ninety-five per cent and more of all one's problems.

Science—the flexible interpretation of inflexible data—lends a hand here. It will manage to breed ('rearing' is the word) the kind of younger generation that suffers from an indisposition in the matter of convictions or attitudes of mind, but is disposed to settle devastatingly on culture, like swarms of locusts, destroying, squashing one another in the senseless, dead-end drive of the temporarily indestructible swarm.

Men of sense will remain unbelieving when science produces homunculus fantasies of that kind; no humanitarian will seriously believe that the only thing a cultured people accepts as true could be the nebulous dreams dreamed by a swarm of locusts.

In fifty years' time, more will be known about it—that, really, is the only comfort we can ever find.

Perhaps the individual in the swarm of locusts also thinks, 'In fifty years' time, more will be known about it.'

But until a decade ago, we musicians knew uncertainty only as it affected our own narrow field. And, even there, analogies proved useful: 'it always turned out so, or so, in fifty years' time, having been quite the reverse during . . .'s lifetime—so this time, too it will turn out as in case X, Y, or Z.'

The presentday musician therefore has no option but to present inflexible data, leaving it to science, in the future, to decide whether it 'flexes' them, and, if so, how. In that sense, the present book strikes me as written from a valuable point of view. Analogy brings inflexible data to light. To us, they are works; to others, they must still become so—for the moment, that is purely a matter of feeling. A matter, though, of the feelings of people whose education in the classical tradition alone made them competent to present, with limitless honesty, a new world of sound, with which the incompetent can make contact only through underhand means and defamation.

So let me here contribute one more fact to the stock of inflexible data. I read, in one of the analyses this book contains, that people have cast doubt on the honesty of Berg's adherence to 'atonal' music (so-called and wrongly called: I believe it is tonal), because in his juvenilia he adopted a completely different musical language, one that absolutely emphasises key, and because, moreover, he has recourse to key at many points in his works. The blame is laid on my 'demonism', which has imposed the 'atonal' style on him against his nature. My demonism! How useful that could have been to me, had I only found out about it while there was still even a little time left! Whoever would have thought it! How I could have terrified my enemies, and laid a spell on my friends! Who knows what I could have brought about, if some kind foe had drawn my attention to it. Too late—by now, there's nothing to be done. What was the spell I laid on my friends? It lay in their talent, their character, their conviction, their attitude of mind, their fidelity, all their good qualities: yes, *all*—because a genuine attitude of mind takes hold of the entire man and automatically produces the requisite but unalterable conviction. So it owed nothing to good qualities of mine, only to my friends' good qualities; it is not my achievement, good or bad, but their ability to acquire

1 Schoenberg would
presumably have
noticed this mistake,
had he finalised the
preface.
L.B.

a conviction and to preserve an attitude of mind. What is
Beatrice without Petrarch[1] and his love? And my religion
needs no God, only faith.

But now the more technical side of the question; before
'atonality' I too wrote music which absolutely emphasised
key, as late as my Chamber Symphony —this fact is (I hope)
well-known; and in my youth I composed songs à la Brahms,
and before that à la Schubert, and even further back, when I
knew only violin music, I composed à la Viotti, and Bériot, and
. . . Singelé! Whose 'demonism' led me to atonality?—since
in my youth I, too, wrote a simpler, more 'natural' music?

I do not know whether people know what Alban once said
to me, when we were discussing the question whether tonal
groupings and the free style could mix. He said that as a
dramatic composer he did not believe he could do without
the possibility of contrasted characterisation, including an
occasional recourse to major and minor. Although in my own
music for the stage I have never come up against this problem, his explanation struck me as completely illuminating.

But, above all, *believeable!*—if the gentlemen whose lack
of talent is all-comprehending, even down to the inability to
believe—if these gentlemen know what 'believeable' means.
Something is believeable when the likes of us say it. . . .

If times were normal, there would have been no need to
go into things in this way, though other troublesome things
would have taken their place. The distinction is merely that
nowadays people aim to wipe out my artistic views with stink-
bombs—stink-bombs of pseudo-scientific and philosophastic
origin. And that when someone lacks the capacity for simple
reception and the ability to see for himself, someone reaches
for a philosophy of life.[2] Once one has seen how a party
badge transforms an underdog automatically and promptly
into a superman ready to abdicate his personal powers of
decision, one will take these philosophies of life no more
seriously than one does other fashionable slogans.

So, if times were normal, we should have to go into things—
other troublesome things—and should presumably do it in the
way which, in the end, we always found the only suitable one:
by 'turning our backs on whomsoever deserves it'—so,
finally, keeping out of things. Which I hereby do.

2 One of Schoen-
berg's untranslatable
puns. *Weltanschauung*
'vision of the world',
usually translated as
'philosophy of life'.
Anschauung, a word
Schoenberg often used
in a semi-mystical
sense of 'vision' or
'contemplation', seems
here to be used in a
matter-of-fact way:
*unmittelbare Anschau-
ung* = 'direct vision',
or 'seeing for oneself'.
'Where simple recep-
tion and *unmittelbare
Anschauung* are lacking,
Weltanschauungen are
brought into play.'
L.B.

Appendix 4 / Alban Berg Dedicates the Opera *Lulu* to Schoenberg[1]

1 Fram a draft of a letter dated 28 August 1934.

Dearest friend!

I know that you, like Dr Schön, would answer my question, Alwa's question, 'May I come in?'[2] with a 'Come along in, don't stand on ceremony!', and that I should then express in my embrace all the emotions that irradiate my soul on this 13th of September. But I can do so only at a distance and that, for me, is one of the painful things about this day! The other is that, all because of the frightful times we live in, I cannot approach you with a true *gift*, but merely with a *dedication*. Please accept it, not only as a product of year-long work, consecrated to you from the depths of my soul, but also as the documentation of my deepest conviction, a document directed at the outside world: the whole world, and Germany too, is to see, from this German opera's dedication, that its allegiances lie[3] in the field of utterly German music, which will for all time bear *your* name.—A third painful thing: that I cannot lay at your feet the score of the whole opera, only a copy of the opening. But the formula 'write it down' also applies, alas, to *Lulu*!

2 The opening words of Berg's opera *Lulu*.

3 Literally, 'it is domiciled in'. Cf pages 93-4 for an example of the importance of a person's 'domicile', to those brought up in the pre-1914 Austro-Hungarian Empire. L.B.

1 From the com-
memorative volume on
Schoenberg's sixtieth
birthday.

Appendix 5 / The Eternal Youth of the Genius [1]

Eternal youth of the genius, eternal youth of the creator!
That is what crossed my mind when in 1933, after many years,
I once again saw Schoenberg (whom I had known as a
seventeen-year-old) at one of his lectures. Yes! It was the same
young Schoenberg with his quality of living unboundedly
in the present—a quality that reveals itself anew at every
moment—and with the elemental power of this timeless
vitality. But I was amazed not by the fact that, at almost
sixty, he was *still* so young: what I then came to realise was
that the seventeen-year-old, living on unaltered in my memory,
had *already* possessed this true youth of the future master—
though at the time I had had no idea of the complexities
behind it all.

Already to be truly young, in one's early years—that is a
gift of grace granted to scarcely one among thousands.

For, all of us, we are not born young, we are born old,
age-old. Like precious seed under stony ground, it lies beneath
the monstrous desert of a hereditary burden going back many
thousands of years—our capacity to be truly young, could it
but come to light: buried under everything mental, spiritual
and physical that our age-old traditional inheritance has
piled up: there it lies, the eternally young germ of our true
being.

And most people among us, before they have identified
what, out of all this rubble, belongs to them, what does not,
what they should take with them and what has to be newly
acquired before it may become their own property and
what must be cleared away—most of them have reached the
end of their life span, are weary in body, soul and mind, and
must leave the world before they have found themselves!

It is a gift of higher Grace (perhaps earned in a previous
existence, through 'constant onward striving') this gift of
being as young, even when young, as others become only on
the threshold of death, for that kind of youth alone is youth
no longer dependent on chronological age, and it can never
pass away, except through some great sin. For youth of that
kind imposes a duty too; a duty to create!; to create in the
spirit of nature, for it is an *executor* of her creative power, and
has become *aware of the fact, and responsible*.

But, in this sense, such creation is as much a wholly

natural function of the creative man as is the bodily metabolism of the non-creative, those who are still wandering under the spell of a dead, oppressive tradition. What breathing is for the ordinary man—inspiration: breathing in; ex-spiration: breathing out—is in the case of the creative man the filling of oneself with the spirit of the world (*inspiration*) and making it known by giving form and figuration to earthly material (*exspiration*).

Nobody caught up in *this* metabolic process can age, unless he neglects his duty; for he is not obeying the dead tradition, he can not be the prisoner of hereditary burdens, nor their pious guardian; he has rather become the living power of tradition itself, the same power that in nature forever re-awakens the living plant out of the *seed*, which is nature's *sacred traditional inheritance.*

It is the tradition of the immortal spiritual seed that represents the creative man's most sacred task in life, and the secret of his youth is no different from that of eternally young nature herself—*natura naturans*, who rejoices ever in giving birth, and who in giving birth constantly rejuvenates herself; it is also the very secret of *music*—the secret of eternal *becoming*, which never *is* and is *forever becoming*!

For just as the musical work is *eternally present*, because it nowhere *is*, but constantly *passes away* even as it builds up before us—just as every note is destined to pass away again, even as it comes into being, in order to preserve the work itself and its ungraspable, omnipresent vitality, so the secret of the creative man's true youth is that he is never there as anything other than the one who is *becoming*, as part of the *eternal* process of *becoming*, a witness constantly reborn each moment. To be a witness to eternal *becoming!* Could one only do that, in full consciousness!—There is a mocking popular phrase applied to the conceited: 'He can hear the grass growing!'

Don't laugh! There has already been more than one man who *heard* it growing, and let others hear it too—those who had ears.

Mozart once wrote in a letter—I quote the sense rather than the exact words—that, as he composed, the work would form itself according to the same laws that govern the growth of the plant from the seed, until it blossoms and then becomes fruit. *He* heard the eternal germinative powers, growing and weaving. The unfolding sound as all life sprouts from the seed of ever-self-renewing life, which will *abide* (*währen*) as truth (*Wahrheit*) itself will abide.

Whoever has become the guardian of such a tradition, whoever serves this *abiding*, has become one of those who may and must be the prophets of *truth*—truth which, like genuine music, never is and always *becomes*: to be a part of which means to be eternally young.

Today Schoenberg's pupils praise their master as the man who teaches one to 'be true': but I praise him as the man who has become timeless. What matter if he is twenty, sixty or a hundred? He has brought mankind a sprig from the tree of life.

OSKAR ADLER

Bibliography

(only publications in book-form have been taken into account.)

1 Schoenberg's own writings

Harmonielehre	Vienna 1911; Third edition, revised and enlarged, Vienna 1921, Universal Edition	A heavily abridged English translation appeared, New York, 1948, Philosophical Library: 'Theory of Harmony', trans. Robert W. Adams
Texte	Vienna 1926, Universal Edition	Texts of Die glückliche Hand, Totentanz der Prinzipien, Requiem, Die Jakobsleiter
Models for beginners in composition	New York 1942, G. Schirmer Inc.	
Style and Idea	New York 1950, Philosophical Library (Some essays originally in German trans. Dika Newlin)	This original edition has been out of print for many years; a greatly enlarged edition including many previously unpublished essays is in preparation, Faber, London
Structural Functions of Harmony	London 1954; new edition 1969, Faber, London	
Selected Letters	London 1964, Faber, edited by Erwin Stein. trans. Eithne Wilkins and Ernst Kaiser	
Preliminary exercises in counterpoint	London 1963, Faber, edited by Leonard Stein	
Schöpferische Konfessionen	Zürich 1964, Die Arche, edited by Willi Reich	Selected essays, aphorisms, letters and extracts
Testi poetici e drammatici	Milan 1967, Feltrinelli. trans. Emilio Castellani	
Fundamentals of musical composition	London 1967, Faber, edited by Gerald Strang and Leonard Stein	

2 Tributes to Schoenberg

Arnold Schoenberg in höchster Verehrung von Schülern und Freunden.

Munich, 1912, R. Piper

Special issue of *Musikblätter des Anbruch.* Erwin Stein's own English translation of his contribution, *Neue Formprinzipien,* was later included in his book *Orpheus in New Guises,* London, 1953, Rockliff.

Arnold Schoenberg zum fünfzigsten Geburtstag

Vienna 1924, Universal Edition

Arnold Schoenberg zum 60. Geburtstag

Vienna 1934, Universal Edition

A Symposium, edited by Merle Armitage

Schoenberg

New York, 1937, G. Schirmer, Inc.

3 Biographies

Egon Wellesz *Arnold Schönberg*

Vienna 1921. E. P. Tal Co. Revised and Enlarged English edition London 1925, J. M. Dent, trans. W. H. Kerridge

Paul Stefan *Arnold Schönberg*

Vienna 1924. Zeitkunst-Verlag

Dika Newlin *Bruckner-Mahler-Schönberg*

New York, 1947, King's Crown Press

H. H. Stuckenschmidt *Arnold Schönberg*

Zurich 1951, Atlantis. (2nd enlarged edition 1957) English translation, same title, London 1959, Calder, trans. Humphrey Searle and Edith Temple-Roberts.

Willi Reich *Arnold Schönberg oder der konservative Revolutionär.*

Vienna 1968, Fritz Molden English: Arnold Schoenberg, London, 1970, London, trans. Leo Black

4 Books dealing with Schoenberg's works

Josef Rufer *Das Werk Arnold Schönbergs*
Kassel 1959, Bärenreiter
English: *The works of Arnold Schoenberg—a catalogue of his compositions, writings and paintings*. London 1962, Faber, trans. Dika Newlin

René Leibowitz *Schoenberg et son école*
Paris 1947, J. B. Janin
English: *Schoenberg and his school*. New York 1949, Philosophical Library, trans. Dika Newlin

René Leibowitz *Introduction à la musique de douze sons*
Paris 1949, L'Arche

René Leibowitz *Schoenberg*
Paris 1969. Éditions du Seuil

Karl H. Wörner *Gotteswort und Magie. Die Oper MOSES UND ARON von Arnold Schönberg*
Heidelberg 1959, Lambert Schneider.
English: *Schönberg's MOSES AND AARON*. London, 1963, Faber & Faber, trans. Paul Hamburger

Karl H. Wörner and Otto Daube *Arnold Schönberg*
Dortmund 1962, W. Crüwell

Karl Heinrich Ehrenforth *Ausdruck und Form. Arnold Schönbergs Durchbruch zur Atonalität*
Bonn 1963, H. Bouvier Co.

Glenn Gould *Arnold Schoenberg. A Perspective*
Cincinnati 1964, University of Cincinnati Occasional Papers No. 3

Wolfgang Rogge *Das Klavierwerk Arnold Schönbergs.*
Regensburg 1964, Gustav Bosse

Georg Krieger *Schönbergs Werke für Klavier*
Göttingen 1968. Vandenhoeck & Ruprecht

Anthony Payne *Schoenberg*
London 1968, Oxford University Press

String Quartet in D major (published 1966)	1897
Two Songs, Op. 1	1897 (or 1898)
Four Songs, Op. 2	1899
String Sextet (Verklärte Nacht), Op. 4	1899
Six Songs, Op. 3	1899–1903
Gurrelieder	1900–1911
Pelléas and Mélisande (Symphonic poem), Op. 5	1903
Eight Songs, Op. 6	1903-1905
Six Songs with Orchestra, Op. 8	1904
String Quartet No. 1, in D minor, Op. 7	1905
Chamber Symphony No. 1, in E major, Op. 9	1906
Two Ballads for Voice and Piano, Op. 12	1907
Friede auf Erden, for mixed choir a cappella, Op. 13 (text by Conrad Ferdinand Meyer)	1907
String Quartet No. 2, in F sharp minor, Op. 10	1907-1908
Two Songs, Op. 14	1907–1908
Fifteen Songs to poems by Stefan George, Op. 15	1908–1909
Die glückliche Hand, drama with music, Op. 18	1908–1913
Three Piano Pieces, Op. 11	1909
Five Orchestral Pieces, Op. 16	1909
Erwartung, monodrama, Op. 17	1909
Six Little Piano Pieces, Op. 19	1911
Herzgewächse, song for soprano, celeste, harmonium and harp, Op. 20	1911
Pierrot Lunaire, Op. 21	1912

Four Songs with Orchestra, Op. 22   1913-1916

Die Jakobsleiter, oratorio (incomplete)   1917–1922

Five Piano Pieces, Op. 23   1920–1923

Serenade, Op. 24   1920–1923

Suite for piano, Op. 25   1921

Two Chorale-Preludes by J. S. Bach, transcribed for orchestra   1922

Wind Quintet, Op. 26   1923–1924

Suite for piano, three wind and three stringed instruments,   1925–1926
Op. 29

Four Pieces for mixed choir, Op. 27   1925

Three Satires for mixed choir, Op. 28   1925

Variations for orchestra, Op. 31   1926–1928

String Quartet No. 3, Op. 30   1927

Prelude and Fugue in E flat major by J. S. Bach, transcribed   1928
for orchestra

Piano Piece, Op. 33a   1928

Three German Folk-songs from the 15th and 16th centuries,   1928
arranged for mixed choir a cappella

Von heute auf morgen, opera, Op. 32   1928

Four German Folk-songs from the 15th and 16th centuries,   1929
arranged for voice and piano

Begleitungsmusik zu einer Lichtspielszene, Op. 34   1929–1930

Six Pieces for male-voice choir, Op. 35   1929–1930

Moses und Aron, opera (incomplete)   1930–1932

Piano Piece, Op. 33b   1931

Concerto for cello and orchestra (after a harpsichord concerto   1932–1933
by G. M. Monn)

Three Songs, Op. 48   1933

Concerto for string quartet and orchestra (after Handel)   1933

Suite for string orchestra   1934

Violin Concerto, Op. 36   1934–1936

String Quartet No. 4, Op. 37   1936

Piano Quartet in G minor by Brahms, transcribed for orchestra   1937

Kol Nidre, Op. 39   1938

Chamber Symphony No. 2, Op. 38   1939 (begun 1906)

Variations for organ, Op. 40   1941

Ode to Napoleon, Op. 41   1942

Theme and Variations for wind band, Op. 43a (version for   1942
orchestra, Op. 43b)

Piano Concerto, Op. 42   1942

Prelude for orchestra and mixed choir, Op. 44   1945

String Trio, Op. 45   1946

A Survivor from Warsaw, Op. 46   1947

Three folk-songs for mixed choir a cappella, Op. 49 Nos. 1–3   1948

Fantasy for violin with piano accompaniment, Op. 47   1949

Dreimal tausend Jahre, for mixed choir a cappella, Op. 50a   1949

De profundis (Psalm 130), for mixed choir a cappella, Op. 50b   1950

Modern Psalm no. 1, Op. 50c (incomplete)   1950

Index

Index

Index

Index

Index